A
Philosophical and Practical Guide
for the
Returning Runner

Return to Running

Richard Benyo

This book is for Max Acker:

> *watcher of sunrises,*
> *bunker-keeper,*
> *drum-beater,*
> *frustrated philosopher,*
> *eternal spectator.*

Contents

Night Moves

*T*here should probably be a law against high school reunions—just like there should be a law against dentist drills, sassy waiters, backed-up sinks and ants at picnics. There is something very unholy about reunions. So it was that in the spring of 1974, when the mimeographed letter clunked into my mailbox with the questionnaire about what I'd been doing to squander my life away for the last 10 years since that hot June night when we'd gathered in the new fieldhouse to sit through seemingly hours of boredom waiting to escape into the real world, I did the only human thing possible: I gave in to my perverse nature, the dark side that comes from witches' caldrons and bat wings, and I filled in the form. I sent my 20 bucks (enough money to get us through four weekends in style back in those fortunately bygone high school days) and waited for the blessedly morbid event to come clomping down the numbered blocks on my wall calendar.

I was—on the logical side of my nature—very apprehensive about going to a high school reunion. Foremost, I didn't really enjoy high school; it was not one of the high points of my life. How great can high school be in a town of 5500 where, as the crest of the post-war baby boom, we were going to constitute the school's largest-ever graduating class (some 72 young, eager bodies straining for release), and where we had to hitchhike or cajole a ride four miles to the next town down the line just to see a movie? How great can high school be where the chemistry lab is still using browned jars of anonymous liquids and crystals that were manufactured in 1936? How great can high school be in a building where there was constant war and strife among the three scholastic divisions of seniors? The conflict and the cliques were so bad that the attempt at a fifth-year reunion had mercifully fizzled, sputtering out like a wet fuse at the launching pad, a victim of infernal combustion.

Even more logically, what was the sense of it all? People, following graduation, manage to keep in touch with the people they want to keep in touch with. The rest of the classmates just sort of drift away, carried out to some sea that is by then long-separated from your own by the shifting of the great land masses of your lives. Why disturb the cosmic flow of things? It was logical that 10 years hadn't made the least bit of change for the better in persons you didn't get along with in 1964. The same amount of time also might have contributed to some acquaintances you'd liked very much having fewer and fewer things in common with you, and therefore fewer things to say once you bump into each other with drinks in hand and un-natural smiles of welcome on your lips.

From the perverse side, it would be interesting to see what had happened to the high school heroes and heroettes—to see if the theory of fast-starters and slow-starters held up at Jim Thorpe Area Junior-Senior High School as it seemed to in many corners of America. (The theory was that fast-starters, much like solid-fuel rockets and Olympic sprinters, were explosive and sensational during their period of activity, but they burned out and fell to earth with a fizzle if they weren't careful to keep something in reserve. Slow-starters, of course, were like liquid-fuel rockets and distance runners, both of which start at almost imperceptible speed, building speed as they go, having a much longer life at the apex. In high school reunion terms: Were the gridiron heroes still on top, or had the tackle been made and were they pressed nose to the ground, a crush of humanity on their back kneeing them after the whistle?)

The reunion, in its way, was anticlimactic. It was held in a rod and gun club hall where club members wandered in throughout the affair and took their accustomed stools at the bar, drinking as though there weren't 75 overdressed people behind them conducting some arcane ritual.

The predominant impressions from the reunion were:

1. The teachers who'd come had aged by a decade, and they

were a bit slower in movement, but really they'd changed hardly a scratch.

2. Most of the kids in no way resembled kids anymore, the most evident mark of their maturity being extra poundage that made some of them—myself included—look not quite like themselves.

3. There were precious few who had not changed at all. Several of the guys looked almost exactly as they'd looked on that hot June 1964 night, while a few girls were almost mirror images of themselves in their white graduation gowns. The guy everyone probably should have been jealous of was the one member of the class who'd died several years after graduation: He'd live on in each of our memories as we'd last seen him; he'd still be 18 when we were 75.

4. Some of the acquaintances from high school I'd most come to see didn't bother to attend the reunion.

5. Everyone gravitated into their own little cliques, just as though the reunion were the same as a sock hop or a victory dance in the school gym (and there were precious few of those).

The evening was, without a doubt, one of the more educational I've ever spent. It brought home the fact that would haunt me even more when my 30th birthday approached: Although as kids we never thought about it, we are all mortal beings and our end begins as soon as we squeal our first protest at life. The reunion also brought Max Acker back into my life.

Max Acker, as a quick run through the little program containing the information from the questionnaire we'd returned revealed, lived only a few miles from my wife and me in Alexandria, Va. Max Acker was one of the last people in the world I'd have expected to leave Jim Thorpe, Pee-A. Max Acker sort of hated Jim Thorpe, Pa., while still sort of loving it.

Max had moved to town when his career as a teenager began. I use the word "career" because being a teenager in the age of the Kennedy presidency was a full-time job for some of us, made more complex by the fact that the job designation had just recently been initiated. Max Acker was something of a throwback from the mid-1950's *Blackboard Jungle* genre of teenagers—one who'd discovered there actually was such a thing. He liked Marlon Brando and James Dean, and while the rest of us were walking around, Max was roaring through town in one souped-up car or another. He'd had a head start on most of us in being a teenager though. He'd been sick or hadn't been paying attention or something one year in his early school days and he'd been kept back, so he was a year up on us from the first day we laid eyes on him.

His mother was Italian, and Max had inherited her dark hair which he'd built into a swirling kind of duck's-ass hairdo that always had a big strand in front the size of a gerbil's tail that kept falling down into his eyes. He'd keep combing the hair up onto its pedestal with a comb that constantly hung out of his back pocket. He wore the necessary leather jacket and cleats on his shoes so that he ricochetted off the walls as he slouched down the halls. He traveled with a bunch of other guys that he apparently had something in common with. They seldom went to any school functions, and when they did they always circled up on the fringes of the activity like a pack of wolves looking for someone in the herd to come down on. They were very good at glowering at people and at waiting until the last moment to move out of the way of an approaching adult. When they wanted to dance at a Friday night YMCA record hop or some such affair, they'd walk halfway up to the intended girl, snap their fingers and point to the floor in front of them. Girls who didn't comply with the summons were summarily ridiculed by the pack for the rest of the week at every opportunity.

Max sat behind me in homeroom, and maybe we got along because he always had so much to say and I had so little, because he didn't feel threatened by me and because I'd once seem him puking his guts out in an alley behind the YMCA after he'd made a show of strength in downing several quarts of mediocre beer and I'd never said a thing about it to anyone. We sort of had a silent agreement that we had nothing in common to be belligerent about. Our paths crossed frequently in high school but always at a glancing angle.

Occasionally, when his car was torn apart in the little yard behind the apartment he shared with his father after his parents drifted apart, he'd walk home from school and I'd waik along with him. He'd tell me about all the neat things he and his friends had been doing, all the girls from nearby towns they'd been porking every weekend. I'd listen dutifully, shaking my head in understanding at the importance of being cool and having the line and being able to snap my finger and get what I wanted. Hell, I couldn't even whistle. (I never let on, of course, that I knew most of what Max said was merely bluster and verbalization of fantasies cockily strutting around in his mind, rather than after-the-fact accounts of exploits to rival Cassanova's expeditions to the boudoir.)

After high school, though, as is fitting, the class drifted apart...at least those who'd left Jim Thorpe for other environments. I lost track of Max Acker like I lost track of almost everyone else. I figured that the sensitive nature he'd been covering with his cracked leather jacket had probably long since been extinguished, and he'd ended up working at a gas station or maybe he was in the Army or something. The night of the reunion, though, I'd no sooner put the program back down on the table after discovering he was still in proximity to my life than I felt a tap on my shoulder. Turning around, there was Max Acker.

Instead of saying, "Hey, lemme borrow a pencil," as he'd done frequently in homeroom, he said, "Hey, neighbor, why haven't you been over to see us?" Behind Max was his wife, Janet, a girl I'd vaguely remembered being in a grade several years behind us. So he'd married a hometown girl, but he'd left the adopted hometown.

After a few minutes of exchanging information and phone numbers and promising to get together back in Alexandria, Max and Janet Acker returned to their clique and we continued with our drinks and conversations. As the talk buzzed around me, I thought about Max. He'd gained 30 or 40 pounds since high school, and he was smoking heavily. But he wasn't in jail, and he'd gotten married and he was settled down in suburban Washington, D.C., with two children, with a pickup truck, living in the same house with his mother, and he was working for the government delivering mail from one federal department to several others in the gigantic federal complex around which the nation's capital is built.

On the way home from the weekend, my wife Jill and I

wondered if he'd ever really call so we could get together. He did, two days later, and we went by the Ackers' house for a Fourth of July picnic. Ultimately, we began to spend almost every Friday and Saturday night at the Ackers' house. A strange pattern was developing, though. Every Friday and Saturday night became much the same, with only slight variations.

We all enjoyed old rock 'n' roll music, stuff from our high school era, everything from Chuck Berry's "Sweet Little Sixteen" to "My Boyfriend's Back" by the Angels. Max had been buying new pressings of the records, and I still had hundreds of my 45s from high school. We'd take boxes of records over, and Max would sit down in front of his J.C. Penney stereo system and play disc jockey. We'd drink copious amounts of beer, sing along with the songs and make tapes as though Max's rumpus room in the basement was an outlaw FM station. We even did silly things like rate the records, hold dance contests and make hypothetical Top 40 lists. Max's two kids thought they had four playmates their age before their bedtime each weekend night. My wife and I would leave at two or three in the morning, and when Max would call the next day he'd tell us how he'd stayed up to watch the sun rise.

The Friday- and Saturday-night sessions with Max and Janet Acker became rituals. Max drank and chain-smoked and stayed up many nights to see the sun rise. There was something gnawing at the insides of Max Acker. The more weekends we put in with him, the more evident his problem became.

Some of Max's conversations revealed that he had been wrestling with heavy thoughts. His vocabulary was extremely wide and varied for someone who'd spent most of his high school days being called onto the carpet; he had turned into something of a philosopher. He'd hated high school, but he loved to talk about it; life for Max Acker had ended on graduation night.

"It'll never be like that again," he'd constantly lament. "If I could go back, I would."

Max Acker was frustrated with his life. He had brains and no opportunity to make use of them, so he'd made use of what he could find to survive. He'd been beaten around as a kid, and he'd lost the momentum some people need to rise to their potential. He'd been cowered by his life, and he felt it was well past the midstride and that it was hopeless. He lived his life in his basement (which he called his "bunker," his refuge against the battleground of modern life) where he had browned and wrinkled photos of his youth hanging on the walls and where he could listen to old records and embellish stories of the good old days.

On several occasions, he became depressed to the point that he spoke of suicide in graphic detail, ending with the conclusion that he wasn't man enough for even that. He saw more and more suns rise, drank more and more beer as he began a campaign to see how many of the plastic six-pack restrainers he could accumulate in a year, and he smoked pack after pack of cigarettes and got little exercise outside of hefting mailbags on the job during the day. Some days, he didn't make it to work because after staying up to watch the sun rise he couldn't move himself to his truck to get to work.

We drifted away from Max. We'd talked ourselves blue trying to get him to pick up his life at that point and make a new start. We'd tried to talk him into taking some courses at the local two-year college, but he contended he wasn't smart enough and that it was too late. He felt he was unworthy and that he was worth more to his family dead than alive.

We'd often get late-night calls from Max as he sat drinking beer and smoking cigarettes in his bunker until the sun came up to put him to sleep. Sometimes, his body would just give out midway through the night. As he was sitting in a chair, his head would go back, his mouth would open, and he'd be dead to the world for as many as a dozen hours.

We drifted farther and farther apart. It was depressing to go to Max's house, and there were problems developing on top of each other as they do when any relationship goes bad. Max called occasionally, the phone conversations getting shorter all the time.

Then, one night early in November 1976, Max was smoking and drinking and wearing his cowboy boots in the bunker. He'd sort of drifted into country and western music and was wearing cowboy outfits, talkin' about bein' a truck-drivin' man. He was doing his usual night underground, away from the real world. He sat down in a chair, a guy 31 years old who was down on himself, and he fell asleep as he'd often done before, his mouth open and the television set on.

His wife, as was normal in such a situation, left him there and went to bed without disturbing him, figuring the sleep would be good for him. The next morning, Max was still sitting there, in the same position. During the night, his life had caught up with him and had flown like an invisible bird out his open mouth.

Max Acker was dead.

As is typical of a small town, there were suddenly all kinds of stories flying around Jim Thorpe, Pa., about how he'd died. The most common one was that he'd died of an overdose of drugs. People just don't die of natural causes at 31 years of age.

There's some truth to that, I suppose. Max hadn't. He'd died of frustration and depression and too much drinking and too much smoking and too much abuse of his body with too many ritualistic waits for the rising sun, and he'd died because his body machine had just run down in a slow suicide. Max Acker made sure that my wife and I never saw life quite the same again.

Chapter One

Doin' What
Comes Natural

*I*t is impossible to begin discussing running without first discussing God. The God a runner finds while making his way—solitary and open to the universe, along a forest trail or across the rim of a mountain or along a beach licked by the ocean—is a topic covered later in this book. But the God that must be sorted out and appreciated first is the God, elemental and huge and beyond the knowledge of mere men, who started things on their way initially.

Any discussion of God or religion is bound to be revolutionary in its way, if for no other reason than two people sitting next to each other in the same pew in the same church on the same Sunday have different versions in their minds of what and who God is. Throw in things like evolution and the allegorical nature of the Bible, and things begin to get sticky. Nothing about life, mankind, the universe or God is simple, and some of us apparently like it that way. So, throwing caution to the wind and without getting bogged down in this portion of the discussion too long, we should get two facts straight:

1. The Bible, especially the Old Testament, is an allegory and should not be taken literally.

2. Each year, evidence mounts that evolution is the road down which mankind came.

Paradoxically, and against the hard-line feelings of people with narrow visions of God, both facts strengthen the role of a God in the lives of each of us.

The Bible was passed down by word of mouth from one generation to another, over a space of many, many generations, by people with little education and many superstitions. It eventually fell into the hands of people who could—and did—take time to write the stories of the Bible down. Word of mouth is an excellent way of making legends, but it is not a very good way of keeping an accurate record of what actually happened.

To see what problems are involved with accepting word-of-mouth stories at face value, watch what happens to a rumor that leaves one person's mouth and is passed to a second. When the second person passes it to the third, there are embellishments added until, by the time it reaches the 10th person's ears, a black cat that Johnny saw last night has turned into an escaped saber-tooth tiger and there's panic in River City. Consider the additions and changes that are tacked onto stories passed down over thousands of years.

Consider, also, the stories of the Bible.

The story of Adam and Eve conjures images of the Earthly Paradise—sort of a Palm Springs without tipping. Everything is perfect. Adam and Eve have everything they want. Adam and Eve are the only people there, so there are no lines. Adam and Eve are, therefore, acknowledged as the mother and father of the human race by people who read the Bible literally.

Yet consider this: If Adam and Eve were the only people on Earth when the human race was begun, where did the rest of us come from? In order to have any children, Adam and Eve and their children had to copulate, which is incest. Simply put, if we read the Bible literally, we believe in and condone incest. We know scientifically that incest is certainly not good, because the mixing of genes too close to each other in structure causes mutations and deformities and insanity. Perhaps, in our moments of depression over the direction the human race is taking and when we read of some ridiculous or loathsome act a human being has committed against another human being, we can believe that there might have been incest within the family of Adam and Eve. But if that were so, how do we explain the occasional stupendous intelligence that finds its way into the human race?

If Adam and Eve were not brought upon the earth full-blown and ready to commit incest to begin the human race, how did we begin? We began, it appears, fairly recently in the scheme of things on earth, and we began—the evidence continues to mount in this direction—not so much as a conscious tearing from the rib of Adam as a casual byroad of evolutionary affairs.

Now, this kind of talk has traditionally brought howls of outrage and indignation from peoples trapped in the narrow alleyways of religion—despite the fact that on some days, with what we read in the newspapers and see on the television news programs, the monkeys have plenty of grounds for suing the human race for defamation of character.

There is always going to be a cult—and I use the word "cult" very carefully and deliberately—of self-centered religionists who believe, because they've always been told to believe and because they are too lazy to consider anything beyond that belief, that human beings are made in the image and likeness of God. Again, as with the Adam and Eve story, some people take this literally; they picture God as a gray-haired old man sitting on a granite throne who does nothing all day beyond listening to mankind's bellyaching.

These people see themselves as the children of God, despite the fact that the Bible God cautions mankind toward modesty. What is more immodest than thinking we are like unto God?

We aren't like God, although some of us apparently think we are either like unto God or that we are God—to the point that He has bestowed His word upon us, personally, and by doing that has told us to go out among mankind and bend and shape other men and women to this version of what God wants and is and means, even if we have to kill or maim or imprison the other fellow to do it.

What people really mean when they say we are made in God's image is that we have made God in *our* image.

The simple fact is that God is so far above and beyond us puny human beings that, at least on this earth, we do not have the necessary mental tools even to begin to understand Him. God is a force that starts things rolling; that—before there was anything in a universe that stretches mightily into infinity in all directions—blew a grain of sand into existence that somehow grew into planets and suns and universes one upon the other; that began planets and destroyed suns; that took hops and skips from our little universe into others whose suns have been born, grown and died, and the light of their exis tence—despite the fact that it travels at 186,000 miles per second—has not reached our universe yet and perhaps won't reach it until our own universe has vanished.

This God, who begins solar systems from a grain of sand that he made from nothing, is made in the same image and likeness of a human being who has trouble learning to tie his shoelaces? To believe that is to throw a puny insult against a force so powerful we haven't begun to learn the extent of His creations, much less their motive force.

Appreciating God for the force that He is makes things like evolution all the more wonderful and opens the possibilities that evolution has not, indeed, reached a dead end with mankind as we know it; there may be wondrous new horizons beyond our current development. I'd hate to think that God's creation of mankind is really a dead one and that, once developed, the human model is arrested in its development. Each year, mankind makes further modifications and improvements on computers, video game centers, toothbrushes, airplanes, shoes, his own mind. Are we to believe that God is less interested in further development of the product than mankind is?

Can we, then, see evolution as something evil? Or is evolution one of God's most complex and wonderful works? And if we have evolved from some other forms of life, what forms were they and where are they now? How did we develop thumbs and complex biomechanical structures that allow us to walk and skip and run? How did a pile of gray cauliflower in our skulls begin to grasp the possibilities of infinity and calculus and lyric poetry? Are we a better ape, or are we aping what we hope we'll eventually become? Let's take a quick run down the evolutionary trail and visit with some races who have traditions that are not entirely alien to our own.

*A*s we've seen in our daily lives and in our dealings with God, mankind has an inordinately large ego. He feels himself the center around which all things revolve. At least to the individual man, that's pretty true on a practical level. Man usually pauses only long enough in his daily romp down the pathway to look at what's within the range of his own sight. Naturally, everything he sees, if he turns around in a circle, radiates from him and to him. (This is nothing new, certainly. Even those wonderfully bizarre ancient Greeks, who gave us so much development of the mind and body, believed that the earth was the center of the universe around which all other matter out there revolved. However, they had the saving grace of understanding, even at that early time, that the earth was spherical instead of as flat as a card-table.)

Before we begin discussing where man came from, we must establish where the place he resides came from. Where'd the earth come from, anyway? Where did it begin? How long ago? How'd it get itself started?

Booksellers in London in 1779 got together to publish a book titled *Universal History*, which firmly set the date for the creation of the earth in the autumn equinox of 4004 B.C. They even went so far as to pinpoint the exact location of the Garden of Eden. Unfortunately, people bought the book and began searching for the Garden of Eden; they also began believing the 4004 B.C. dating. They never found Eden, and pretty soon evidence came along that there were a lot of things lying around that were apparently on the earth before there was an earth. God, then, didn't set the planet earth down in its orbit like a father sets the plastic house down on Main and Sycamore Streets in a Christmas decoration.

Since it all happened so long ago, well before television was around to record the event on videotape, we have no eye-witness reports of the creation of the earth. Our evidence is in the record of the rocks that form the earth. They tell stories by their age, formation, by their piling one atop the other. They are like a book with pages that weigh tons; the first pages of the book are on the bottom and have to be dug for in deep places.

Originally, God blew his nose, and out in space a huge mass of gasses and other matter was formed. It got denser by degrees and therefore developed a gravitational pull which hauled in other matter to itself. This other matter joined together in the caldron of tremendous heat and over a period of millions of years began to spin. The spinning caused huge chunks of this mass to be flung off from itself, like in the game where a line of kids joins hands and spins around faster and faster to see how long it will take until the end kid is going so fast he can't stay on his feet anymore—at which point he loses his grip and goes tumbling up against a tree or a parked car or something.

One of those "kids" that was flung off was slowed in its headlong tumble and settled approximately 93 million miles from the swirling mass. Other kids did the same thing and these planets settled at various distances from the central mass. Some of the smaller masses were still spinning and, like Charlie Brown when he gets a baseball hit back at him, the force of this spinning knocked all their clothes off. The pieces of clothing became moons. Apparently, the earth only got its baseball glove knocked off, because it has only one moon. Jupiter, with a face as round as Charlie Brown's, got every-thing knocked off and has 12 known moons.

The newborn earth was extremely hot, of course, and there was no way anything could have lived on it.

When did all this happen? Well, for people who live to be about 65 years of age, it's hard to comprehend the numbers.

However, stopping to think for a moment about the numbers listed here will give us a little humility the next time we think we're in God's image and likeness—or that He's in ours. (Consider also that the advancing scientific measuring devices may find that these numbers are woefully inadequate as research into the birth of suns continues.)

Our sun had reached a point where it could qualify as a star some five quadrillion (that's five plus 12 zeros) years ago. The earth has been separated from the sun and on its own for two trillion years.

With ages like that flying around, just when did discernible life of any kind (in this case, plant life) appear on earth? Well, life first appeared in the waters of the earth approximately 300 million years ago, give or take a century or two.

When did mankind's ancestors begin walking about the earth, littering it with refuse so archeologists could find it many years later and reconstruct it into a partial history? Less than 50,000 years ago but more than 25,000 years ago.

How did all this life stuff begin, and what does it have to do with running. Well... That "well" is used as a pregnant pause that, in the grand scheme of things, may last for 50 million years, but in this context it is merely a way of putting off an explanation that begins with the very inconcise words: "No one knows." It is, literally, one of those mysteries in the Grand Scheme that makes God so much more than many people picture Him, because life was seemingly begun in such a casual fashion.

The earth, as it cooled, consisted mostly of water. Then, as it continued to cool and as matter became more solid, very tortuous land masses with pox marks of volcanic activity began to erupt at various places. The molten material of the land masses that had blown their way from the center of the forming mass began to cool in the air because, although the air was hot enough to take the paint off the side of a battleship, it was cool compared to the center of the earth. The rocks were twisted and bent as they cooled, and new masses came to the surface next to them and twisted themselves against the already established land masses. We began to have the birth of the continental mass, the super-continent.

Millions upon millions of years later, as the land masses

began to cool, and as the air began to cool, and as the incredibly fiery caldron of gasses and liquids and fledgling land began to take form, the earth was like a gigantic chemical hotpot that likely will never be duplicated—at least not in the vicinity of our solar system.

In this huge phial, chemical things were happening as temperatures fluctuated and as water began to quiet itself and as more and more land masses appeared. At some point, several chemicals got together and, perhaps struck by a stray flash of static electricity (there was a lot of it around in those days), life was formed—a marvelous accomplishment. Despite the fact that the life we're talking about was less intelligent than bread mold and about as mobile as a rock, it was life.

This bit of probably brownish slime lived because it fit the main definition of life as we know it—including its capacity to die. For everything given, something must be taken away. A rock is forever, in one form or another, but if you wanna live then you gotta be willing to die. The brownish slime lived, and died—and (another necessity of being defined as life) it reproduced itself, in this case by simply Xeroxing itself so that there would be others similar to it that would carry on after it died.

I use this word "similar" because in talking of the tremendous amounts of time involved here, millions upon millions of years in which the earth was undergoing changes (the earth's temperature was lowering, its spinning upon its axis was slowing, and its axis was shifting, etc.), the slime wasn't staying the same. It was, through succeeding generations, altering itself to fit its changing environment.

Now, let's say that the slime was the Universal Slime, meaning it was all over the earth, because it had perfect hot-house conditions in which to thrive once it started. Universal Slime didn't fly or walk or run or think. It lived, and it bred, and it sort of swam in that it allowed itself to be carried with the currents wherever the currents happened to be going. By this means, it was carried to all points on the earth—which is why it was Universal Slime instead of *Regional* Slime, whom we are about to meet.

With the earth undergoing so many changes, the Slime that was a common factor at the beginning was finding itself trapped in parts of the earth that were not exactly like other parts. It was getting cooler at the poles than at the equator, mountains were still springing up and trapping some of the Slime in lakes. Universal Slime, in order to survive under the constantly changing conditions, made compensations by becoming Regional Slime.

The Slime at the North Pole (which was nowhere as cold as it is now but was still cold relative to the rest of the planet) began to develop a tougher and thicker outer covering in order to hold in its warmth and to keep out the bad elements. On the equator, the particular Regional Slime sent out extra filaments in order to absorb all the sunshine and heat and to provide for proper ventilation of body functions, although they were very basic and primitive. Each Regional Slime colony developed along different lines over the millions of years the earth took to adjust itself. Those infant Slimes who failed to develop what was needed died before they could reproduce and so were weeded out of the colony.

*O*ver more millions of years, the Slime developed other attributes, and at some point actually went from plant to animal life—still very small and very basic, but now mobile. Once animal life—even in its basic form—was introduced, things began to happen more rapidly. It wasn't rapid by today's standards but rapid in the context of the whole world picture. Fish developed and became bigger; some fish developed lungs and spent some time (especially cool nights) on land, laying eggs. Some of the things that came from the eggs liked the land, and began spending more and more time there. They developed softer scales than their fish ancestors, and they became amphibians. Some branched off and became reptiles. Some became *big* reptiles, like we often encounter in Grade B prehistoric films. There were yet no men; in fact, there never were men while there were huge reptiles like Tyrannosaurus rex.

There were all sizes of reptiles, from little squirrel-sized beasts to some the size of tractor-trailers and larger. Some of the reptiles began to develop rudimentary feathers instead of scales, and eventually began to jump off rocks and glide. Later, the feathers were developed enough to allow them to lift their bodies into the air and actually fly up off the ground. Other fleet-footed little reptiles went in different directions, becoming rudimentary mammals. They were clever little buggers—the epitome of brainpower to that point. While the huge reptiles would lumber about terrorizing movie sets along the countryside, these little buggers would creep into the nests the big reptiles had made, and they'd tear open the eggs and have a breakfast of two sunny-side-up eggs. They supposedly contributed to the end of the age of reptiles by destroying them before they ever hatched. The mammals were too quick to get caught and too little probably even to be seen by the huge dinosaurs unless they were equipped with corrective lenses. The dinosaurs were not especially protective of their young, anyway; they were more interested in finding the huge trainload of food they needed every day to stay alive.

A twist in the earth's axis that brought cold to the land of the dinosaurs, and the little mammals having omelets and poached eggs every morning effectively killed off a group of animals that had lived with immunity. The thunder lizards were gone, and the little rat-like mammals, who'd developed fur coats to protect themselves against the cold, lived on.

Development began to speed up. There were still species of fish and birds and amphibians and reptiles that had adapted to the changes in the earth, but mammals were beginning to get the upper hand—not because of their size, but mostly because of their increased brainpower, their cunning and their adaptability.

One species branched off to become several other species and we eventually had woolly mammoths mixing it up with saber-tooth tigers. The theory is that at this point the highest form of intelligent life was the ape family. And this is where all the controversy comes about, because man's ego balks at thinking he came from apes. (Apes probably have the same controversy, as they sit around a circle in the jungle at night trying to argue that they didn't become that voracious destroyer, man.)

The evidence is that man did *not* come directly from the apes, but that at a point in evolutionary development man and apes had a common ancestor, then they developed down different paths. For the apes, there were two basic types, ground apes and tree apes. Tree apes went swinging through the trees like monkeys still do. Ground apes ran around the forests and jungles and sat around on their haunches more like today's gorillas.

Although there were some pretty silly conclusions drawn by early anthropologists that certain races of humans came from different species of apes, the most universally-held contention is that ape-men eventually developed (through many, many stages) from the *running* ape of the Cenozoic Period that lived on the ground among the rocks. The running ape ate fruit and vegetables, and probably spent more time running from something that was going to eat it than running after something it wanted to eat. It was a communal ape similar to the present-day ground apes of the Gibraltar area.

Some wonderful changes were taking place in the animal kingdom, not the least of which was the increase in brain-size among those apes. It did not happen rapidly, of course, but the first we see of proto-man (a definite transition from apedom) comes roughly 50,000 years ago. The proto-man was the Cromagnon of the Reindeer Period; they followed the reindeer herds and chased down the weaker reindeer when they wanted food. They were not especially swift, but they were persistent runners, using a method of outlasting their quarry and running their hooved meal into the ground. They were accomplished artists, doing cave paintings of such complexity that they were not matched at the height of the Greek and Roman civilizations. They seldom if ever drew pictures of themselves, but rather drew the animals they saw and needed for food. The Cromagnon Man or Reindeer Man was very adaptable; when the reindeer and horse and bison herds diminished, he took up fishing.

These accomplishments and advancements should not overshadow the fact that the Reindeer Man had many shortcomings. Although they had much time to develop (they lived in Western Europe for 10 times the length of the Christian era), they never made pets of animals; they had no dogs; they domesticated no animals; they did not cook their food and had no cooking utensils or pottery; they did not farm; they were naked, painted savages with great endurance for running on the part of the men, but who had a tradition of fattening their squaws and starting them on child-bearing at the earliest possible time. The Reindeer Men watched life passing in front of them, drew it when they had the urge, ran after and killed animals when they were hungry, and did very little else. They were the hippies in the development of man.

The Reindeer Men were proto-men; they had developed some of the qualities we like to associate with men. It should be remembered, however, that the Reindeer Men were still removed from modern man—and this as little as 12,000 years ago. During their period, there were still many strange and awesome animals roaming the earth that are now very much extinct. For instance, there were still lions in southern Germany twice the size of the modern lion. Consequently, men were still very much involved in running as a way of life.

This, for the most developmental pockets of man, was about to change, though. The new form of proto-man that came into prominence about 8000 B.C. was the Neolithic Man. He was very much like what we consider modern man, in that rather than running after game for his food he domesticated it. Therefore, he could just walk up, give a cow a good whack between the eyes with a heavy stone and have all the meat he wanted for several weeks—at least all he could eat before it decayed. Neolithic Man also began farming and settling down in one place, no longer traveling thousands of miles in a year following the caprice of a herd of reindeer or bison.

Man had suddenly become a suburban farmer and rancher. This change seemed to come about rather rapidly. It should be stressed that the Neolithic Period constituted only about one percent of the time span of the previous Paleolithic Period.

It was during this period that the race of man was introduced onto the North American continent. But again, owing to man's perverse and accidental nature, the men who were domesticating animals and planting gardens in Europe did not come over here. Man kind of came in through the back door after taking a wrong turn through Asia and crossing the Bering Strait. While man was coming into America by the back door, the camel, a beast developed in America, was exiting in the same manner.

This getting away from running and settling down with farms and domesticated animals standing around dumbly waiting to die, this gathering together into rough towns and cities, happened relatively fast on the calendar of life. It also heralded what we like to call civilization, a period during which the newly-enlightened man turned to herding so he would have time to contemplate the stars and think about forming religions.

The religions he formed were in his own image and likeness which, basically, was violent and cruel. During this period of dawning civilization, contemplative man, armed with a brain he didn't know how to use properly, felt that the harvest would be better if human sacrifices were made to the power that made things grow one year and that caused famine and plague the next. These were not human sacrifices of crippled or deformed members of the society; they were the pride of the race, raised, as though a fatted cow, to be sacrificed in ritualistic ceremonies to the good of harvest.

Later, as man became more civilized, he developed better and more efficient means of doing away with people, while his inventiveness managed to provide *too many* religions, so that as B.C. turned to A.D., the pagan Romans were killing the Christians, and a thousand years later the Christians were killing anyone thought to be an infidel—all in an attempt to save their souls.

Of course, with the earth being as large as it is, and with mankind being as diverse as it is, advanced forms of civilization passed certain pockets of people by—so that in some remote sectors of the world, people scratched out a meager living without the benefit of TV dinners, air conditioners, Oldsmobiles and fluoride in their water.

Civilized man was on a different track, though. He was into developing artificial means of transportation: horses, ox-carts, railroads, pickup trucks, jet planes. Primitive tribes that managed to sneak into the 20th century primarily depended on their legs to carry them through, while at the same time managing to avoid some of our traditions.

*T*his is a good juncture, before speaking of the Tarahumara Indians of Mexico, at which to talk about primitive vs. civilized pleasures. We can talk about them by comparing two items. For the Primitives, it's running as a lifestyle and as a simple pleasure; for the Civilizeds, it's the development of the pocket calculator.

Pleasure is something all of us say that we seek—yet apparently get too little of, because we continue to seek more. For primitive peoples, pleasures are very simple and basic: it is a pleasure not to be eaten by a lion today; it is a pleasure to have a few minutes in a day filled with trying to find enough food to live on to be able to sit down against a rock and feel the sun warming the weary limbs; it is a pleasure to take part in a good—and successful—hunt; it is a pleasure to travel from village A to village B quickly and efficiently along rugged trails, there to visit friends, barter for some goods or woo the chief's daughter. Pleasures that are simple have no barbs along their sides to slow them from getting right to the pleasure centers of the person enjoying them.

Pleasure emanates from the pleasure centers of the body, whether we look at the pleasure centers as purely physiological or psychological. If we were not housed in a body that was equipped to enjoy pleasures, we would probably call what we were experiencing something else—because it is our bodies that have senses to tell us we are enjoying something. When we find our senses functioning at a low heat, but functioning all at once and at about the same level, we call it a feeling of contentment or a feeling that all's well with the world. When one sense begins enjoying something more than the other senses, we have words that escape our lips to describe the sensations. A banana split tastes good and we say, "Mmmmmm!" The tactile senses respond when we stretch first thing in the morning and our comment is "Aaaahhh!" We hear a bit of haunting music and our answer to it is something like, "Oooooh!"

Primitive people and children have less sophisticated senses of pleasure than civilized adults carrying sacks of duty and responsibility and "culture" upon their backs. Primitives and children are much better off because of their uncomplicated appreciation of simple pleasures—because less is more, and because simple is almost always more complex than what we call complex when what we really mean is "confused."

The simple pleasures revolve around the body, and no matter how Puritan man later tried to confuse the matter, there is nothing wrong with simple pleasures that stroke the body. Primitive man (and, again, children) finds great pleasure in simple body functions: the bending of a knee; the curling of a toe, the winking of an eye, the moving of the bowels, the smacking of the lips, the process of walking, running, jumping, bending. Observe the fascination with which a primitive or a child (for they are closer to each other than they are to us) wiggles his or her toes, curls the hand around a stick or dashes down a road. There is a certain glee and concentration on their faces. (There is a similar reversion to such pleasures in elderly people, although there is a mixture of awe with them that such acts are still possible.)

Primitives will play simple, strenuous games for hours, seemingly determined to make the feeling to the body that the game provides last as long as possible. Similarly, children will run around a tree for an hour until something breaks their concentration. On their faces are looks of pleasure that they don't completely understand but that they aren't about to ruin or lose by questioning. Civilized adults occasionally suffer from this simple pleasure when engaging in weekend softball or volleyball games. Unfortunately, because it is not a daily part of their lives, their unused bodies usually revolt on them the next day.

Use of the body in simple (but strenuous) activity should be a basic pleasure. It is with primitives and with children; it is with most animals. It isn't with civilized man, however, because of the pocket calculator syndrome—which is simply this: there is the novelty quotient to consider when dealing with civilized adults.

The novelty quotient is the point at which something that was extremely fascinating when first we encountered it turns to ashes in our mouth and just downright bores us because of overexposure.

As sophisticated adults, we are supposed to appreciate sophisticated things. Some of us don't always do that because some of us don't consider sophisticated what others do. This is a problem in our psyches that makes it possible to have four major automakers in America instead of one. In that sense, in the sense that many of us still retain some cynicism about our sophistication, we are primitive—and that's to our credit. Too often, though, we find ourselves being dutifully fascinated by the things that other people decided for us are sophisticated, and therefore worthy of our attention and interest. By contemplating the object of sophistication, we are supposed to derive some unexplained pleasure.

For instance, when the first automobile belched its way along the roads, our primitive cynicism rose to the surface, and we said things like: "Get a horse!" "It'll never catch on." "Who wants a bucket of bolts like that?" What we were saying from the increasingly hidden depths of our beings was: "I've got two good feet that'll get me where I want to go; who needs this?" Well, the novelty of the thing caught on, almost everyone bought a car, and soon became bored with it but out of habit continued to use it, foresaking the feet and legs.

The same thing happened with the pocket calculator. People used to figure up the amount of money left in their checkbook by making columns of figures on a scrap of paper and then subtracting what the wife had used up. Along came the first bulky, expensive but fascinating pocket calculators, a product of the space age. It was suddenly possible to have an adding, subtracting, dividing and multipying machine a fraction of the size of an adding machine, and it gave you your answer not on a slip of paper but in cute little lighted numbers. We were enthralled, fascinated and overcome by the thing after our first reaction of, "Who needs something like that? I ain't no accountant (snicker)."

The calculators became more and more fascinating, capable of doing functions in a microsecond that it took Albert Einstein years to figure out on a bulky slate blackboard. And, since they were being made by many, many companies, competition set in. The calculators began to do more and more things while costing less and less, while becoming smaller and smaller. Now, the original calculators look like bulky dinosaurs, crude things with scales. But the calculator has become so common in our society, so pervasive, that we take it for granted, because we are sophisticated.

Therefore things like this, though wondrous at first, lose their novelty, while additionally taking away one more basic function—and pleasure—from the modern man. He or she no longer has to know how numbers work with or against each other. All that is required is to push a little button and the machine will give you the answer. There is no need to learn how to figure out numbers in your mind. High school graduates, with a holster on their hip containing the newest calculator on the market, go out into a hostile world ready to finger their way to the top. Should there be a battery shortage, Wall Street, the American school systems and the local supermarkets would have to close down for lack of knowing how to add five and seven.

Sophistication, then, robs us of simple pleasures—things like walking to the store on our own two feet and, when getting back home being able to whisper to ourselves, "Hell, that felt pretty good"; or like figuring out numbers in our head or on a scrap of paper, and being able to whisper to ourselves, "Hell, that felt pretty good."

Sophistication and civilization rob us of certain pleasures generated by our bodies. We do, of course, pay the price. On the other hand, primitiveness (and the accompanying pleasures of the body) also demands its price.

Take, for instance, the greatest runners in the world, the Tarahumara Indians. (And let's put their credentials right up front: the young Tarahumara boys are not considered men until they can cover approximately 100 miles between sunrise and sunset, over some of the roughest ground the earth has ever vomited up and forgotten.) The Tarahumara live roughly 350 miles south of El Paso, Texas, in Chihuahua, Mexico, in an area roughly 40,000 miles square; there is one Tarahumara for each mile of rocky desolation. The most primitive of North American Indians, the Tarahumara live in a depression in the earth known as the Barranca Urique, 4½ times larger and 2000 feet deeper than the Grand Canyon. They are miserably malnourished, suspicious of civilization, fall victim to any disease that happens to be passing by, and they die with great efficiency.

In Jonathan F. Cassel's book on the Tarahumara, written after two extended stays among them, he describes their plight this way: "Tarahumara vital statistics are startling. Two out of three babies, and many of the mothers, die at birth. Death comes from uncontrolled hemorrhage and postnatal infection. Three out of five babies who survive the primitive birth process will succumb to disease and malnutrition before they are five years old. The survivors will rarely live to become 45 years of age."

Birth is accomplished by the solitary mother, whose time has come, walking off into the wilderness where she finds a tree with a branch that is slightly higher than she can reach. She painfully constructs a rough nest under the tree and then reaches up for the branch, grasps it to pull her up onto her toes and then awaits the arrival of the infant, which dutifully falls into the nest. The woman is unattended during the birth process. If she dies, the child dies with her because it is then unattended. If she lives, the child may have died in the rough process. If she lives, she may die weeks later from infection.

The Tarahumara are a people similar to what all people were several thousands of years ago. They are morose, suspicious and by all rights should be one of the most depressed people on the face of the earth—or rather, in a pock-mark on the face of the earth. Yet, although happiness is a stranger to the Tarahumara, they do find a feeling of nobleness and accomplishment and almost joy at their running—and especially at their stick-ball game, *rarahipa*, a rough, fast-moving game in which two teams compete to see which can push their wooden ball around a course first. The courses are sometimes

150 miles, and the game continues after dark with runners carrying torches.

What resistance the Tarahumara have for death is not given them by civilization. What allows some of them to survive to be 45 in a land that attempts to kill them at birth is a toughness and a persistence augmented by their running great distances in incredibly short periods of time.

In their adherence to the basic pleasures and accomplishments of the body against a hostile world—or rather, in their refusal to approach life in any way other than with what they find within themselves—they are much like children. And a child is essentially the perfect runner.

Consider, for instance, the fact that when learning to walk, a child does not really attempt to walk. Any parent who has squatted on the living room floor while the other parent launches their child across a few impossible feet of floor-space on its inaugural trip on two feet knows that the infant does not *walk* those steps; it runs them. It hurls itself with a primitive ferocity from one parent to the other. If the infant makes the trip successfully, it is googily happy. If it does not make the trip, and if its parents are not over-protective, it is trying to make the trip again and again and again, and perhaps practices while the parents are out of the room. But the first steps are never at a walking pace; they are always an infant sprint.

The normal child, once mastering how to "walk," finds that he or she likes to get from one place to the next at a pace faster than is considered feasible for a person at such a young age. The child wants to run to get from one place to another, and its natural tendencies are at work to propel it rapidly from one new discovery to another. Of course, civilized as we are, we caution the child to *walk, don't run.*

The litany increases as the child's curiosity and adventuresome spirit intrude: don't run near the pool; don't run on the sidewalks; don't run through the house; don't run across the lawn; don't run, don't run, don't run. The child's efforts to get somewhere fast are frustrated, and then parents fail to understand the obsessiveness with which the child wants to get the family car when he or she is old enough to drive. The child has been frustrated in getting from one point to another as quickly as possible all during childhood, and that frustration is being saved for the car, which is the civilized valve for all the running the kid has stored up.

What the perfect formula for human happiness is may be impossible to predict. It certainly isn't the completely automated world of modern civilization where we are transported from one place to another by some machine, whether we want to be or not. But neither is it the miserable lifestyle of the Tarahumara Indians, no matter how accomplished they are in getting from one place to another on foot, because it is impossible for man to invent a vehicle that will efficiently and economically traverse their hostile land.

It is, perhaps, somewhere in between, a ridding ourselves of the shortcomings of the primitive life by introducing and accepting the good things civilization has brought to us—such as advanced knowledge, medicine, the capacity for longer life—yet a holding onto the primitive pleasures in the bodily sensations that we apparently feel obliged by civilized standards to deny ourselves.

Perhaps there is a need to allow the primitive, simple, savage pleasures to run their course in children by allowing them to run—by, in fact, encouraging them. Perhaps such a practice would allow them an outlet for their incredible amounts of energy—energy that is too often forced inward by constraints arbitrarily forced on a rambunctious kid. Let the kid get his frustrations out, use some of his energy, get together between his body and mind by running down the street or by running through the yard. Maybe the kids have something the Tarahumara have that saves them from going insane in a world that does everything it can to push them over the edge.

Maybe the trip to teenagerhood would be made easier if the run were encouraged.

Chapter Two

Prosperity's Children

There is a lot of discussion about what the first rock 'n' roll song was—where it all started. The best bet is that it began in June 1954 when the Cords released a song on the very minor Cat label that claimed, "Life is but a dream," and emphasized the dream by the nonsense chorus of "Sha-Boom," which became the title of the song. Within a few weeks, a cover version of the song was done by a white Canadian group, the Crewcuts, and the song began working its way up the pop charts. Rock 'n' roll had evolved from rhythm and blues, rockabilly and pop, with some gospel thrown in, and America would never be the same.

It is even more difficult to pinpoint an equally important date that paralleled in many respects the introduction of rock 'n' roll. This other phenomenon was something called a "teenager." Somehow, before the 1950s, children just seemed to walk into a dark closet at some prearranged time in their lives and, like a caterpillar doing strange metamorphosis inside a cocoon, when the door opened they walked out as miniature adults. There was no middle ground. There was infancy, childhood, young adulthood, adulthood and then into the twilight zones of middle age and beyond.

For many reasons, perhaps the most important being the economics of the era wherein young people were a new money source businesses could aim at, the 1950s saw the emergence of a new class in society. The term "teenager" became a quick and easy way of referring to those children on the way to adulthood who were in junior or senior high school, and who seemed to have suddenly popped up everywhere doing the jitterbug and piling a dozen of their awkward, developing bodies into a $75 wreck resurrected from some junkyard—for the purpose of getting in the way of adults who had lives to live and jobs to do.

When rock 'n' roll hit, the new breed, the teenagers, had been primed for it. Besides being outlaws from the traditional social structures, they now had a unique sort of music that was 100% their own. No more Frank Sinatra or Frankie Laine or Tony Bennett borrowed from the previous generation's life-style; it was more like the college crowd of the 1920s—faddish, outlandish clothes, jive talk, hanging out and fun, fun, fun.

Besides the obvious war dances of rock 'n' roll, and the teenage costumes of black jackets and tight sweaters, tight pants and ruby red lipstick, there was another ritual borrowed from ancient and primitive societies. There was the matter of getting from point A to point B.

In certain societies fortunate enough to have domesticated horses, the great turning point in a boy's life comes when he is judged old enough, smart enough, and strong enough to set out on a hunt by himself to track down, capture and train the horse that would be his transportation as a man. The horse made the man when the boy was ready.

In America of the 1950s, with prosperity allowing adults to purchase more and more new automobiles, the used-car lots of America were backing up with languishing horsepower that the law in most states allowed to be reined in by young men (and women) who had reached the age of 16. With money in their pockets and parents who were operating under the philosophy of "I had to suffer as a kid, and now that I've got money I'm going to see that my kid doesn't have to put up with what I had to," there was an influx of teenagers becoming men at age 16 whether they were ready or not for their first mount. It became a ritual that on the 16th birthday the keys were solemnly placed in the sweaty palm of a pimple-faced little tyke who suddenly became incredibly mobile—more mobile than any 16 year-old in history.

This ritual did not encompass every 16-year-old, of course, because the majority of the parents saw their child driving his or her own car as a sure case of putting a gun to the kid's head and pulling the trigger. There were enough teenagers who did get cars at 16, however, to make most of the generation mobile.

In one decade, the youth of America was knocked off its feet or snatched from the seat of its bicycle and put on wheels that ran by internal combustion power—power that required

merely the exercise of turning a key with the right hand and stepping on a pedal with the right food. With the increasing prominence of automatic transmissions, it was possible to drive a car without ever using the left foot, and using the left arm only as a means of waving the left hand at friends on a cruise through town.

Like most teenagers of the late 1950s and early '60s, I very badly wanted a car. But even though my brother and I both had part-time jobs and had the money to buy a clunker, our parents refused to give us permission to make the big jump from foot-soldiers of the teenage army to a mobile division. We bummed rides from friends whose parents were more liberal minded. Our contribution, of course, was buying the gasoline to power the battered beast through a weekend of anxiously anticipated debauchery to neighborhood towns that never seemed to work out and that usually ended up as a tour of the country with frequent stops for burgers and pizza.

For the most part, though, we walked—and sometimes ran. Hell, it was that glorious age that none of us appreciate until it's over. You have the energy to accomplish feats that now seem comparable to Superman leaping tall buildings or Lindbergh flying the Atlantic.

A typical Friday or Saturday night for my brother and me when our automobile connection had a heavy date was to walk back and forth from the Olympian Dairy-Mart, the hangout on the extreme east side of town; down six blocks to Joe Brown's Newsstand, another hangout; over two blocks to the Baby Doll Pizzeria; then down five blocks to the bridge that crossed the Lehigh River; over the bridge to Jim Thorpe proper to check out Pete's Newsstand, and on up Broadway to Dugan's Cigar Store; from there up the Back Hills behind the Capitol Theater (which had been closed by this point in our lives) to the Heights, a nearly vertical climb of about a thousand feet, to check out the playgrounds and Corky Witt's store where some of the kids from the Heights hung out; then down Centre Avenue to what was known as the Donkey Path, a nearly vertical drop of a thousand feet that brought us back to the bridge, where we'd cross it and retrace our steps back to the Baby Doll, Joe Brown's and ultimately the Olympian. The Olympian had a big gravel parking lot where we could sometimes get a lift to Lehighton, the next town down the road, after refueling on pizza and root beer.

We'd make the circuit on foot, sometimes as often as three times in a night. We developed formidable calves, massive appetites and walked off much of the emotional frustration that was building up in bodies looking for some action.

This was partially because, like many small towns, our high school had only three sports in which to expend all that extra emotional and physical energy: football, basketball and baseball.

It is better not to talk about baseball. No one in school even knew who was on the team. It was sort of a phantom team that somehow showed up in its uniforms on our very rough baseball diamond behind the high school and went through the motions of somehow representing JTHS against other similar teams. It was a phantom team because none of us ever got close enough to the baseball diamond to see who was hiding under the caps. We'd long since gone sour on organized baseball. If it wore uniforms and carried a bat and glove, it was suspect. Real baseball to us was a bunch of kids choosing sides, running their low-cut sneakers ragged, trying to swing bats two pounds too heavy for them, featuring half the team without gloves and a hardball covered with electrician's tape. Any other kind of baseball (excluding professional ball, which began to go to hell in a golfcart after Mickey Mantle and Richie Ashburn retired) was counterfeit and avoided.

Football at our school was something of a joke. Our team was traditionally undersized, it had no depth, we were in no organized league so that all games on the schedule had to be quilted together from open dates on the schedules of other teams (many of whom had three and four times our student body and whose linemen were always twice our size), and we had some seasons where it was a moral victory to get on the scoreboard. When we occasionally found another emerging school in some rural county that was as bad at the game as we were, we treated them with all due respect—just to make sure they stayed on our schedule.

Our football field was subject to drainage problems. The corner of the field where the linemen practiced (I was a 147-pound tackle) was the same corner of the field where kids came at night to break their soft drink bottles when they didn't want to take them back to Joe Brown's store for the deposit. To complicate things, none of our equipment fit, so when we ran we rattled and parts of our uniforms fell off. And we did run, sometimes for hours.

We were required to run wind-sprints down the field, two players at a time. The one who got to the other end first without losing his hip-pad didn't have to repeat the exercise.

The loser had to jog back to the upper end of the field and start all over again against someone else. We also had to do laps of our "track" when we goofed up. Some of us goofed up on purpose, because if we got a couple of us clunking along in our pads and jock and too-large football cleats, we could spend a good half-hour shooting the breeze while the rest of the team continued to pound the crap out of each other.

For those of us who weren't too fond of getting thumped and thumping back, plodding along around the rough dirt road that circled the field was like a vacation. It was meant as

punishment, but we saw it as a reward for being too smart to stay there in the glass-pit and get scarred up. One of our football coaches, in signing our senior yearbooks, went so far as to put this cryptic admonition under his picture: "One More Lap! The punishment that refreshed."

Our town was a basketball town—a small school, yes, but with all the moves. In the early 1960s, the basketball team won the state championship in its class and the following year got to the last game before losing by one point when a player from Rothrock, seeing the clock run out and his team down by a point, took a lucky throw from midcourt and sunk it. He shot with his eyes closed.

Basketball was big because, well, there wasn't much else to do. There were schools all over town because, before the early 1950s, the town had been two separate towns that had separate school systems. Playgrounds abounded, and every playground had at least one basketball net. Guys would be running up and down those basketball courts from morning to night in summer. Games would go on two and three hours after darkness came, because the guys had been playing on that court for so long they knew by instinct where the basket was; the sound of the big round ball striking the chain net (chain nets were used because rope nets wore out too fast) indicated whether it had gone through or had merely brushed the sides.

During the middle 1960s, though, the authorities began putting chain-link fences up around the playgrounds to keep kids out during hours when the schools were not in operation. The town's basketball prowess correspondingly went flaccid.

Although track-and-field was a recognized spring-time sport in schools surrounding our little town, it was never instituted as a sport at our school. The nearest we came to track-and-field was in the annual intraclass track meet, for which we practiced two weeks during gym classes. Because the town was surrounded by mountains and because most of the kids had spent their childhood walking from one end of town to the other to find a baseball game or to meet some kid for a hike or to get into some mischief, there were some good natural runners. Most of us had played enough outlaw baseball at the high school field, too, that we knew where the swamp was in the third turn of the track, so we lost very few runners during the intraclass meet. Those we lost were usually sophomores, anyway, and the battle for points was always between the juniors and seniors.

Those meets were quite an occasion, because the entire

school got a period away from class to sit on the bleachers to cheer or jeer us on. The best kind of crowd is a crowd that's happy to be there, because they're getting away from something less tasteful. Our audience then, for our one track meet a year, was larger than the audience we'd have had at a full schedule of interscholastic meets.

The lack of a track team at Jim Thorpe Area Junior-Senior High School raised a nagging question in my mind that has never been answered. The question, in talking with other people who've grown up in small towns and who also went to small schools without the benefit of a track team, seems to be raised frequently—but with no logical answers. Why was there no track team?

A track team takes an incredibly small investment from the school board—certainly much less than a basketball team. What's needed? Some shoes, matching shirts, gym trunks (which the kids already have), a few hurdles, jock straps for those who want or need them, and a place to run, a coach and some volunteers to officiate and to drive the team to away meets. Track allows for a variety of talents to be used in non-contact sport—sprinting, running, jumping; things that come natural and that, at least in a small town where it's practical to walk or run from one end of the town to the other, are probably already highly developed. A cross-country team takes even less material and time, and doesn't even require a track; it also offers an alternative to football in the fall.

The problem, at least in our town, seemed to be that the school board never bothered to ask the students what sports they wanted. It had always been the ball games and so it would remain, despite the fact that the town had been named after Jim Thorpe, one of the greatest track-and-field men in history. (The representation of old Jim that was most seen in our town was of him posed with a football uniform wrapped around his broad shoulders; maybe someone thought it would be in bad taste to picture Jim Thorpe in a sleeveless shirt and shorts.)

It was rather sad, really. The lack of track passed over the possibility of getting students who weren't involved in other sports to involve themselves in *some* sport—especially since many of them had developed certain natural tendencies toward the disciplines of track. Sad, too, because caught at the age when running and jumping and sprinting and doing long-distance walking and jogging are on the threshold of being discouraged by the increased interest in becoming super-mobile by owning a car, we were never encouraged to continue to develop an interest in track-related sports.

There was a paradox present: Although many of our parents refused to allow us to have automobiles, they never really encouraged us to develop mobility within our own bodies. We were told to walk, but we were never encouraged to run. Running was still thought of as an unseemly thing to do. As children, we were told to walk, don't run. As teenagers, we were encouraged to accept the values of our parents (which included depending on a car) and were further discouraged from running—even by coaches in high school, who continued to see running as a punishment for doing badly in some other sport.

It was unnatural, in its way, for my brother and me to run up the mountain behind our house, clamber down the other side and then run *around* the mountain to get back home—just because it was there. Luckily, no one ever saw us do it, although our parents would occasionally ask us where we were going. When we'd tell them, their comment would be: "That's a pretty silly thing to do," or "What do you want to do that for?' We didn't quite understand why we wanted to do it, and we'd been taught not to argue with our parents, so we'd just shrug our shoulders and be off for a wasted afternoon.

I'll always have to wonder, though, growing up in that environment with all those mountains and all those miles covered on foot as kids, whether if we had fielded a track team we would have gone as far as the basketball players who could drop balls into baskets in the dark.

Chapter Three

Days of Books and Beer

*C*ollege in the middle 1960s was something of an experience—even at a small, state-run, mid-Pennsylvania institution. On the first day of school in the fall of 1964, it didn't look as though it was going to be much more than a pleasant four years. There was no intimation that next April there would be one of the first East Coast sit-ins protesting everything from restrictive curfews for women to banning, by school officials for the students' own safety, the use of skateboards on the hilly campus; or that within the next two years an outlaw underground alternative newspaper would appear on the campus that the official newspaper would support and that the administration would attempt to squash by infringing on its First Amendment rights; or that the school would grow from 1800 students in 1964 to 3200 in 1968; or that guys would begin marrying whomsoever they could find in order to stay away from the draft that wanted to send them away to a country they'd never even heard of and had no right being in if they did get drafted.

The first weeks were taken up with what's called Orientation. At other colleges, it's called hazing or initiation or Freshman Month or whatever. What it means is that there are these naive, stupid, cattle-like freshmen students coming into school who thought they were big deals in high school because they were seniors and at the top of the totem-pole, but now they're back down on the bottom of the pole and the upperclassmen (and in particular the sophomores, who went through this ritual the previous year) go out of their way to make sure they realize it.

Of the roughly 900 freshmen students at Bloomsburg State

College in the fall of 1964—900 students that the dean of education told us would be whittled down to 300 by the time graduation ceremonies rolled around in 1968—some began jumping ship during the Orientation phase. We began believing that at this rate, the dean of education's estimates were a bit conservative.

Bloomsburg State College was a part of the 14-college Pennsylvania State College educational system. The system had originally been established to train teachers for the Pennsylvania public school system but had begun initiating liberal arts into the curriculum around 1960 because there was a change in emphasis in the state-supported educational system. As with all governmental organizations, however, the 14-college system was sluggish in coming out of its teacher-education mode. As teacher factories, the colleges had specialized. A few of them were very heavily into physical education, specifically West Chester State, East Stroudsburg State and Loch Haven State. Bloomsburg State College's specialties were special education and business education.

Despite this de-emphasis on sports, some of the Bloomsburg teams did very well—especially the wrestling team. It helped, though, that the czar of physical education in 1964 was Russ Hock, one of the US Olympic wrestling coaches, and BSC's wrestling and football coach. Coach Hock made his teams feel they were equal to or better than their opponents, and often they were. Unfortunately, they also felt they were better than the run-of-the-mill student, continually taking their place at the front of every line that formed on campus. Every other sport at the school was, if not de-emphasized, at least overshadowed by wrestling and football. Women's sports were confined to field hockey. Running sports were not only overshadowed, but in fact literally buried.

On an October Saturday morning, in order to escape the blues of Orientation and the depression of a chilly, dark-cloud-scudded sky, I wandered to the lonely upper portion of the campus—that bleak place where the president lived and where any future physical development of the campus would commence, as soon as the legislature could vote the funds. I was walking toward the upper campus because I'd read in the school newspaper that there was going to be a cross-country meet at 10 a.m., and, having come from a high school that did not even offer track, I was curious to see how cross-country was run. (Additionally, I'd read in the paper where the annual intramural cross-country meet was going to be held during the next week. Since I'd placed first in the half-mile in our annual high school intraclass track meet, I thought that if it didn't look too difficult, I'd give it a crack.)

I kept my eyes peeled for the crowd that would be gathered to watch the cross-country meet. But as I reached the gym and the parking lot beyond, where the affair was supposed to start, I found nothing except two guys in a deserted corn field doing some warmup running. The weather began to turn brisk, the clouds darkened, and the first flakes of snow for the upcoming winter presented themseves. It was a damned bleak day to have guys out running around in their underwear. I crawled down farther into my windbreaker, letting my eyes peek above the collar.

A few more guys wandered out from the warm gym and began doing exercises in their sweatsuits. The opposing team was doing its exercises down at the far edge of the gym, on a small patch of grass. Everyone looked pretty serious and dismal. It was almost 10 o'clock, and there was still no crowd. I began to think that maybe the meet was being held somewhere else, that a bus would come to take the teams to the real course, and that I'd be left behind because I'd been a dumb, naive freshman and didn't have any idea where the crowd was supposed to gather.

A few moments later, a guy wrapped up much like I was approached and asked if I was a student here. I mumbled that I was, afraid that maybe it was a secret meet and no students were allowed to watch it. Without another word, the guy grabbed my arm and pulled me toward a battered 1962 Rambler. I was too chilly by that time to take my hands out of my pockets to defend myself. I was sure he was taking me to the campus security office and that I'd be before the dean within the hour.

Instead, he drove me out Lightstreet Road, reached across me and opened the door a second before the hulk screeched to a halt, pushed me out while pulling a stick with a red flag on it from the back seat and tossing it to me.

"When they come up this road," he said, pointing back in the direction from which we'd just come, "point the flag in that direction." He indicated the direction of Interstate 80, several miles away. "Then, when they come back this road, you point them down there." As his car wheezed and shivered in the building wind, he pointed behind me to a foreboding country road that cut off Lightstreet Road and went downhill at a steep angle, disappearing into a grove of trees. Where it went from there, I had no idea. Being a dumb freshman I nodded my head in agreement to his commands.

Shivering in my corduroy jeans and windbreaker, I began questioning the meaning of life as the snow flakes whipped around me. I moved the stick with the flag from one hand to the other, giving the free hand time to warm up in my pocket before pushing it out into the cold again. I stood there for what seemed like hours, wanting to run across the road to the bushes to relieve myself but afraid that while I was there, "they" would come by and find themselves faced with a decision of direction that only I could solve for them.

Finally, way off down the road, I saw little figures working their way toward me. I forgot about my own discomfort for a moment, took my position, gritted my teeth against the cold wind and pointed my flag down Lightstreet Road. The two sets of runners, our guys and their guys, filed past at ever-decreasing speeds. It seemed remotely exciting to be part of this grand thing. Coming up behind them was the battered Rambler. The guy who'd shanghaied me waved and continued to follow the field. I had no idea how long it would take for them to come back, but I could see at least a half-mile down the road and knew they weren't coming yet. I ran across the road, took care of business and was back in plenty of time to freeze some more.

Finally, the field began coming back toward me. The runners were very much strung out, and their breath was making clouds in front of their faces like horses do. We had a guy in the lead, but our second-place guy was way back in sixth place. I pointed my flag down the lonely country road that went god-knows-where and consigned them to their fate—one by one, glassy-eyed, ragged-breathed people filing past oblivious to the snow falling around them.

It seemed to take forever for the roughly 14 guys to make it past my point. And sure enough, still following them was the Rambler that looked as though it was having trouble keeping up with their pace. Again, the guy in the car waved at me and smiled around gritted teeth. He didn't make the turn down the country road but continued down Lightstreet Road, back to the college. I put the flag under my arm and shoved my hands back into my pockets, bouncing around in an attempt to keep frostbite from my toes. I didn't know whether I should wait or go back to the school on foot. I waited—and waited.

Finally, the Rambler chugged up the hill again, and the guy collected me. I later learned that he was concerned that I'd run off with his flag. I also learned later that Coach Senor Brady was always as bizarre as he was that day. I immediately decided that if I was going to freeze my butt off for the old maroon and gold, I was going to do it while I ran rather than standing around waiting to be found in the spring.

Cross-country is, at the best of times, a lonely sport. At a college where the athletic director is only vaguely aware that there is a cross-country team, and where he wouldn't think of recruiting runners even if he were coaching the team himself, it was also a strange sport to which a bizarre mixture of people gravitated. From the coach on down, the team was two points west of strange.

We never knew how Coach Senor Brady got involved with the team. Maybe he raised his hand to scratch his head at a faculty meeting and found himself cross-country coach or something. He didn't seem very athletic, although he took all of us rather seriously, as though we had been appropriated for him and he was bound to return us in as good a condition as he received us, or perhaps even better. He taught Spanish, and each summer he would hop into his battered car and head south of the border—either to Mexico or farther south to one of the South American countries where he could practice his Spanish and raise hell with no one knowing where he was from, other than that he was a gringo who knew where the action was.

From negotiating the mountain roads in every Spanish-speaking country in the Western Hemisphere, the old Rambler had terminal shimmy. Everything shimmied. The shock Colombia, the front end alignment had seemingly been kicked apart by some rabid donkey along a Mexico trail, and we always kidded Senor Brady that he never got the car fixed because he was lazy, that the shimmying steering wheel wound his self-wind watch.

Fair-haired Senor Brady was no fool when he went to southern climates to speak some Spanish, though. He wasn't about to get caught with his pants down like Humphrey Bogart did at the watering hole in the conclusion of "The Treasure of Sierra Madre." No way, hombre! Senor Brady traveled with a .45 under his shimmying Rambler seat. When not using it to discourage pesky bandits down south of the border who tried to prey on him as his wheezing car struggled up mountain passes, he'd use it to pick off groundhogs that sat along the side of the Pennsylvania highways as we shimmied along to cross-country meets early Saturday mornings. He'd pull out the gun when he saw a groundhog minding its business along the right side of the road, put the gun out his window, aim across the windshield and *blam!* . . . a groundhog would take the eternal sleep on each three out of five attempts.

Like my high school football team, our college cross-country team was almost required to overturn rocks to find opponents to fill the schedule. We added Pennsylvania teams like Susquehanna and Kings College and Bucknell, and some state college from New Jersey to our schedule to beef it up. There were only so many other teams in the Pennsylvania State College system who were willing to lower their standards and run against us.

We occasionally won a dual meet. In fact, one year our team took second place in the state championships. But we all knew those things were flukes and accidents. Our real mettle showed in our teamwork and our dedication to preserving the life and limb of the next guy on the team rather than in our efforts to be winners. The most flagrant example of heroism came at a meet against Kings College in Wilkes-Barre.

Now, Wilkes-Barre is a precarious town built along a river that has a tendency to overflow its banks. In order to discourage this practice, there are levees built along both sides of the river. Just across the river, on the western side, is Kingston. Kings College took the Kings thing to heart and laid out its cross-country course along the Kingston levees. They also arranged to borrow the town park's storage room for the visiting cross-country team's locker room. The room featured a nice selection of used gardening equipment, spiders the size of toupees and two showers that, because of the dampness, were apparently being used by some biology students as a culture try for algae and mold samples.

It had been raining all Friday night and was still raining Saturday morning. The trip up to Wilkes-Barre had been dismal. The rain was keeping the groundhogs in their burrows, and Senor Brady was despondent. After changing with the spiders watching us and feeling as though we were clammy enough to be dead, we piled back into the cars (the cross-country budget was something like $600 for the year, so we traveled in Senor Brady's car and a second car if we could borrow it) and headed for the levees. The rain had made the land fronting the levees a quagmire. It was very cold, there was a wind of about eight miles per hour, and some of the puddles had pretensions to becoming small lakes. We saw a bad race ahead.

The course was two laps through the valley of swamp, up over the levee, along the town side of it, back up over the levee and through the valley again. On the second run through the valley—after finding it almost impossible to get up the grass-covered banks of the levee but possible to bring enough Kings College runners down with us into the mud to keep the race about even—our number two runner, Big Charlie, decided that it was time to make his move and pass a guy who wasn't giving him room to pass. Charlie decided to get around the guy by running through one of the puddles. (He knew he couldn't get his shoes any more wet than they were. We were issued good shoes and uniforms from the track team supply room on the day of the meet, you see, and the guy in The Cage at the college locker room made sure to instill in us the knowledge that these pieces of equipment would have to last through about 10 years of use before the next requisition came down.)

Charlie made his move while Chuck Bowman and I approached the puddle, figuring to skirt it as we'd all done on the first lap. As Charlie began sending up a spray with his high-dollar shoes, figuring to be past the Kingsman by the time he reached the other side, he suddenly realized that maybe he'd made a bad move. It was one of those situations where the mouse knows as the snake's coils tighten around it that maybe

it just isn't his day. Well over six feet tall, Big Charlie was now 5'6", then 4'9", then 3'4". The dark waters were closing around Big Charlie, and he was still making running motions, hoping that his momentum would carry him across the puddle before the puddle closed in over his head. He was only halfway across.

Chuck "The Preacher" Bowman and I took only a moment to scurry about collecting branches and sticks we could stretch out to Charlie as Ramar of the Jungle did every Saturday morning when trying to pull something from a quicksand pit. We finally found a branch long enough to reach Big Charlie, and we began pulling him across the surface of the clammy pool.

"Oooooh" was the only thing Charlie was uttering.

"Ooooooooooh!" he said to us as we dragged him from the pool, where black slime had covered his maroon-and-gold uniform. "Oooooh!" he said, and before we could restrain him, he was back in the race, apparently trying to get warm by running. He got one of the two showers all to himself back at the mold room. All the way back to school, he sat wrapped up in a blanket in the back seat of the rattling Rambler saying, "Oooooooh!" over and over.

Although it did not take us long to realize our place—or lack of place—in the athletic scheme of things at Bloomsburg State College, we tried our best to have the spirit and supportive stance for the football team that are necessary to form the brotherhood of collegiate athletes. We sort of felt bad when, given the status of professional wrestlers, we were occasionally billed as the football team's halftime entertainment—while the crowd left their seats to get a hotdog or neck under the bleachers.

It worked like this: Whenever possible, our athletic director (football coach) would squeeze one of our cross-country meets into the traveling schedule of the football team. Apparently, Coach Hock had gone to too many Olympic Games and was fascinated with how they ended the marathon in the stadium so that the last, painful quarter-mile of the race would be within full view of the assembled multitudes. In any case, some of our trips corresponded with the football team's trips. We were not taken along on the football team's bus, though. We weren't even taken along on fan buses; we were sent on our way in Senor Brady's Rambler and whatever second car we could scrounge up. We weren't allowed to change in the football team's dressing room, either, because we were much lower on the totem pole.

I believe it was at Cheyney State College, down in the south-eastern portion of Pennsylvania, the predominantly Negro state college in our conference, where we had to hike to an upper portion of the campus and change around the corner of a building, literally out in the open air. The start of the race was timed so that it would finish its tour of the local country roads just as the band got done giving its halftime entertainment. Cheyney had a cross-country team that traditionally had very little depth, but that had two or three first-class runners who could really take off. I was always fascinated by their methods of running, which included lacing little bells to their shoes so that they could more easily judge their pace by sound.

Midway through the race, in my usual middle-of-the-pack position, I keyed on the back of a Cheyney runner 10 yards in front of me. For the rest of the race, it became a battle of inches as I came up on his shoulder just as we made the turn from the street into the football field. In true Olympic fashion, we had to make a tour of the track once inside. Since they hadn't given us a tour of the course in advance, I'd saved more than I should have, and when we hit the track I began a feeble attempt at a kick that put me up next to my quarry.

I still don't know whether it was because halftime was really boring and they wanted something to liven things up, but as we rounded the track to head down the backstretch to the finish line a dozen Cheyney coeds began cheering *me* on. Now, cheering to a cross-country team that would have been able to fit its entire season's crowd into a telephone booth was all that was needed. With a spurt, I edged the home-teamer at the finish line. Unfortunately, as I did, I turned to glance at the vanquished, and he wasn't any too happy about the outcome.

Faking as though I were doing a cooldown jog, I went past my cheering section, got a round of applause and ran right into our football team coming back onto the field. Since I wasn't wearing a football uniform and was as thin as a car antenna, they didn't see me and I got knocked out of the way—only to be saved from being trampled into the turf by Ed Niege, the team's most ferocious lineman who was in the same drawing class I was in and who was probably one of the most sensitive guys on campus when out of uniform. My Cheyney opponent, who'd been stalking me at a safe distance, saw Niege and casually walked the other way. I wonder if he ever got back with his girlfriend.

Even though football players wouldn't walk across campus to see us run, the cross-country team wasn't so lax in its faithfulness to the maroon-and-gold. One beautiful fall Saturday morning, we "entertained" the Loch Haven State College cross-country team on our course, which ended in a half-mile hill. By entertaining, I mean we allowed them to beat us because they were our guests. We were a very hospitable team. After our showers, we went down-campus to the college lounge to have a Coke and to celebrate Preacher Bowman's accomplishments—he'd run the best race of his cross-country career, and, although we'd lost as a team, we easily shared in Preacher's victory.

Unfortunately, when we walked into the lounge there was no one there. Everyone had left campus to go to the football game at Mansfield State. Our elation over Preacher's accomplishment faded. Being in possession of a VW micro-bus and being a little daggy to start with, I suggested that we get aboard my wreck and make our own fan bus. Everyone was so senseless from the beating we'd taken and the loneliness we'd found in the lounge that they agreed.

Now, a VW micro-bus, especially a 1963 VW micro-bus, was nothing short of an analogy of our cross-country team: it was top-heavy, awkward, didn't handle in the slightest breeze, and it was underpowered. With a 35-horsepower motor, it could just about reach 35 m.p.h. on a level road with a strong tailwind. Unfortunately, there were some formidable hills to climb on the way to Williamsport before we proceeded on to our destination. We almost had to let some of the guys off to push us up the hills. Going down the other side, we found that not only did the bus have a bad motor; it also had bad brakes. We made note of that fact for the trip back, where we'd have to go down the hill we'd just struggled up. Our descent into Williamsport did have its compensations, however. We got the bus up to a personal record of 56 m.p.h. (Fortunately, Preacher Bowman was from Williamsport—or Billtown, at the natives call it—and he got us through side streets that helped us make up a few minutes.)

We arrived at the football game in time to hear the kick-off as we were buying our tickets. After a pretty dry first half, BSC edged ahead and won the game. Everyone was in a victorious mood, so we decided to get the hell out of there to beat the buses from the school to a place to eat. Preacher led us to a great spot in Williamsport, and we were on the way out of town just as the fan buses came through.

Our feeble-motored bus climbed the hill out of Billtown at an incredibly slow pace. The fan buses were catching up. The team was egging me on as we topped the hill and tipped down the other side. One of the buses had built up too much momentum, and it caught us as we began to build up speed.

"It passed!" yelled Vic Keeler, our expert on heel bruises.

I mutely shook my head, trying to keep our bus on the road as the wind from the passing monster tried to dislodge us from the side of the mountain.

We were picking up speed, being sucked along behind the big fan bus, sucking up diesel exhaust fumes that seemed to be making our engine cough.

"Oh no!" Vic Keeler called from the back. "The other one's caught us."

Indeed, the lights of the second fan bus had pulled up on our rear end, and Vic was trying in vain to signal them to give us more room. Preacher Bowman was kneeling on the floor, asking for a passage into the Big Gates for all of us when we got clobbered. Big Charlie was sprawled across one of the seats; he'd eaten too many hot cinnamon rolls at the restaurant we'd just left, and he didn't know if he was going to be sick from having played glutton or from plain, unadulterated, old-fashioned fear. Dick Yost sat in the front passenger's seat trying to hold his eyes shut but too curious to manage it.

"I'll try to get out into the passing lane so the bus back there can close up," I said.

The suction from the bus in front of us had our bus up to 61 m.p.h., an unheard-of speed for a breadbox on wheels with about as much stability. I tried to turn the bus into the passing lane and safety. It wouldn't go, even though the steering wheel was turned all the way left. The combination of the two huge buses had created a vacuum between them, and we were trapped. There were all kinds of moaning and groaning going on behind me, but I was too busy to check what it was. I heard Preacher's cries of lamentation above all else, and it was a comforting sound in the maelstrom.

"He-he's passing us!" Vic sputtered.

Sure enough, the bus behind us was making its move. When it moved into the passing lane, it disrupted the very tenacious vacuum that had been holding us between them. I fought the wheel to try and find a point where the front tires would establish some traction on the road surface.

As the fan bus pulled alongside, some of the students saw who it was in the micro-bus and they began waving and laughing and giving school cheers, totally unaware of our acquaintance with death. The brakes on the bus began to smell, but mercifully with the bus behind us past, they also began to bring our speed down. We wrenched our way out of the first bus's draft. By dropping the VW into a lower gear, we slowed and pulled off the road. Big Charlie was into the woods before the thing stopped. Preacher Bowman began offering prayers of thanksgiving. Vic Keeler, for one of the first times in his life, was completely silent, and Dick Yost, who hadn't uttered a word during the whole episode, summed it all up:

"I never liked football."

He probably spoke for most of us. At that point in my life, I was as bored by football as I'd always been—even when I'd played it in high school. Within a year, I'd be actively hating my high school football career. . . if collecting splinters can be called a career.

My college cross-country running had not been punctuated by any great accomplishments. I sometimes finished near the middle of the field and picked up more points than I'd have liked. More often, however, I was struggling in toward the end, my race punctuated by acute pains in the sides at any speed above a walk.

My solution to the problem was more training. I was merely out of shape and needed more time on the road, more miles, more workouts. It was fairly easy to get what I thought I needed. There were the afternoon workouts with the team, which included a brace of calisthetics and stretches (Senor Brady was not familiar with any of the great coaches of the time, but he did believe that a warmed-up body was a properly-functioning body), some interval work under the leader-ship of our captain to warm us further and then a quarter-mile run across Lightstreet Road to the golf course, a deserted country club that had been purchased by the college years before as the site of future campus development.

The golf course wasn't your usual rolling-hill kind of place—it was like a saddle over the back of a horse, occupying the top of a rather pretentious hill. Our afternoon workouts often took us to that hill, where we did repeat sprints up the dirt road leading to the top until the sprints had degenerated into drunken staggers. After nearing the point of complete exhaustion, we'd make one more run to the top and hang a right to cross the crest of the hill, connecting with a back road farther down the hills where we could come back toward the campus along Lightstreet Road.

In addition, it was almost always possible to hook up with one or two of the guys for a night run, which usually came about eight o'clock, after our evening meal had time to settle and when the drivers were less likely to see us in our gray and red training outfits. We'd run four or five miles, shooting the bull and dodging cars that chased us back onto the shoulders of the road without even having the satisfaction of knowing they were doing it. I also managed to sneak in a morning run, hoping that the three workouts a day would put me into some kind of condition that would get rid of the cramps in my sides. Occasionally, the stitches would occur during workouts, but they mostly saved themselves for racing conditions. My three workouts never did seem to overcome my conditioning short-comings.

An additional complication arose from my three separate workouts—besides the fact that my roommate couldn't stand to be in the same room with my sweaty training uniform. My style, by the evening run every day, deteriorated terribly. By Saturday when the race rolled around, I'd use up every re-maining ounce of energy just to keep up with the mid-pack runners. Our course was a pretty complicated affair, with plenty of hills to go up and down. The downhills were my un-doing.

At the point where I'd been shanghaied to hold the direc-tional flag during my freshman year, the course dropped several hundred feet in the space of three-quarters of a mile. Coming around the turn to go shooting downhill, it was imperative that a runner hold his speed back or face catastrophe if he ever encountered a pebble that might throw off his stride. A tumble along that gravel road, and he'd be out of running for the rest of his life. Consequently, it was necessary to put the brakes on just a mite. The strain of the feet sliding forward in our Adidas and Puma running shoes, which we weren't allowed to wear during the week for fear of wearing them out, gave us classic textbook cases of black toenails.

Perhaps, if we'd have been allowed to train in our Adidas and Puma shoes, we could have become used to them and could have made proper modifications to them, but that was unheard of. We had enough trouble getting the track uniforms signed out for a meet, much less being allowed to wear good shoes during the week just for training runs. Those downhills gave me a complete set of black toenails. One by one, they dried out and fell off. All except one grew back.

The great toe on my left foot refused to come in correctly. After four trips to a general practitioner who fed me aspirins and then cut away some of the toenail while I sat in a chair holding onto the underside of it so I wouldn't go through the roof, and after three similar unsuccessful attempts by a foot specialist to do the same thing (the foot specialist had a nicer chair for me to hang onto and he charged more), I decided to go to a surgeon. A year and a half of butchering my toe and spending an hour before races freezing my foot in ice just so I could run poorly in races was getting to me.

Over the Easter vacation in my senior year, the surgeon put me on the table, put me to sleep, fixed the toe, and it's been perfect since then—although it's minus 20% of the nail. In the rather thorough examination the surgeon, a gigantic bull of a man with purple skin and fingers the size of Polish sausages, gave me prior to doing the surgery, found that I had two rather veteran hernias that should have been causing me distress.

"Have you been having pains in the sides?" he asked.

"Sure have," I answered.

"These have been here a while," he said. "Did you do any heavy lifting or straining some years ago?" he continued.

"I supposed I did," I said.

"We'll fix them for you as soon as you get through college."

Heavy lifting? I tried to envision what kind of heavy lifting I'd done prior to the stitches in my side. For the first few days following the knowledge I had double hernias, I didn't manage to dredge up the source. Then, back at school, making some jokes about playing football in high school, it came out. Our coach, always looking for some edge to benefit a very under-sized squad, had read somewhere about isometric contractions. He latched onto it like a cat onto a screen door.

Unfortunately, he didn't bother doing any research into what the proper method of doing isometric contractions was. His incredibly brilliant method of getting the entire team to do 15 minutes of isometric contractions per day that would turn them into a race of gorillas was to have us line up under the bleachers, extend our hands above our heads until they contacted the undersides of the seats, and then, at his count, to push against the bleachers with all our strength until we became blue in the face. It made some of us walk like gorillas afterward, but it never really turned any of us into creatures of incredible brute strength. It also did a mighty good job of popping a pair of hernias. I never pass a set of bleachers with-out thinking horrible thoughts at them. As it would turn out, I'd seldom again watch a sporting event from bleachers.

Fortunately, under non-race conditions the hernia problem did not occur as regularly. Something about the competi-tion—perhaps the tension and apprehension that the hernias *were* going to flare up under race conditions—seemed to bring them out as regularly as day turns to night and one race follows another on the schedule. Three-a-day training with calisthetics in the afternoon session probably did not greatly improve the condition. By the fall of 1968—in fact, during the 1968 Olympics—the hernias would be excised.

Back at the campus, though, there had been something big going on that would keep me interested in running beyond an arena in which to meet other people as marginally sane as myself.

On Saturday mornings when we had no cross-country meet scheduled, or when cross-country season was over for the year or had not yet begun, I developed a ritual of taking a casual, solitary 18-mile run. Leaving the campus by Lightstreet Road,

I'd sort of pretend that I was a car and was going on a trip. I-80 had only recently been opened, and apparently no one had told the motorists of Pennsylvania about it. There were a few semi tractor-trailers using it and some Greyhound buses but very few cars. There was a very, very wide shoulder that was paved in rough asphalt, and the roadway hadn't had time yet to accumulate obstructions like chucked retread tires from the big semis or dead rabbits and dogs or abandoned cars.

The stretch of road between Lightstreet and Route 11 was almost like a fresh snowfall; it was exquisitely peaceful and in its way refreshingly dull. Once onto Route 11, the scenery changed. Connecting Berwick and Bloomsburg, Route 11 is one of those old 1950s strips of fast-food chains, local imitations of fast-food chains, two-bit flea-bit motels with an occasional quality motel thrown in just to break up the monotony, and deteriorating concrete roadway where occasionally some weed or itinerant tree would stick its head up through the buckling cracks of road surface. A rough path ran along the side of the road, and a set of railroad tracks ran parallel, as did a sluggishly-flowing river. The closer you got to Bloomsburg, the more tightly-packed were the neon-signed attractions: car dealerships, farm equipment franchises, a gravel pit, more motels, dairy bars, an out-of-place house—Americana of the Highways.

Like some of I-80, Route 11 was incredibly straight, and on 11 the telephone poles seemed to go on forever. The boredom didn't much matter, however. On Lightstreet, I had put myself on what amounted to an automatic pilot. The slap of my training flats (they were plain black canvas with three white stripes in those days) on the asphalt was pretty much like the steady hum of an air conditioner in a motel room after a very hot afternoon. It lulled me like a seemingly gentle hand on the forehead into an otherworldliness—a sort of drumming peace that hypnotized the strictly conscious portion of me, allowing me to literally separate at the upper lip.

Everything from the mouth on down became a vehicle to carry the senses of sight and hearing and smell and general observation. It became similar to riding atop a big guy with stilts. There was the very real sense of swaying rhythmically and of moving, but it was as though from an observation plat-

48

form. We used to call it simply "separating." Some of the
other guys on the team experienced it; some didn't. Those who
didn't always thought it was some sort of in-joke the rest of us
were pulling on them. During the separation, though, there
was probably as close to a mystical experience as I've ever felt.

The first time it happened, I didn't realize it was going on
until I stopped in Bloomsburg, to cross Route 11 and head up
the hill to the college. With the stopping, there was a physical
jerking of my body as though I were running with an automatic transmission that had, with the stop, just shifted from
an overdrive gear I didn't even know I had, back down into the
gears everyone who's ever run a step in his life is very familiar
with. I can still remember standing there, on the rough grass
atop the curb, the depressing railroad tracks behind me and
traffic running past in front of me, knowing that I wanted to
cross the busy roadway when it cleared enough to make it
safe—but not being able to do it because I was preoccupied
trying to figure out just what the hell had happened.

I'd just run 18 miles in roughly 100 minutes, and most of
the run I didn't remember unless I consciously went back and
picked through my memory. I pushed myself across Route 11
and up the incredible hill that ended our cross-country course,
walked the block to my dorm and went into the shower. It was
probably one of the longest showers of my life as I tried to reconstruct, under the narcotic spray, just what I'd been doing
during the hour or so I'd been striding along I-80 and Route
11.

Little by little, I reconstructed what I'd been doing during
that time, something like an alcoholic trying to piece together
a lost weekend. I constantly surprised myself as I came up
with one thing after another that I'd covered during the run.
Thoughts strictly philosophical and ethereal, cataloging impressions and smells of animals along the road, rumina-
tions on the state of the country through reading its garbage
along the roadway, small solutions to small problems that had
been nagging me; just on and on.

I found that I'd covered more than 18 miles of the roadway
in my mind—I'd gone thousands of miles and covered several
file drawers of thoughts and problems and questions. On the
tip of my mind hovered the knowledge that I'd covered some

things that I was never, at this moment, going to be able to reconstruct—things and thoughts that I'd probably never again be able to duplicate.

I became a Saturday morning junkie, ritualistically going on my 18-mile runs. Occasionally, I'd vary the runs to try some different back roads where cars seldom went and where Saturday morning traffic was virtually nil except for a kid on a bike. I became very conscious, however, of my separations, and I looked forward to them. Then, because of my increasingly painful great toe, I began to lose stride with my Saturday runs. The separations did not come, because they need a smooth pool of running in which to ferment and grow, and my runs were becoming ragged affairs that were almost limps.

Depression set in and I began giving up my Saturday morning runs because running was becoming too painful. It was my senior year; most of it and much of my junior year had been characterized by pain caused by doctors failing to be doctors, failing to send me to someone who could take care of my pain once and for all.

The running just plain stopped because it was too painful to go on.

I thought longingly about those Saturday morning separations on occasion. But at Easter vacation, when I finally did have my toe fixed, my running was gone. I had to stay away from running several more weeks in order to allow the toe to heal properly. Graduation and its attendant concerns intervened, and so did looking for a job. Running became the last thing on my mind, and the only separation I was thinking about was separating myself from the island that a college is and set sail for the real world of the gainfully employed. The decay had begun.

Chapter Four

Got Decay,
If You Want It

*I*t seems that at some prearranged moment between leaving school and entering the real world, a plug is pulled and many of our illusions are drained away like so much used bathwater. School—whether it is high school, college, the military (for that's a form of school, too, complete with dorms and classes)—is something of a guarded island. What happens on that island does not necessarily reflect what's happening in real life—in fact, in most cases what happens there has little to do with anything. This is not said to sound cynical but to reflect a very simple observation: high school, college, the military are controlled environments, in some way attempting to help us build up safeguards and skills to survive in the real world, which is seldom as controlled.

True to human nature, most of us never realize the advantages of the controlled environment. We are anxious—very anxious—to get outside of it. We are anxious to leave behind the protection of the institutional island, because in exchange for the institution taking care of certain of our needs without our ever having to worry about them, we feel that we have to give up certain freedoms—and that ultimately we will be better off looking after ourselves, earning our own way, being our own boss.

No more going to the messhall for often unappetizing but almost always nourishing meals, or to the school cafeteria for nutritionally sound if sometimes bland trays of food. We look forward to the days when we can either prepare or buy our own foods. No more sergeants to make sure we're in bed at lights-out, and no more hall monitors to keep us under control in the dorm. When we get out into the real world, we'll take care of all those functions because we're big enough and smart enough and mature enough to handle our own lives. No more mandatory physical education classes and endless calisthetics and swimming classes; no more 20-mile hikes. Our bodies are at the height of their prowess and they'll stay that way because, hell, we're in the 18-22 age range when anything is possible, when we can go all day and go all night and never skip a beat.

We look forward to our freedom—freedom to do what we feel is in our best interest instead of having someone else decide what's best for us. We anticipate that magic moment, that climbing the wall to the land where the grass is greener, the meals are better, the nights are longer, and where we'll exercise in our own way, on our own schedule, for our own satisfaction.

The moment comes when the gates of school or the military are left behind and we're on our own. We become intoxicated with the sweet aroma of freedom. The great, wide, wonderful world is before us, and it's ours to conquer.

We enter what sociologists call the Decade of Decay.

Our prime productive years are almost unanimously used in struggle with a world we passionately embrace. We must find jobs, and once in the job we must work hard to advance so that things will be better financially and emotionally than they are now, because there are so many more-established workers above us in the organizational structures. Not all of us had a business to inherit when we reached the age of majority, so it means hard work and struggle and often strife. If marriage did not come the day after graduation or separation from the military, we enter the rituals of preparing to get married—even if we don't really know it.

During that period, our promises that we can take better care of ourselves than the institutions could become so much wishful thinking. We eat on the run, when we can, or we indulge ourselves eating junk that we would dutifully snatch out of the hands of a little brother or sister if we saw them eating it. We keep incredibly bad hours and don't even attempt to make up lost hours. The nearest we get to exercise is dancing at a night club until it closes, or going to parties and holding up a bottle of beer or a mixed drink. If marriage came quickly, we find ourselves saddled with a mortgage, a spouse, maybe a child or two and an inclination to keep the job we are holding down at the moment because we've got "responsibilities."

None of this is affecting us, though. For the first year or two, the wonders of youth spill over into the world of self-indulgence and struggling upward mobility. Like mountain-climbers making their way to a base-camp site, we feel that all is still within our grasp.

Unfortunately, like an automobile that is run without attention to oil changes and battery water levels and tire pressures, our youthful bodies (recall that we began to die the day we were born) begin to show signs of wear that a new paint job or set of clothes aren't going to hide entirely.

There is perhaps a nervous twitch developing, a reliance on cigarettes to keep the nervous hand occupied, too much caffeine in coffee and colas, maybe too much booze without proper exercise to burn the alcohol off, too much tension that has nowhere else to go but inside the nervous system. Life becomes a roller-coaster that you swear you're going to get off as soon a it slows down. Maybe you even make attempts to do something about it, taking up "sports" that will let you feel you are fighting the spreading belt-marks—sports like bowling or darts or fishing that actually expend about as much energy as sitting in front of a television watching the world go by in soap-opera fashion. They are perhaps worse for you because they provide another opportunity to eat more and smoke more and drink more; at least when dulled or asleep in front of the television the body is receiving some much-needed rest and isn't ingesting anything.

This is a dismal picture for the 18- to 22-year-old who could lick the world, who played basketball like a demon in high school, who played a wicked game of football in college, who was star of the base softball team in the military. It's a dismal picture but a common one—a picture that is not painted entirely by choice but is rendered in good part by the society in which we live, where manual labor is being downplayed and where we are headed toward more and more clerical-type jobs, where we spend our productive years servicing machines that service other people who'd be better off doing it themselves. (Fortunately, there seems to be a break in the pattern of fitting oneself into the niche society makes for us, but that does not always help those already ensnared.)

But let's back off for a moment from the dismal picture that is going to move us, like a slow-moving but determined locomotive, toward a 10th-year high school reunion, the outcome of which we already know.

Let's trace the decade of decay a little closer and see how it applies to most of us, how most of us have shared it, how one life released from the institutional life parallels another, how there is the attempt to grab a lifeline as the social structure pulls at your ankles from the depths, and how the crossroads are reached where the decision must be made to settle back into the easy chair or to get up off the spreading ass and slim down. The more Life-After-Institutionalization is different in our wide, highly-diversified country, the more each of us is a brother and sister to the experience it presents.

I don't know why I ever wanted to get out of college. I'd seen my father struggling to make ends meet and to find a job that would provide us with security—not a job he would like or that would necessarily give him some satisfaction from life. If the post-World War II period were the post-Vietnam War period, where people are more free to choose occupations, my father would have become a forest ranger or a Montana hunting guide or a prospector in Alaska, any of which would have better fit his temperament and given him at least a passing acquaintanceship with the term peace-of-mind. He'd have taken some consideration of his personal rewards from his job instead of doing what everyone after the Second World War did, which was to look for security in a world that said security was the important ingredient to happiness and never mentioned that even security may not be all that secure—especially if you can't enjoy it.

No matter how much we mutter and curse about the job we have, the largest part of our waking existence revolves around that job, and most of us bring the job home with us at night. Seeing how my father brought his job home with him every night, and how it set the tone for how the night at home was going to be, and how it only aggravated any and all short-comings his disposition might have had to start with, I decided early on to find work that I'd enjoy—even if the pay wasn't any too great.

This is a very good philosophy for peace of mind but, like the person who hates his job and comes home to settle down with the job's residual problems until it weighs him to distraction, having a job you like can help you decay just as fast—because it can get you so involved with it that it leaves little time for anything else.

I graduated from college on a Friday and the following Monday morning I walked into the newspaper offices of *The Times-News* in Lehighton, Pa., and was promptly given a key to the door by Nate Dermott, managing editor. I was also given the title of associate editor.

"Here's the key," Nate said, "take over."

Between the newspaper and a cable television closed-circuit network that the holding company owned, I found 70-hour weeks to be common. The newspaper grew like a spreading amoeba. We took over the *Lansford Record*, and in order to keep the loyalty of the Lansford readers we became *The Times-News & Record*. We took over the *Tamaqua Courier* and once again hired most of their people in order to keep good relations with the town of Tamaqua. We secured the services of Ed Gildea, an able editor, just before that takeover of the *Courier*, he had seen the writing on the wall and had jumped ship. There was talk of trying to make the newspaper's flag reflect our most recent purchase by changing it to *The Times-News, Record & Courier.*

Ed Gildea was made editor of the newspaper, and I was moved up to managing editor when Nate Dermott discovered he had cancer of the lungs and removal of one lung only delayed his death by a few months. To the holding company, which had begun newspapering only five years before, the word "managing" in my title made me higher than the editor on the totem pole, something Ed Gildea and I never discussed because we'd have gotten along beautifully if they'd have thrown us in a cage with one dog biscuit between us.

We put the local newspaper, *The Lehighton Leader,* out of business. The owner wanted us to buy them out, but we were tired of buying newspapers, so we just hired their people away when we killed their paper in order to keep good relations with the town. Someone in the back shop made up a trial flag that read: *The Times-News, Record, Courier, Leader & Fill-In-The-Blank.* The right side of the flag took a sharp right turn and ran down the extreme right column of the front page. We all thought it was funny; the owner of the holding company didn't.

Working on a newspaper back in the area I'd grown up in, and seeing what was happening to me because of my long hours on the job and little time to do anything truly physical (other than manhandle video-recording equipment), I'd made the attempt to stage a comeback. It was 1969, a year after I'd begun working on the newspaper-with-the-expanding-name. I pulled out my maroon-and-gold gym clothes from the back of a drawer, purchased a pair of Adidas running shoes and began running at night.

The gym shirt was reversible, with gold on one side and maroon on the other. I always ran with the dark maroon side out in order to blend with the night, because Jim Thorpe, Pa., has always been a rather conservative town. Anything slightly different is suspect and the topic of conversation for weeks and months afterwards. I ran at night so that word would not get around town that there was a nut on the loose. I also didn't want to have the word getting back to my employer that I was a mite strange. He already had his suspicions, but he wasn't about to get rid of someone who worked for so little and put in so many hours.

At Bloomsburg State College, although the town was also conservative, they'd come to expect that people who went to the college up on the hill were bound to be a little different from them. In Jim Thorpe, with no college for miles to house weirdos, and with the nearest mental institution 30 miles away, I ran at night to avoid ridicule and taunts and beer bottles and motorists having fun with me.

At that point in my life, however, with my body decaying because of not putting it to good use, I realized that Jim Thorpe was not a good place to make a comeback.

First of all, since air conditioning is generally unheard of in Jim Thorpe and similar northern climate areas despite the fact that it can get hotter there in the summer than it does in the Deep South, as soon as it gets warm people sit out on their front porches every night to drink beer and talk and take advantage of the cool breeze that comes marching down the streets at about that time most nights. Even running with the dark side of my shirt out, there were too many street lights that illuminated a runner just enough to make a murmur run down the street behind him:

"What was that?" "Did you see something over there?" "What's he done? Who's he running from?" "Where's my gun?" "Why doesn't he grow up?"

It was also very possible to startle some of the folks out of their night-time walks. And anything strange like that is bound to bring some calls to the local coppers.

If that isn't enough to discourage a runner, someone sitting atop one of the surrounding mountains after dark with his eyes closes could tell exactly where the runner was in the town a thousand feet below. Every other house has at least one dog, and many of the dogs aren't chained. The mountaintop observer could follow a runner's progress by the sound of the dogs barking. It was like a chain reaction. Run past the first dog and he yelps to tell the next dog down the road that there's some idiot coming. The message is passed on and, like a bunch of gossips, the dogs you've passed sit there whining and moaning about what just happened on their street. I had to take to running with a stick to ward off the more enthusiastic canines. I began to like cats very much. They sort of adopted me as their patron saint, because my passing gave them temporary freedom from the dreaded dog population.

The third and final straw that discouraged my comeback as a closet runner was the very thing that had started most of us kids on a life of running around town despite our elders' orders to quit running and walk like a normal human being. And that was the hills. In Jim Thorpe, it's impossible to run a half-mile in any direction without coming up against a hill. Those hills had given us incredibly strong legs as children, even the hills I'd faced and daily conquered at Bloomsburg were nothing to the aged ruggedness of Jim Thorpe's hills.

There was every conceivable type of hill—from almost completely vertical (like Fisher's Hill, Center Street between Sixth and Eighth Street, the best damned place in the mountainous town to go sleigh-riding) to long, extended hills; from just plain mountains to very plain hills, they were everywhere. There was no mile run that could be made without puffing my way up a mountain or hill. It became discouraging. Even running around the block involved some elevation changes.

I'd allowed myself approximately two years to get out of shape between when my toe became too painful to run on and a year into my career as boy editor. The two years had added 10 pounds to a 158-pound running weight in college, and it had taken most of the sprint out of my legs. Hills and mountains, which I'd once enjoyed, were destroying me. I'd end up walking to the top of hills I'd dashed up three years before.

Combined with everything else that was going on in my life, I aborted my return to running at that point and hoped something would happen to bring my vitality back. I even played with the theory that maybe I was doing too much too fast and that if I laid off a little bit I'd be better able to make a comeback later...

The things that made it almost possible to make a comeback were Ed Gildea and a gravity railroad that hadn't been operational since before I was born.

It would probably not be too far from the truth to say that Ed Gildea has been a newspaper man and family man for most of his life. He's worked in editorial positions at several current and now-defunct newspapers in the central-eastern portion of Pennsylvania, usually relatively small newspapers that would not take him too far afield from his home in Lansford where he has been putting together quite a large family. He's always been a guy who loves to be outdoors, whether it's just taking a walk or riding some of the most battered and over-used bicycles in the Panther Valley. He just likes to get out and go, and look at things along the way, and get some fresh air and exercise.

When the *Times-News* began staging the battle of the newspapers, and consequently became victorious over other competitors and began absorbing them, Ed Gildea saw the way things were going and applied for a job with the *Times-News*. He was, at the time, the editor of *The Tamaqua Courier* which, with The Other Paper snapping at its heels, was not the best place in the world for a good-natured guy like Ed Gildea to be working. He joined our staff as editor, which on a small local newspaper (for it was still small no matter how much it was growing and gobbling up other newspapers) gave him the opportunity to plan each day's issue, write editorials and answer telephone calls from irate readers who were a little ticked off because the newspaper hadn't sent a reporter and photographer to their granddaughter's birthday party the previous night.

Through it all, Ed Gildea remained unperturbed. When something threatening would happen to him, like a huge guy with a hard-hat bursting into the office to demand to know why the New York Yankees' box-score had been left out of last night's paper, Ed would stand up from behind his desk in the far corner, face the threatening person, laugh nervously, smile and five minutes later the two of them would walk out together telling jokes and slapping each other on the back. After ushering his new friend to the door, Ed would put his hands in his pockets and walk nonchalantly back to his desk where he'd pull out a sandwich from a huge bag his wife would pack for him.

It would probably be conservative to say that Ed was an easier guy to work with than any other journalist I've ever met. It helped that we had a lot in common, of course, including our slightly left-field view of the world in general. We were both blithely naive in some things, but both of us knew that you're kidding yourself if you think you can change the world or change the mind of someone who's already got his mind set. We were together from the start on the feeling that the county needed to be revitalized, and, incredibly, there were a lot of people against us.

The Carbon County/Schuylkill County area had been on top of the world back at the turn of the century. It was supplying badly needed coal to New York and Philadelphia, and there was plenty of work for everyone who had an interest in working—and almost all of the immigrants had that interest. Little by little, however, the area began dying as the need for coal decreased. Coal was dirty and uncouth as a heating fuel; it was being replaced by cleaner-burning gas and very clean electricity. Even homes in the coal-producing sections of the state were occasionally removing the "I Burn Coal" stickers from their windows and quietly changing to alternate fuel-sources. By the 1950s, the area had become badly depressed. There was less call for coal, and men were out of work and unwilling to pack up and move their families. It became common to find a job in Allentown or Bethlehem, towns approximately 30 miles away, and commute every day.

Whether from a lack of momentum or whatever, some people seemed to want to keep the area sliding in that direction. Others, however, came up with some radical ideas to revitalize the counties. They wanted to take advantage of the natural beauty of the area (it is located on the southern edge of the Pocono Mountains, a well-known resort area) and turn it into a tourist attraction.

A battle was joined. Those who wanted to keep depression in Carbon County lined up on one side, and those who wanted to bring prosperity through tourism lined up opposite them. Ed Gildea and I were in the middle. We wanted to see tourism come in as long as it didn't destroy what was good with the area.

The symbolic battle for us centered on the right-of-way of what is known—or rather, what *was* known—as the Switch-back Railroad. It had been the first gravity railroad in the country. Cars loaded with coal would be shoved over the edge of the mountain in Summit Hill, then they'd free-wheel down a grade about four miles long until they entered a valley, where they'd roll until friction slowed them down. Then, a cable from the next mountain (Mt. Pisgah) would be attached and the car would be pulled up to the top of that mountain. The car, once atop Mt. Pisgah, would be emptied down a chute. The coal was collected at a site along the Lehigh River at Mauch Chunk, where it would be loaded either on barges that would be floated down the river by a series of canal locks until it arrived in Philadelphia, or it would be loaded on coal cars and taken by rail to New York City. The Switchback Railroad was some 7.6 miles long—down one mountain and up another, very simple, very effective.

With the demise of coal's importance in the area, the railroad fell into disuse—but not for long. Enterprising people turned the railroad into a sightseeing attraction. Instead of sending coal down the tracks, they sent cars loaded with tourists. But that, too, waned. Eventually, the cars and the rails and the giant steam engines that pulled the cables up the mountain were broken down and sold to Japan as scrap iron. The local quip is that we got it all back in World War II.

Now, a development company wanted to build housing plots along the portion of the old Switchback Railroad right-of-way that ran through the valley. It was a good plan, basically, although the land was very rocky and would normally have been unappetizing to a developer. What made it attractive was that right across the road that ran through the valley a huge artificial lake was being built—a lake that would hold back flood waters from washing away (one more time) Jim Thorpe proper, and that would provide a valuable recreational area for the county midway between Summit Hill and Jim Thorpe. The watershed was a project both Ed Gildea and I supported. We didn't support the developer's plans, however, and unfortunately the developer had more money than we did to mobilize for war.

We dropped back a few miles, considered our mode of attack against the despoiler's plans, gathered our resources (which at that point consisted of our positions on the newspaper and the fact that both of us liked to run and get out in the open air) and charged!

We'd hold a race to draw public attention to the Switchback

Railroad right-of-way. That'd fix them dastardly developers. That'd save the historic site. Well geeze, when you're short on money, you've got to rely on desperate measures.

Plans for the First Annual Switchback Scamper were developed during our coffee breaks at the newspaper office, which worked out pretty well since neither of us drank coffee. Everyone else sucked in their morning caffeine, and we blew out grand plans for a gala event with a budget of $00.00.

We had the means and method of getting the news out, but we didn't know if we could motivate the local folks to take part in our affair. In order to ease local people in, we decided that instead of calling the event a "run," the word "scamper" would be more appropriate. It allowed us to encourage people to walk the trail, or to ride their bicycle on it, or to run it. It covered all the bases; it opened our event up for anyone from infant to cane-wielding veteran of many campaigns against life.

Ed set aside every Sunday and cajoled his entire family into coming along with him to the trail to help clear it for the Scamper, which we'd set for the early part of October with decades of disuse behind the trail, Ed's job was literally cut out for him. He and his family chopped down brush that was overgrowing the trail, removed fallen trees from across the path, smoothed especially rough spots along the downhill portion, removed some of the weathered railroad ties that had been left in the ground that might trip someone up and came up with quite a collection of old railroad spikes. There are always some folks in small towns who go against the grain and who become enthused with plans that are thought to be a bit daffy by most. One of the people who got involved was a former miner who took one of the spikes Ed had resurrected from the right-of-way and painted it a brilliant gold.

Over a coffee-less coffee break, Ed decided that since he was from the Panther Valley (the western terminus of the railroad) and since I was from Jim Thorpe (the eastern terminus), our contribution to the Scamper would be to symbolically relay the golden spike. Ed would run it downhill from Summit Hill to the point known as the Five-Mile Tree, the point where the two sections of rail crossed, with me running it on toward Mt. Pisgah overlooking Jim Thorpe. That made a great deal of sense since Ed was older than I was, and he deserved to run the downhill portion while I ran the uphill 3.7 miles. Unfortunately, while Ed was out with his family on weekends foraging through underbrush and getting to know the trail rather intimately, I was tied up with extra work at the company helping televise high school football games.

When the day of the first Scamper came, I never got to see the ceremonies at the start of the affair at the park in Summit Hill. I never got to see the politicos making speeches, or the bands marching and forming a golden spike, or the mounted policemen keeping the throng back from the massive press of runners and bikers and hikers. (Later, Ed would be kind enough to tell me that none of those things had come about, that there was only a meager crowd, a few local dignitaries who made no real speeches of any consequence, and that the only horse was the statue with the Civil War guy astride it. I knew better, though: with the amount of promotion and publicity we'd pumped out through the newspaper's columns and on the evening news on the company's television station, I knew that there was a crowd of thousands—the magic element that had traditionally been missing from my college cross-country days.)

While all the speeches were being made and all the beauty queens were giving the entrants a good-luck kiss, I was swatting several varieties of fall flies that thought I had been left there as an afternoon snack. I wished I'd have worn jeans or something instead of being a lug and wearing white gym shorts and a white T-shirt and my trusty Adidas running shoes. My light coloring in the bright fall forest was giving the bugs something to home in on. I continued to walk around, swatting and wondering if I'd have any energy left to run by the time Ed arrived with the golden spike. I fantasized about having brought along a golden fly-swatter.

For what seemed like an eternity, I sat and paced and leaned there, 150 yards up the side of a mountain from the road we knew as Lentz's Trail (Lentz's Bar and Grille was at the Jim Thorpe end of the road), hidden amidst the crumbling ruins of what looked like ancient stone battlements but that were, in reality, merely stone foundations and trestles where the railroad cars coming from Summit Hill passed under those coming back from Jim Thorpe. Fears entered my mind that some drunken hunters out for a day of sport might mistake me for an albino rabbit that would bring them fame and fortune for its 175-pound bulk. Visions of myself as rabbit stew began to arrive, and I began to welcome the possibility after a while just to escape the bugs.

Then, off in the distance toward Summit Hill, I heard voices and underbrush being snapped. I did some quick stretching exercises in order to be ready to make a run for it if it were hunters wielding shotguns and ready to sprint up the 3.7-mile grade to Mt. Pisgah if it was Ed Gildea. It was neither. A kid on one of those little bicycles that do wheelies and have incredibily high sissy bars on the back came zooming down the trail.

"They're coming! They're right behind me!" he shouted, like a bicycling Paul Revere.

"By land or by sea?" I asked him.

He looked at me as though I'd been lost in the forest too long and went zooming on to the point where the trail wended its way upward, jumped off his bike and stood there, ready to point runners and others in the right direction. Bob Thomas, a Panther Valley runner, came down the trail, and chomping right behind him was Ed Gildea.

Now, Ed Gildea is not your usual runner. There's nothing fancy about him. He manfully plods along in cutoff shorts, hunting socks and hiking boots, looking more like a port-a-john or a hiker running through the woods than a runner. He was making some grunting noises and perspiring some, but he was moving well, his usual smile very much in evidence. I took my position, accepted the sweaty, golden spike from which the paint was wearing off, and took off after Bob Thomas.

Ed Gildea's last words were: "You can catch him."

Ha! What I hadn't told Ed was that I hadn't had enough time to get back into shape, which he should have been able to tell just from looking at me. I'd never run this portion of the trail before and therefore knew nothing about where I was going, and there was no way I was going to catch Bob Thomas—especially going uphill for 3.7 miles.

At first, some bicyclists pushed their way past me on the narrow trail, but I would have my revenge on them later.

Then, other runners approached me—and passed. I kept going, more out of pride at that point—and out of a sense of duty to Ed's dream of getting the damned spike from point A to point B—than out of a competitive nature. Even doing it as a relay, we weren't going to catch some of those younger guys. I knew I was lost; I was already thinking of myself as an older guy. What I didn't know was that, after passing me the golden spike, Ed Gildea had continued on and he was back there somewhere, closing on me.

I came to a brightening spot along the trail and saw all the bikers standing around, cluttering up the trail. I soon learned why. At that point, a landslide had allowed some of the mountain to fall away. There was no longer a railroad right-of-way at that point; there was a field-mouse right-of-way along a ledge three inches wide across a sheer rock face—a distance of some 20 yards and a drop of better than 50 yards.

I grasped that golden spike in my left hand, ready to stab it with all the power I could summon into the sheer cliff-face if I began to slip. Huffing and puffing, I carefully crossed the ledge, leaning into the cool rock face. Once on the other side, I felt a satisfaction at having beaten the bikers, although I could see some of them had walked their bikes to the bottom of the cliff and were crossing down there in an attempt to head the runners off.

Within another mile, the race was over. The trail came to a portion of Mt. Pisgah I was familiar with from spending many a summer day hiking up the mountain to go swimming in the strip mines. I pushed the button to pour on a little more speed and make the finish look good for the crowd, but I found I had virtually nothing left beyond a lot of obscene noises telling me I was in terrible shape for someone who used to spend Saturdays running 18 miles.

I crossed the line, shook hands with Ed and official timer Jack Yalch who'd started the wind-up alarm clock at the beginning of the race, hopped into his jeep and four-wheeled it up to the top of Mt. Pisgah and was now busy reconstructing the tape across the trail so that everyone who made it got the satisfaction of breaking the tape.

My satisfaction came from struggling down off the mountain, getting a ride to my little apartment and soaking in a hot

66

tub for an hour. I had trouble walking for three days afterward. At about the time I was healed enough to move, and at
the moment I was thinking I should either give up running
entirely or do something to get back into shape sensibly, the
man who'd made the golden spike presented Ed Gildea and
me with the spike mounted on a varnished slab of the original
railroad tie from the Switchback Railroad. That was all it
took. I swore to myself and to Ed Gildea, with my hand on the
golden spike, that I'd be ready for the 1972 edition of the
Switchback Scamper.

Little did I know that no one was going to be able to
properly cope with the 1972 Switchback Scamper, and that my
best resolve was little better than no resolve.

The time imposed by work continued to edge the 80-hours-
per week mark and left little time for anything else. A
month following the First Annual Switchback Scamper I met
the woman I'd marry the next April, and work combined with
domestic responsibilities conspired to further put my grand
plans for a comeback behind. I made a feeble attempt to get
out during the evenings of the late summer and early fall to get

in shape for the Second Annual Switchback Scamper scheduled for Oct. 28, 1972, but my training was haphazard. I was,
it seemed, facing the beginning of the end of my attempt to
ward off the expanding belt-line and diminishing prowess of

youth. I was caught in the talons of the decade of decay and was not strong enough to resist it.

The night before the Scamper, it rained. The morning of the Scamper, it was still raining. It was one of those miserably cold autumn rains that chills to the bone no matter what clothes you're wearing.

George Harvan, a very able professional photographer who'd sort of become the official Scamper photographer, had trouble taking photos that day, it was so miserable. I still have one of George's photos of the start of the Scamper. It is a graphic reminder that there are things worse than death. The picture was shot adjacent to the park in Summit Hill. There is a timer, a starter (using an ancient Springfield rifle to send the runners off into their misery), a crowd of three people standing to one side to watch the festivities, and one of the saddest-looking groups of 24 people anyone's ever about to assemble for a photograph.

The group looks like the survivors of some catastrophic natural disaster, complete with running noses and fogged eyeglasses, trying to muster a wan smile for the camera as they take that first tentative step. Even in this group of 24, there are those in the middle and at the back who, caught in that forever trap of the camera's eye, have not taken their first step while the rest of the field is already moving. It is a picture Goya would have treasured.

It becomes, then, impossible to fairly describe what that meager group of 24 "runners" looked like at the end of the run—partially because words are inadequate, and because, as they struggled in to the top of Mt. Pisgah, still faced with the task of getting from the top of the mountain down to the bottom before they ever approached civilization, they walked away individually and were never again gathered in the same place at the same time.

Even with a mere 24 runners to clutter the course, it was still treacherous. The fall had already shaken the leaves from the trees, the leaves had littered the woodland path, and the rain that had been falling since the previous day had thoroughly wetted those leaves so that they were like flat ball-bearings, ready to slide out from under a runner's foot. Apparently to further complicate things, the starter's gun had pricked the low-hanging clouds and allowed the waiting water to come down in torrents; there was one downpour after another. Not yet out of Summit Hill, most of the runners were soaked to the skin; water was even leaking in around the edges of those who'd worn foul-weather gear. The dogs that had accompanied us during the first Scamper had sense enough to stay home.

The run was an agony of trying to avoid particularly slippery spots, trying to see over, under or around glasses that had become thoroughly fogged, and the mere struggle for survival—a struggle to make an end to it, to get it over and to get thee to a hot bath and some warm and dry clothes.

In what seemed a never-ending run that was broken by the high adventure of traversing that extremely narrow ledge along the landslide near the end of the run, where a few inches of slippery rock provided the avenue to keep going while a yawning drop of shiny rock-face waited for anyone who slipped, all somehow survived. A pack of damp mongrel human beings no self-respecting dog would allow in its hovel, we limped from the mountain and were never to run the course again.

Considering the dangers of the ledge that needed crossing, the decision was made to cut that portion of the run from the Scamper and to run it, instead, as an all-downhill course, ending up at the KOA campgrounds above Jim Thorpe—which featured showers and a parking lot where the survivors could gather and where any crowd that had an inclination to form could be accommodated. It also featured the added attraction that the last two miles were run along a road, out of the woods, where it was possible to pass other runners without danger of twisted ankles and bruised shins from python-like thorn bushes.

The first era of the Switchback Scamper had ended. Among all but myself, there were no laments. By ending atop Mt. Pisgah, I theorized, no one except those suffering equally could see my halting attempts at being a runner. With the course running all downhill and the last two miles along a public road, all accomplishments or lack of training would be laid bare for any and all to see. I left town a little more than a month later.

I've always been wary of people who pass themselves off as experts. I've always hated to listen to sermons. I've always been bored by most editorializing, because it is often more pompous than the topic it's castigating and much less interesting. What I don't like most, I suppose, is a self-professed expert who sermonizes me in print about something I'd rather ignore.

Ah, ha! you say, now that he's set me up like that, he's going to do exactly what he says he hates others to do, because that's how people who get in front of a typewriter are. They can be perfectly nice people at any other time, but when they're on a crusade, look out.

Well, I hate to admit it, but you're right. This is one of those pauses in a book where the writer intrudes himself upon his readers, because he thinks his editor has probably become so snowed down with manuscript at this point that he isn't reading as closely as he should so something can be slipped past. It is one of those vehicles or gimmicks being used by our modern novelists who no longer want to tell their readers a story, but who want to be preachers with an audience that can't pump his hand until it breaks after the sermon ends. About the only people who pull things like this off successfully are Kurt Vonnegut (who still contends that he doesn't write science-fiction but does) and Norman Mailer (who contends he's a novelist but who is still the best journalist going). I know before I start that this isn't going to work, but I've done so many other bad things in my life that one more won't destroy everything, I suppose.

In order not to lose readers who've been patient to this point, we'll have a short preview of coming attractions featured later in this chapter:

Twisting Mountain Roads Were Their Lives,
A Successful Moonshine Delivery Their Goal;
Love, Death, Screeching Tires and Broken Glass
As the Stock Car Circuit Erupts
In a Blaze of Unleashed Horsepower,
Powerful Loving, and Fender-Bending Madness!

I've always wanted to do those teasers they flash on the screen for previews of upcoming movies. They used to be an art-form—almost as good as the real movie because they contained all the important scenes and characters. But, like everything else, they're now a mere shadow of their former selves. Let's do a couple more so you good folks stay in your seats until the end of this chapter:

Meet the Skinny and Wily Hal Higdon,
See Him Run the Beach at Daytona,
Hear Him Expound the Virtues of Running,
Watch Him Create His Frankenstein Monster
And Then Snicker Behind His Hand at His Handiwork.

And, the final one:

A Gripping, Gut-Wrenching Tale That Will Inflame
*   Your Heart;*
Friends, Brought Together after Years of Separation,
Only to Find that Life Is Like a Cookie in the Rain!

That last teaser, of course, is another reference to Max Acker, the guy I went to high school with whom you were introduced to back in the opening chapter. I wasn't going to introduce Max Acker so soon in the original plan. In fact, what I'm going to be getting into here would have probably been the opening chapter if everything were right in the world. But when thinking about it, I found that Max Acker's death was the push I needed to wise up and fly right, and it seemed that to introduce you to Max would be beneficial. It would also allow me to bring Max back into this chronicle at the end of this chapter—to sort of pick up loose ends and tie them neatly together, since talking about him up front and finishing with him before getting into the strictly practical portion of this book would make it seem as though the book were extremely well-planned, when actually much of it is being written while the things related here are actually happening.

I was also going to use Max Acker's death and my consequent realization that I could very easily be next as a sort of parable that would lead me into a book that could, for all intents and purposes, be titled *The Runner Reborn*. This is similar to the I-Met-God-And-He-Saved-Me school of writing, which I understand is doing very well in the money department lately. Everyone wants to be reborn. I guess we aren't always happy with what we were originally born as.

It would have been easy to do that. I may even take a trip to a high, wind-swept mountain someday, and fast and talk to the eagles and cockroaches and other creatures who know what business they are about, in order to find the true meaning of running so that I might write it up as a religious experience and as a new, true religion. I could become rich and not have to do anything but run around in robes and things for the rest of my life preaching running.

I think that running, approached properly, can be as vivifying an experience as religion and can bring a person closer to the forces that move the worlds and shape our lives. Honest. As with every other great idea, though, someone else will beat me to it. But just to guard against that, perhaps I'll get the preliminary thoughts on that aspect of running down in the next chapter.

But enough wandering of the mind and diarrhea of the typewriter. On to the self-proclaimed expert sermonizing and editorializing:

Modern man allows himself to be manipulated every day—by advertising, certainly by peer pressures, by family, by desires he has implanted in the brain at infancy. Wear a Brooks Brothers suit, or you'll look like something from the Goodwill store. Be an individual, but wear the same clothes and think the same thoughts I do. When are you going to grow up and get a steady job like your father?

One of the great things about the generation I grew up with is that it has made at least an attempt to be truer to itself than most generations before it or since. True, many of the grand ideals that the generation born after the attack on Pearl Harbor rallied around in the 1960s have since been let tarnish a bit. True, that strange generation of The Bomb has been almost entirely assimilated into the society it didn't trust and has, indeed, accepted many of that society's values as its own. True, many of the radical elements of that generation are now prized employees of the system they criticized. But that's a natural osmosis as the new generation filters itself through the society it was born into. What comes out on the other side of society is not so much a new generation made into the image of the old but a slightly discernable alteration in the basic fabric of society through which the generation passed.

It would not be too far off the mark to claim that the more casual lifestyle many older people are finding pleasure in these days was instigated by the children born in the 1940s and '50s. Many older people are becoming more and more aware of themselves as individuals, with individual needs and with pleasures that can be arrived at by taking greater care of themselves, than ever before. It is no longer accepted as good and proper to see yourself as a simple, lifeless cog in the machinery of society.

By the same token, however, many young people allowed their individuality to be submerged once they reached their 20s. We've already made note of the 20s as the decade of decay, primarily because people at that age are struggling, usually on the bottom of the totem pole, to make a place for themselves in life and in society. They are concerned with accumulating possessions, with developing value as an employee in the job market, with "settling down" after what must be assumed was a stormy and tempestuous youth.

The 20s may be biologically the prime of life, but in actuality—especially in the American society—those 10 years are the foundation blocks on which the rest of a person's life will be built. The need for a bigger car, a bigger house, a frantic vacation once a year, a family with all the trimmings, takes over the person's sense of his or her individual needs. Although we are all born pretty much the same, a factor that separates us from the animals is that at least mentally we are all potentially individuals in thoughts and in words. Our lifestyles can reflect that individuality.

Some people realize this in their 60s—and they proceed to do something about making proper use of the years ahead of them—so that they aren't years spent waiting for the inevitable but rather years spent ignoring the inevitable. It is unfortunate that more people don't come to a realization of their individuality earlier in life. Sadly, some people never find themselves at any age.

A realization that a person is an individual, the only person like that ever seen on the face of the earth and ever likely to be seen upon the face of the earth, is important. The further realization that the individual is housed in a body that is a wonderful machine, but is finite and much less capable of reaching through time and space the way the mind does, is all the person needs to begin taking giant steps toward understanding and enjoying his life more fully.

The superfluous thing about a sermonette like this is that those reading this book are already very much aware of the correlation between health and happiness. They've done something either to bypass the decade of decay or they're taking positive steps to repair whatever damage their 20s have done to them. In some cases, however, that wonderful human quality of curiosity has prompted someone to pick up this book. If it has any lasting value at all for those who read it, it would be nice to think it lies in the realization that if you've survived the decade of decay or are going through it now— and are taking positive steps to set a new course—you're certainly not alone in their journey.

You've got a traveling companion down the road to ruin and up the mountain at the other side. Listen to what one idiot let happen to him during his decade of decay.

To supplement my income at *The Times-News*, I began writing articles for *Stock Car Racing Magazine*. I came into it through the back door when Dr. Dick Berggren, a college-level teacher of psychology and a weekend racer, contacted my former college roommate, Paul Allen, who was working as publicity director for the fledgling Pocono International Raceway in Pennsylvania. Berggren asked for a story on the raceway. Paul Allen didn't have time to do the piece, so I did it—with great misgivings. I was still very much convinced that sports cars were the only kind of true racing machines in the world.

Dick Berggren began bothering me for more and more stories, and I began getting more and more into stock car racing, appreciating its rather unique appeal and the talents required to be successful at it. Going to the tracks and doing interviews was a nice way to escape my increasingly depressing workload at *The Times-News* and affiliated enterprises. Stock car racing was primordial, vicious, noisy—sort of like the press-room at the newspaper, the huge offset presses setting up a thunder and a din that is somehow awe-inspiring. I felt more akin to stock car racers and stock cars than I did to the local town council meetings and flower club exhibitions. I was getting rammy—which is another way of saying that when you've got to leave town to have a good time, you'd best consider leaving town.

When, in late 1972, M. Denis Hill, editor of *Stock Car Racing Magazine*, wrote and said he'd been made publisher and that the editorship was open and would I like to have the job, my wife and I hopped into our wheezing 1964 Rambler and took a flit on down to Alexandria, Va., to look over the situation. By the end of the weekend, we were making plans to move, and by December 7 we were in Fairfax County, Va.

One of the first people I came in contact with once I assumed the editorship was Hal Higdon. Hal stood out head and shoulders above many of the other people who were sending stories to the magazine. He was professional and knowledgeable. He was pitching us to buy the rights to a chapter in an automotive book he'd just written called *Finding The Groove*, a collection of stories on every conceivable type of automobile racer, from street drag racers to Formula One types. Hal represented the kind of person I saw the sport of stock car racing needing to pass on to readers the excitement and drama that most of the submissions we were getting just didn't catch. Everyone was trying to sell us "Gee whiz, you shoulda seen the race; it was exciting!" stories.

Hal was trying to sell us quality writing about stock car racing. For his quality, he wanted more money than our average contributor. Somehow, I managed to clear it through the tight hands of the purse-strings, and we began using Hal's stuff whenever he could find time to pump something out for us in conjunction with a book he was working on. In that arrangement, we managed to have Hal's work at a fraction of the price *Sports Illustrated* was paying for the same thing.

The subject of Hal's running came up occasionally, and we'd compare notes on our respective careers. He had a lot to report while I had very little. I was occasionally getting out for a painful run of about a mile, but I was unable to get myself committed to the point that I was doing it as a regular thing. And I knew from college that if it isn't done as a regular thing, the discomforts of running are never gotten through and it's very discouraging.

Hal sent me a copy of his book, *On The Run From Dogs*

And People. It was inspiring. For two weeks after reading the book, I tried to get my running program off the ground. It fizzled out in the face of the mounting workload at the office, where the magazine was set up so that one person constituted the entire editorial staff. There were no flunkies to shift any of the work onto—each editor did everything on his magazine. Between races to cover almost every weekend and long hours at the office (especially during deadlines), running was again forced to the background.

My wife and I had gone to the fateful 10th-year high school reunion, and we were spending an inordinate amount of weekend time with Max and Janet Acker. On several weekends, we'd stop and ask ourselves if we hadn't perhaps gotten into a rut. We agreed that we just might be in a rut, but it was easier to stay in it than to crawl out.

The stock car racing seasons continued to be colorful and exciting. The NASCAR Grand National scene, particularly, was fascinating. Hal Higdon was writing a book on the 1975 Daytona 500, and we got together briefly in Daytona Beach. While we were there, unfortunately, our apartment in Alexandria was being broken into, and we had to cut our stay short. Hal took over our motel room (they're at a premium in Daytona during February) and turned out a great book, *Showdown At Daytona.* He also went running on the beach. I didn't.

I had convinced myself somehow that stock car racing was an invigorating sport. The drivers who were successful were generally trim and hard-skinned men. They were incredibly fit from wrestling 3800-pound, 600-horsepower stockers around huge superspeedways with the banked turns tripling their weight, with the sun beating down on a continuous ribbon of asphalt that got to be 130 degrees, while they sat behind an engine producing 1800 degrees of heat internally, and the 180 m.p.h. gust of air rushing through the engine compartment blasted 160-degree air into the cockpit for better than four hours without any relaxation other than a 17-second pitstop every 80 miles.

They were rugged men who spent better than four hours in a wiltingly hot car 30 weekends out of the year. Some of them had been doing it for 20 years. Only the best ever reached the top, and only the greats stayed there—Richard Petty, David Pearson, Cale Yarborough, Bobby Allison, Buddy Baker, Benny Parsons, and up-and-comers Darrell Waltrip and Lennie Pond. My respect for their dedication to their profession was monumental.

Unfortunately, it led to a vicarious feeling of ruggedness that was not reflected in the grandstands or in myself. The drivers were rugged and tough. Most of the fans were overweight and spreading into the seat next to them. I was very perceptively becoming a spectator, like them, to a fascinating sport—and there is a huge abyss between the spectator and the participant. I wasn't Richard Petty or Bobby Allison, and I never would be. I didn't want to spend the rest of my life being someone watching someone else doing something.

A feeling of discontent began spreading its tendrils through me. I still loved stock car racing and many of the people actively involved in the sport. But it was frustrating being a spectator. Life should hold more than the splinters from a grandstand seat implanted in your rump. I began trying to fathom my discontent.

And then Max Acker died. My discontent spread and

became almost a mania. Nothing I'd come up against had quite the effect on me that Max Acker's death did. I began having dreams of Max Acker where there'd be this summons in the middle of the night. I'd get dressed and go looking for him, because he had something important to talk to me about. I'd travel miles and miles until finally I'd come to a bleak and desolate land that seemed to go on forever in every direction— except straight ahead, where a giant mountain of granite rose to a leaden sky. Atop the mountain, I'd find a chair carved into the rock and on it Max Acker would be slumped, his head back, his mouth open in a snore that would never end. I'd stand there for long minutes, hoping he would wake up and tell me what he had to say. After having the dream a third time, I began to understand my own growing uneasiness, and I began to understand what Max Acker was saying to me.

Chapter Five

Running, Almost A to Z

A-Advice

When Max Acker died, his slack mouth told a story that gave a caution to anyone who would take the time to listen to the silent words. They were words that had been spoken from other mouths at other times—but that had been ignored, lost somewhere on their way from the ear to the brain, because they came from the mouth of someone suspect, someone older, someone who had no connection with our lives. Besides which, those of us for whom the words were meant were too invincible in our youth; we would live forever.

We didn't say it in those words, because we could never believe something like that, but we merely failed, in the cockiness of youth, to let the concept of growing old and dying worm its way through our shield of brashness with the world. We knew we were not invincible. But youthful people died in car accidents, from being struck by lightning, from drowning at summer camp. Those things were not beyond the ken of our understanding—they were abrupt interruptions in the agelessness of youth that could be accepted. But people under 40 never died of "natural causes." Sure, after 40 you were open game to everything...cancer, disease, old age. But nobody died at 31 unless by violence.

Max Acker said that was bullshit. And he meant it. And I knew he meant it. Because he'd proved it.

A move so loaded down with massive realizations as one from invincibility to susceptibility takes time. There is a certain inertia to overcome, a certain sloughing off of the shock of both what has happened and at finding that your beliefs are now totally outdated, mere fantasies that can end up killing you, and a crock of shit.

Max died in early November 1976. We heard about it in

mid-November from people back home in Jim Thorpe who'd read about it in the newspaper I'd once worked for. Janet Acker, Max's wife, called in early January to tell us, "so you can never say I didn't tell you." The chip on her shoulder was apparently easier to flaunt with Max's death behind it. Until March, my wife and I really didn't think about Max being dead. We still expected his late-night phone calls to come at inopportune times; we still expected that unexpected knock on our door with a whiff of blueberry cigar smoke seeping in around the door; we still expected his blustering question of, "Hey, you guys got your clothes on?" to accompany his pounding on the door about two inches to the right of the knocker.

In April, my own 31st birthday approached. And although I'd gotten through my 30th birthday with none of the attendant trauma that many males feel at this loss of their 20s (I found no difference between 29 years, 364 days old and 30 years, one day old), Max Acker was intruding on my anticipation of a birthday cake and ice cream. It had literally taken from November until the following April to push through to the realization that, yeah, Max Acker was dead, he wouldn't be calling anymore, he wouldn't be knocking on the door, he wouldn't be talking about all the beer he'd consumed that night, he wouldn't be telling us about the new pair of cowboy boots he'd bought. He was gone. We had suspected that he'd be gone well before his time, yes, but now he was really gone, he was dead, he'd died in his damned chair with the television insulting the little dignity of his death with a test pattern. He'd died, alone, in front of the flickering blind eye that had told him all his life of the wonderfulness of life.

I don't remember what the show was that was on the television, but the realization hit me as I, like Max, sat in front of the little screen while it burped inanities at me. Max Acker was unnecessarily dead at 31 years old. I would be 31 years old in a few weeks. Would I be next? Although I knew that, barring an accident like an airplane falling out of the sky and crushing me under it, I'd probably make it through to my 32nd birthday, I wondered how far I'd get beyond that.

For my age, I was relatively active. I was working on my master's degree, taking one course at a time, and that was keeping me at least marginally active mentally. I was putting full days in at the office and spending most weekends running around from one stock car track to the next, lugging camera equipment over miles and miles of burning-hot asphalt. I was going to the Holiday Spa two and three times a week and was building my upper body, which had always been a bit behind my leg development.

But I *did* have an office job where I sat much of the day, although I balanced it out by making innumerable trips up and down a set of steps to the art director's office. I was 207 pounds on a 5'11½" frame, a good 49 pounds over my average college weight. My waist was spreading considerably, but I consoled myself with the realization that it wasn't with flab but with that strange consistency a male sometimes develops where his stomach feels like a bag of cement.

I knew that if I tried to run I'd get winded, even though I didn't smoke cigarettes. Hal Hidgon, occasionally writing an auto racing piece for *Stock Car Racing Magazine*, would invariably include a line in his cover letter asking if I was getting any running in lately. In my answer, I'd either tactfully avoid answering his question or I'd use the excuse that the job just didn't allow enough time.

At about that time, he began pitching me about a job opening in California where I'd really be able to get back into running if I was serious about it. Joe Henderson, Hal said, was attempting to move over into the company's book division, and the job as editor of *Runner's World* was going to be open. Hal would put in a good word with Bob Anderson, owner and publisher of the magazine, if I was really serious about wanting to get into running again.

The idea of my applying for the job apparently began to become rather fascinating to Hal because he called a few days later, giving me Bob Anderson's address and telling me to send a resume, some examples of my work and a letter expressing interest in the job. I'd seen *Runner's World* on numerous occasions but never subscribed to it, because I knew that having it clunk into the mailbox each month would be like having a great aunt who insisted that I eat my carrots. "Get off your ass and get out there and run," it would say silently, in the same way that Max Acker was saying it.

Becoming disillusioned with the office in which I was working, where the publisher only presented himself approximately one day out of every three weeks—and then only to cause more problems than he solved—I told myself that I wanted out and that Hal's suggestion was offering a possibility. When I examined my motives closer, though, I found that the predominant image of myself that I was trying to resurrect in order to hold off feelings of approaching age was the image of running along I-80 on Saturday mornings, 158 pounds of solitary wanderer at peace (at least for 100 minutes) with himself.

I sent about a 10-pound package to Bob Anderson and waited for his reply. Meanwhile, shocked by the 207-pound lump I'd become, I started upon a program of running and dieting.

Bob Anderson wrote back that there'd been a change in thinking on the position available. What he was probably looking for more than an editor was a managing editor to handle the day-to-day business of the magazine, while Joe Henderson stayed on as editor and also became editor-in-chief of the book division. I wrote back and told him to give me details. Weeks went by with no word.

I had decided by then to get out of the world I was in as a means of regaining my sanity. Our office people were a great group to work with, but there was absolutely no direction there, sort of one of those frustrating situations where there's responsibility but no authority. I took an interview with an advertising agency. The job opening was a good one where I'd be doing the ad copy for magazine and television ads for Chevrolet. Then Bob Anderson finally called; we got together in June and I agreed to start on August 1.

There were enough meshing gears turning now that I couldn't put off a return to running even if I'd wanted to. I began imagining, while I was running at 6 a.m., that Max Acker was watching the sun rise with me and that he was laughing at how long it had taken me to get the message.

April 20—Thirty-one years old today. As with each birthday, the day after the birthday seems very little different from the day before. The difference with this birthday is that the resolution to begin doing something about my weight and my health (which I vaguely began formulating when Max died last November) starts today by way of dieting, in order to drop some of the 207 pounds I'm carrying in order to be in more sane weight bracket when I begin running again. To start running at 207 pounds would be too demoralizing. Must drop to below 200 before I start. Birthdays do bring on contemplation of days past. Can remember in high school eating chocolate malted shakes and pizza in an attempt to add a pound and not being able to, getting stalled at about 158 in college, and then, at some point around 24 years old, finding that a few pounds had crept in. The first few extra pounds looked pretty good. But somewhere, as the metabolism slowed and the weight gained, they stopped looking good. I both dread and look forward to the first day I take the initial step onto the roads.

B-Eats

*T*he return I'd made, in anticipation of securing a job at *Runner's World* and literally having to become a runner again, was a return sprinkled with some lessons the hard way.

I'd started by telling myself that I'd make every effort to run every day, that I'd keep a diary of my progress—or back-sliding—and that I'd make an effort to make my running effort easy on myself by doing something about all the extra pounds I was carrying around.

For most people who are beyond 25, the most common complaint is that they've put on a few extra pounds. On some people, the few extra pounds, if they've arrived in the right proportions in the right places, look rather good—especially if they're people who had a tendency toward looking anemic. The extra pounds just seem to find comfortable spots to sprout, and in many cases the lament is heard that, "Oh, there's nothing I can do about that; it just comes with age." The lament usually is voiced around a chocolate bonbon finding its way into the mouth of the offender.

Extra weight does not necessarily have to come with the accumulaton of age. The weight comes usually because, as we grow, our metabolism changes along with our lifestyles. We are less apt to expend a lot of energy, while our bodies are less apt to burn up the food we're shoveling in. Both factors contribute to making the weight rise rapidly.

If the two contributing factors are slowed metabolism and

slowed body use, the answer to battling the weight problem would logically be either to cut down the volume of food since the body isn't burning up as much now as it used to, or to become more physically active—or, ideally, both.

It seems like a good place to make two points that are eminently important to losing weight:

1. People who use all types of exotic excuses why they can't lose weight are merely lying, hoping that they'll eventually begin to believe their own lies, because essentially they are too lazy to lose the weight.

2. If a person trying to lose weight does so by going on a diet, the diet is only going to be as good as the person's will-power to stick to it. It is absurd to hop from one fad diet to another as they are extolled in the tabloid newspapers sold at the supermarket checkout stand.

And to that I'll add the admonition that virtually all diets are worthless in the face of the simplest formula for weight loss and improved muscle tone we'll get into here. I say that because diets of any type (and there are *some* diets being expounded that are downright dangerous) are merely stopgap measures—temporary measures that end as soon as you cheat, undermine, give up or forget the diet. The program that will become evident in this chapter is one where you will ultimately be able to eat any damned thing you want and it won't add a pound. But at first you've got to sacrifice.

Here's the logic that gets you going: Any pound over and above the amount of pounds you'd like to have on your body is like carrying that one-pound weight strapped to you. In other words, during any running or activity you engage in, you are doing it with an invisible knapsack of pig-iron weights strapped to your back.

So, in order to make the running more palatable, some weight must come off as soon as possible. Later on, the weight will come off at its own leisurely pace, but by then you'll be more able to carry some of it until it vanishes.

Your diet should be simply this:

Breakfast—Coffee or tea, no sugar, one piece of toast with butter and jam.

Lunch—Very light; half a sandwich and a diet soda or some fruit or a salad without salad dressing.

Dinner—Normal dinner, no dessert. Make sure dinner comes well before five hours prior to retiring, since anything eaten within five hours of going to bed almost automatically turns to fat; all it does is lay like soft concrete in your stomach all night, gurgling, while most of your other systems turn themselves off.

No snacks while you're watching tv other than one diet soda per night, preferably 2½-3 hours before bedtime. No hot chocolate before bed, no beer or wine, no nothin'. Learn to crochet or something to keep your mind off eating and drinking at night, because that period between dinner and bedtime is where you're putting on most of your weight.

Now, the good part of the diet. From the evening meal on Friday to the evening meal on Sunday, eat and drink anything you want. For most people, a seven-day-a-week diet is exasperating because they haven't got the will-power to stick with it. With the weekend set aside for ingestion of food in your normally voracious way, you can get through Wednesday and Thursday muttering to yourself that Friday is almost here. It's like driving across the desert knowing that there's a filling station somewhere up ahead.

While you're doing all this dieting, make sure to keep a chart of your weight loss. Weigh yourself first thing in the morning every day and jot the weight down on a chart. You'll notice two things: the weight sometimes back-slides and it sometimes plateaus.

You'll find that following the weekends of debauchery, your weight will shoot up a bit but that it will again begin dropping once you approach the middle of the week, once you're on your diet again. This will serve two purposes: it will give you graphic proof that your weight is being caused by your ingestion of great amounts of food (which some people seem unable to realize until they have some mathematical proof of it), and it will prove to you that cutting back on that food intake during the week is having positive effects on your weight.

The weight loss is not going to be dramatic. It may come out to being only a half-pound or a pound per week loss. But it is a trim and solid pound you've lost, not a plastic pound from some fad diet that's going to pop right back on, full-blown, the minute you pass a candy store.

The plateau I mention is a point where for some weeks you'll have a net loss at the end of the week of absolutely nothing. This should not be discouraging. During your weight-loss program, there will be some weeks when your body will be making internal adjustments to the new regimen and to the loss of weight up to that point. Don't be discouraged by reaching an occasional plateau; it's just a rest stop your body's taking before the next plunge.

Now, the main ingredient that will make this "diet" work for you (I hate the word diet; let's use regimen, since the program goes beyond abstaining from certain foods, and since it, in fact, allows you to eat anything you want over the weekends) is the other half of it, which is the running. Let's talk about the aspirations you should nurture toward being a runner and toward the beginning of your running program. They're both essential to make the weight-loss work and will, in the end, be more of a factor in your life than the loss of 20 or 40 or 60 pounds of unnecessary fat.

June 13—The 13th of any month seems like a good day to get projects started. Any project negates the supposed bad luck associated with the day. Today is more than a good day, because besides being the 13th, it is also Monday, when every week actually starts. My first run on the road back to being myself went down Rose Hill Drive, with a left onto Telegraph Road, then another left to head back toward Rose Hill, and a turn onto Rose Hill Drive near the school. The first half of the run was more a shuffle than a run, and the second half degenerated from a shuffle to a gasping stumble. But I did make it. Checking later, I found that the course is almost exactly two miles. No one out to see me suffer at 6 a.m. except the dogs.

June 14—Tuesday. Sore in the legs. I'm moving okay but very slowly. After first two blocks, soreness turns to soft ache in legs; breathing ragged.

June 15—Wednesday. Still sore, but 6 a.m. running time, although only three days old, is already beginning to seem routine. Slow drizzle today made the running feel better.

June 16—Thursday. It occurs to me to run the course backwards and to take the resulting long hill gradually rather than fighting that one-block-long ball-breaker of a hill every morning. Backwards might be good for mornings when psychological part of runner needs a lift.

June 17—Friday. Garbage truck is out today. Very quiet for some reason. Same paperboy at same place at same time, same people waiting for same bus. They are less awake than I am, because even clomping up like a horse behind them I can approach and be upon them before they know it. Hope startling them doesn't cause heart attacks.

June 18—Saturday. Breathing still a problem. Had run-in with two dogs, but by barking back at them they retreated. Run again in afternoon after a few hours at apartment complex swimming pool. It's 86 degrees and about 95% humidity; legs feel rubbery. I feel like an overloaded airplane trying to get off the ground; fag out on the killer hill and walk to top; start running again and pick up pace in parody of kick to help me feel better for the effort.

C-Aspirations and Goals

I know it sounds better reading "Goals and Aspirations" and that's how Rotary Clubs and such use the terms, but let's face it, you need the aspirations before you can set the goals.

As someone who hasn't run since childhood or as someone who hasn't run since the days of high school or college, your aspirations in life have altered considerably since then. There are new priorities in your life. Different things are important. You've obviously at least halfway decided that your health and well-being are of importance to you at this juncture, and you want to recapture some of your youthful energy and exuberance before it vanishes all together. You want to lose a few pounds or tighten up the muscles and maybe, if something else beneficial comes along with the process, that'll be just fine.

It might be a good time to examine what other aspirations are involved with your decision to make this rather radical move into weight control and running. Are you approaching this as a flippant thing or as a serious project? Do you already have visions of the person you figure you'll be when you come out the other end at a furious pace, or are you just going to kind of play it by ear and see what happens with each step?

The caution here is that you should, by this point in your life, know yourself better than anyone else knows you. You should know the directions your aspirations take, and you should know how easy or difficult it is to make a grab for the realization of those aspirations. The best way to approach the entire thing is to allow flexibility in your aspirations, because some strange things happen to people. Seemingly the most shy, retiring little guy can turn into a fierce competitor, while someone who, in the business world, is highly competitive on a day-to-day basis may find himself just loping along enjoying the scenery and smelling the flowers. You know yourself best; examine yourself, what kind of a person you are when it comes to visualizing things over a long period of time future tensely, and then sit down and make some short-term goals.

Actually sit down and, with a piece of fresh paper in front of you, write down what you want out of this whole thing. Make some short-term goals and maybe some long-term goals. Don't be afraid to put time limits on the short-term goals, but keep the long-term goals open-ended. For instance, in June 1977 when I started watching my weight closely and getting back into running, I set the short-term goal of losing two pounds per week for the first five weeks and, at the end of those five weeks, running better than three miles without being exhausted.

My long-term goals were eventually to reach, at a reasonable time in the future, a base weight of 160 pounds, while being able to run 18 miles on a Saturday or Sunday morning under two hours. (I don't figure that at 31 years old I'm going to match the 18 miles in 100 minutes that I was capable of when I was 19 years old... yet who knows?) On the morning this is being written, Nov. 1, 1977, I'm down to 181 pounds, and I ran 11 ½ miles in one hour, 33 minutes on Sunday, on top of another 5.7 miles to my log last night. I'll probably do about 7-10 miles tonight. But I'm a long way from coming close to doing 18 miles in two hours. It will, perhaps by the time this book is finished on Jan. 30, 1978, be a reality. If not, it still qualifies as a goal, and whether it happens on March 20 or July 4 of next year, it makes little difference. The fact will be that it was a goal on a long-term basis that was realized.

If you've never run as an adult, keep the goals reasonable. If you have run before in some organized team structure, evaluate yourself since you stopped and figure out how long it will take you to come back. Obviously, if you haven't put on much weight, you don't want to set a goal of losing two pounds per week for five weeks; you'll end up walking through doors without opening them.

Get yourself a loose-leaf binder and lots of loose-leaf paper to keep a diary and a running log. Do this for several reasons: Initially, it will give you a place to put down in writing what you want to accomplish, what your aspirations and goals are. It'll also record the day you started all this, sort of the Day One for your new self. If you're shy about starting such things, I'll start it for you.

Today, I decided to lose weight and take up running, to become more fit than the average person and to live longer, to get to know myself, and to record my thoughts and feelings and impressions for later reference.

There, you've got a start. Look at all the things you've already embarked upon: weight-loss, running, fitness, longevity, self-knowledge, realization of the body/mind connection, and diary- and log-keeping, in the best tradition of James Boswell,

Ben Franklin, and other famous log-keeping people.

You'll eventually find yourself coming home after a run, anxious to jot down your impressions and your performance.

You'll feel great pride when you log your current weight. And, when you get a little discouraged, all it takes to pick you up is a peep into the early pages of the diary/log to realize just how damned far you've come.

Okay, now that you've got your resolution screwed tight and ready to work for you and your diary/log is primed, let's get you out the door and into training.

June 26—Sunday. Going to try my first longer run. May be too early after beginning running, but will give it a try. Will run down Rose Hill Drive to Telegraph Road, and from there to Franconia Road, and then up Franconia to Rose Hill, a distance of 5.2 miles, with Franconia almost all hills. Run downhill, along Telegraph Road, feels pretty good, but as soon as I turn up Franconia the hills kill me. Walk/jog home along Franconia. Legs are very weak and breathing is tortured. My J. C. Penney shorts rubbed the insides of my legs raw, which I didn't notice through my pains until I took them off. Some baby powder applied liberally to the raw areas seems to help ease the pain when my balls bump them. Need new shorts—maybe silk. Maybe will begin running without jock, too.

June 27—Take the day off to recuperate from the attempted 5.2-mile run. Perhaps I'm trying too much too soon. I don't have enough sense to realize that I don't make a comeback in a week, but the pain when my legs rub will keep reminding me of my folly.

D-Starting

Whether you are a prospective runner who hasn't run in 20 years or one who lettered in track two years ago, there are certain aspects of human nature that are universal. It will not help to explain that this is as much a book of *don't* as it is of *do*—and to explain that in the interest of science and this book's authenticity, I experimented on myself, subjecting myself to many extreme hardships so that I could sit here, propped up on my sickbed, to tell you the horrors of taking the wrong road down the path to good conditioning. I could—and probably will—relate the pains and aches and extreme discomforts that I suffered by doing certain things wrong, with an eye toward saving you from falling into the same traps. But I still realize that people are people are people.

I know, you see, that as you stand there in your doorway, looking out at the strange world of 6 a.m., with the sun just vaguely struggling up to the edge of the far hills to peek over and announce morning; I know that as you shift from one foot to the other in your ill-fitting gym suit you found in the bottom of a long-forgotten drawer in the attic, your swimming trunks on under the gym suit, your tennis pumps tied haphazardly to your feet, wiping sleepiness from your eyes while trying to make sure you got up early enough so that no one sees you take your first steps; I know, you see, that if I tell you to go very easy the first day you're going to completely ignore me. That's human nature.

So I'm not going to do that. I'm not going to tell you that you're not ready to blister the asphalt in quest of the four-minute mile on your first day. I'm not going to ask you if you've set up a course for yourself or if you've rationally evaluated your goal for your first week. Because I'll be ignored— which is to be expected, I suppose. On June 1, 1977, my first real day back, I ignored common sense, too.

Go ahead, wing it. Give it a shot.

While you're doing that, I'll start explaining what happens when you do, and you can catch up when you get back.

The urge is, initially, to overdo everything. Later on, there will be a shifting back and forth, a constant seesaw, between doing too much and doing too little. The first day out, it's a new horizon. There is a certain feeling of accomplishment at just thinking healthy thoughts at 6 a.m. while the rest of the world is still getting its last couple of winks in before the alarm puts them into their shoes to meet their day. This feeling of exhilaration is coupled with a feeling of impatience to get into the thing.

The combination often results in the new runner sprinting down the block as though in pursuit of a missed bus connection. This reaction is more prevalent in people who are returning to running after having run in high school or college. They feel that because they did it once, some years ago, it should be no big thing. Unfortunately, running is like a straight-razor: if it isn't sharpened regularly, it becomes dulled very quickly. Actually, four weeks away from running and you almost have to start over. This is why, in order to do it properly, it must ultimately become part of a person's lifestyle. The runner, then, returning from track and cross-country glories will likely overestimate his prowess and will go out too fast on the first day. day.

The new runner who hasn't really run since childhood or high school gym class is a bit more cautious. Some cautiousness is the best attitude to adopt when starting up your running lifestyle. Go out slowly, at a simple jog. Don't worry about being considered a mere jogger. Everything comes in stages, and the actual running will come later.

Just get out there and jog, as calmly as you can, from point A to point B, and back to point A—or around the block once, which may be a distance of a quarter-mile. Just get the feet shuffling and the breath coming and maybe work up a little perspiration.

In most cases, it's not necessary to go through a series of elaborate stretching exercises at this point, because I suspect stretching tightens up important muscles more than it relaxes them, and relaxation is of great importance at this point.

Just run the block lap or whatever you feel confident with (some returned runners might want to take on a mile or so the first day), come back inside (making sure not to hang around outside in the chill, damp morning air savoring the accomplishment while you catch pneumonia), maybe do a few little calisthenics, and then go about your business. Make sure you write an entry in your diary/log detailing how you felt and congratulating yourself on starting.

If you went out like a shot instead of playing it cautious, you're probably feeling very tired and sore, having realized that the muscles of youth are passing things and do not stay supple forever. If there is an evident soreness, give yourself a little rubdown on the tightness in the legs and take your morning shower or hot bath. Make sure you keep moving about so that the muscles don't tighten up on you. If you went too fast, you're probably tasting that blood flavor in your throat, too. It'll go away, if it hasn't already.

Go about the day as normally as possible. If someone asks you why you're walking funny, tell them your shoes are too tight. For those of you who overestimated yourselves, tomorrow is when the real stiffness will set in, and getting up out of bed will be as much of an accomplishment as running around the block was today. The lactic acid that your muscles pumped out is settled in the niches of your muscles, and it'll make them stiff and sore until it's once again removed. Walking around somewhat after running helps get some of the acid out of the muscles, but your muscles are so unused to what's happened to them today that they are surprised—and overcome—by the army of acids that have invaded them.

Some soreness and stiffness are to be anticipated, even if you didn't tear out of the door as though it were a set of starting blocks. For the fast-starters, the soreness will work itself out as you work yourself more. My re-entry to running was characterized by a first half-mile in which I was really moving along until my body realized what was happening to it against its will. The next mile was run with a ragged breath that felt as though it were burning a hole through my throat, and the final half-mile was covered at a stagger that was slower than a walk. I took one of history's longest showers, letting the hot water loosen up the muscles somewhat, and then I proceeded to limp for about a week.

The important thing, no matter how much or little the body hurts after the first day, is to make certain there's a second day.

June 30—Thursday. Tried a new course today for a change of pace, and also because I'll be leaving for Daytona tonight and won't be able to run tomorrow morning, because I'll still be behind the wheel when the sun comes up. Ran along the Vepco right-of-way near Rose Hill that contains their huge, steel high-tension towers. It is like a game preserve back there, like the veldt, with dogs, a deer, some cats, cardinals, many rabbits. It also gives you a chance to see the rear end of people's homes and offers a really supreme aloneness at 6 a.m.— except for the presence of the sun, which you run into, and which can make the run interesting because it cuts down your vision to about 10 feet, and the terrain sometimes drops off almost vertical. A really challenging diversion with almost too many short, steep hills.

E-Gear

After my own foolish sprint into the wonderful world of strains and pains on my first day back into the running world, I spent a lot of time soaking in a tub of hot water that the shower had filled, trying to coax my muscles into enough suppleness so that I could go to work that morning. While soaking, as the water began wrinkling my fingers into prune-like things, I had time to reflect on the topic of the running gear. No, no—not that overdrive gear I mentioned earlier whereby you begin running automatically while your mind goes on its own roadways to who-knows-where. I mean things a runner wears.

I must admit that I've always been rather a slob runner. I'm most comfortable in jeans and a ratty-looking sweatshirt that is ready to fall apart. In shoewear, I'm always comfortable in training flats, because while running cross-country in college I found that they were about the most comfortable shoes this side of Hush Puppies. Our team would wear the things as everyday-walking-around shoes. The habit is hard to break, and hard shoes are like those foot-squeezing devices they used during The Inquisition.

Comfort in running has always been of prime importance, and the simpler the comforts, the better. This is a matter of choice, however. I knew a runner in college who used to send one of those laundry mailing boxes home to his mother each week to have his seven different running outfits washed and pressed. He never wore a shirt again until it was properly washed and perfumey new. So there are different tastes. Maybe it all depends on the time of day you run, how many people are going to see you and what kind of neighborhoods you're going to be running through.

I pushed my aircraft carrier up behind my rubber duck and tried to sink the duck, but he kept bobbing to the surface. My legs began to move almost normally, but I knew that as soon as I got them out of the hot water they'd once again revert to being stiff and tight.

Clothes in running seem to be optional. I don't mean by that

that you should sometimes prefer to run in the nude—although I understand there's a guy who's working on promoting a marathon with just that option written into it. (I wonder where you'd pin your car keys or your number.) I guess I've kind of been a victim of the inverse of the clothes-make-the-man theory. Having been in the company of runners for many years, I've found it to usually hold true that a real runner doesn't much care what his running clothes look like. (Since there weren't many female runners when I was doing most of my running, I can't speak for their preferences.)

Usually we'd say, "Hey, let's go out for a run," and a couple of the guys'd say, "Yeah, let's," and we'd rummage around in our room, looking under the bed for something to throw on, and we'd go zipping out the door and do eight or nine miles and maybe use the same clothes again the next day.

My wife hates it, but I sometimes use the same sweatshirt and shorts for a week at a time. Especially if runs come first thing in the morning, when it's difficult to wake up. I've found that nothing makes you want to run out that door and get down to business more than pulling an old dried-sweaty shirt over your head. It wakes you up in a startlingly short time and gives you incentive to run to stay ahead of your own stench.

I love to shower when I come back in to wash off the fresh perspiration (hell, let's not be drawing-room proper: *sweat*), but I'll stand my clothes up in a corner and let them dry for the next run. Their odor tells me in a not-too-subtle way that I was running yesterday and I'm going to be running again today as soon as I get my shirt past my nose, and it gives me a little flavor of where I've been in the last few days. Maybe it's a sort of perversion, but it makes running just a little more elemental, more primitive, and that's basically how I like it.

For the new runner (referring to people rediscovering running that they'd forgotten since childhood) and the returning runner, I'd advise going as casual as you can without being downright disgusting to anyone you happen to pass on the street. You can always buy Fancy Dan-style togs later on. To start your program, though, it seems most logical to me to wear something you're already friends with, since the first few weeks of running are going to be so much out of your normal routine that a little reminder of normalcy (like that old sweat-shirt you use when you cut the grass) can be like Linus' security blanket.

My wife's been after me to buy one of those $60 sweatsuits with the cute piping around the edges, but I've resisted. It makes everything seem so damned faddish. I can understand, however, how for some folks a new, high-buck sweatsuit could be an inducement to get out there and make use of it. Too often, such expensive gear ends up in the back of a closet, because it sort of puts running in a rather suspect light, as though it were a fashion parade, which it most certainly shouldn't be.

The major caution with clothes is that, once you begin doing major amounts of roadwork, invest in a good pair of running shorts—they'll cut down on the agony of chafing between the legs. The chafing problem can be solved in long runs by apply-ing some petroleum jelly in the crotch area. As for the rest of your attire, it is essentially optional.

The one item that is not optional is the shoe. That's the one item of running gear that should be chosen carefully, should be extremely comfortable and functional, and should never be picked because you like the colors. The right pair of shoes can help make running a very refreshing experience; the wrong pair can make it one continuous misery.

In childhood, when our bodies were closer to the ground, shoes weren't all that important. There wasn't very much of us as far as body weight went to give the feet a pounding when we ran, and we ran just as often in grass and on dirt as we did on concrete and asphalt. As adults, it's a little different. We have more weight coming down on the foot with each step, we find we're stuck running on concrete and asphalt more and more, and our feet are a bit more tired than they were when we were young. They need some babying.

Back in the 1960s, when the first running boom hit and when we were running cross-country meets, there was one major running shoe company—Adidas. They made the shoes with three stripes, and they made them in several models. They made a high-buck shoe for competition and a low-buck canvas trainer for everyday use. We never got to use the good shoe except for races, which was awkward because we never got a chance to get our feet broken into the shoes before time to race in them. Many of us opted to use the canvas trainers for races. They were simple and comfortable and broken-in.

Things have changed since then. At the time when I write this, there are 19 serious running shoe companies and dozens of companies making shoes in imitation of the real thing. The imitations prove the theory that you get what you pay for. And what you get with the imitations usually isn't worth the money you may think you'll be saving. The imitations (i.e., white shoes with *four* green stripes) are made from lower-quality materials, the workmanship is usually shoddy, and it doesn't take them long to fall apart.

Just for completeness sake, I'll list the 19 major running shoe-makers in alphabetical order: Adidas, Braun, Brooks, Converse, Eaton, E. B. Sport/Lydiard, Gola, Mitre, New Balance, Nike, Osaga, Patrick, Pony, Puma, Reebok, Saucony, Spot-Bilt, Tiger (Onitsuka) and Uniroyal.

Never let someone else buy shoes for you. Go try the shoes on yourself, in the store. And *never* buy a shoe for its color or design. The next caution is against developing loyalties to any one shoe company. Your loyalties should be to your feet. Any shoe company loyalties may prevent you from finding the just-right shoe for you, because it is made by a company you wouldn't normally consider in your camp of loyalties.

Also, as with cars, due to the influx of companies involved in making shoes these days, you'll be finding so many models with so many arcane features on them that the whole thing can become very, very confusing. The best advice, it seems to me, is to start with a simple shoe. Don't bother buying a shoe with all types of fancy and complicated features added to it until you find out if you've got a foot that needs some kind of complicated feature to accommodate it.

I've tried some of the new, complex, over-engineered shoes and have found that, at least for my feet, they're going in the wrong direction. I seem to have fairly normal feet (apart from having Morton's foot, which is a condition many people have where the second toe is longer than the great toe and therefore prone to being bruised when running; I also have flat feet, but that's another story), so I prefer a fairly traditional, simple shoe.

Since 1973, I've worn Adidas Countries. They're very simple, leather shoes. Having come from Pennsylvania, where it snows and does other mean things to a runner, I find that I prefer leather shoes to nylon, although they don't make many leather shoes anymore, because nylon is "in," which is fine if it never rains or snows where you run. I've got three pairs of Countries, one of them usually off at Jeff Sink's shoe shop getting new soles because if you run even a moderate amount, you've got to count on the shoes wearing out.

I've got a 1973, '75 and '77 pair of Countries. Although the Adidas factories pride themselves on workmanship and quality control, the materials going in the soles and the leather the shoes are made from have had a noticeable decline between 1973 and '77. This shortcoming can usually be rectified the first time the soles wear out by sending them off to be resoled. A good resoler usually puts better soles on the shoes than the factory did.

Another simple shoe that is very traditional in its design, and that works very well for people with simple feet is the Tiger Montreal II. It's nylon, though, so it should be used only on good-weather days.

It isn't being with-it to go into a shoe store assuming you have complicated, deformed feet just because the year's shoe innovation is a chrome doobie off the side of the shoe that makes you run funny. (For the ladies, who generally have narrower feet than the men the major shoe companies are finally manufacturing shoes in your sizes and to handle your unique needs.)

Another caution with shoes: when you go to buy them, don't always trust yourself to the hands of the sales clerk. Some sales people are good at what they're doing, the best being clerks who are runners themselves. But many clerks, we've found, would be better off slinging hash at the corner greasy-spoon, because they're already slinging bull in what they're telling their customers.

Many of the world-class runners (Frank Shorter, Marty Liquori, Bill Rodgers, Don Kardong, etc.) are in the running gear business. If you live within a reasonable distance of their shops, it would be worth your while to buy your first pair of shoes there, because their stores are staffed with runners who know shoes the hard way—from wearing them every day. It would be worth it to go the extra miles, because it'll make your extra running miles all that much more comfortable. Remember, it's better to spend an extra half-hour or hour trying on various shoes at the store than to spend hour after hour pounding the pavement in shoes that hurt. They're your only protection against a very hard, cruel world waiting for you out there.

Once you learn what your feet like, you can literally shop at home from one of the good mail-order houses. But for your first pair, get some expert advice.

If you have problems with your feet, start your search for a cure with one of the good books on the subject, such as *The Foot Book* by Harry Hlavac. You may find your problem solved in the book and may save yourself a visit to a podiatrist. Runners can often solve minor foot problems by using various across-the-counter foot devices, such as Dr. Scholl's, to alleviate irritants like heel bruises, arch pains and blisters. In most cases, you should take every means to try to heal yourself before resorting to a doctor and, if a doctor is the next step, make sure he is a runner or knows the problems runners face. If a doctor ever suggests surgery to correct a foot problem aggravated by running, make sure you get a second opinion from a running podiatrist.

Shoes for running have come light years since we ran in the old canvas training flats in 1964. There is great pleasure in wearing hard shoes all day long and then coming home and slipping on a pair of running shoes; it's one of the great pleasures in life. If you have a job where you can wear your running shoes all day, there's certainly nothing wrong with that; they'll likely keep your feet happier than regular shoes.

Keep in mind when shopping for your training flats that your feet might be most comfortable in something simple; they'll tell you so when you put the shoes on at the store. Don't get complicated unless your feet specifically ask for it, because in running, your feet are king. Buy some books on feet and foot care, and get to understand them. Also understand that many of the pains you'll encounter from the ankles up to the lower back can sometimes be traced back down to the feet.

For the most complete lowdown on running shoes, read *Runners's World*'s annual October shoe issue.

July 2—Hit the beach at 6 a.m. at the Days Inn Shores, running south to the fishing pier and back. Few people here to bother a runner. Sun comes up behind purple clouds. The pelicans are out early like a flight of medium bombers on a low approach. Seventy-five years ago, Stephen Crane was out in a dinghy beyond the surf here after the Commodore sank. But it was January then, and there was a shark, and the people here, on shore, thought that his frantic waves for help were merely sociable waves to say, "Hello there, beautiful morning for a boat ride, what?"

F-Pain

*P*ain to the normal person is either a depressant or a stimulus. It is often both. Get a toothache and you become deeply depressed—but you also find yourself stimulated to do something about it by making the trip to the dentist's office.

The aches and pains that are earned from the first day's return to running are usually a curious combination of sensations.

Hopefully, unless something was sprained or broken, there should be no *pain*. Pain, at least when talking in running terms, is an acute sensation, a knifing in the side, a splintered feeling in the knee, something serious and likely to cause disability for a few days to a few weeks. Pain, in simple terms, is *painful*.

Most of the discomfort one encounters in any strenuous physical activity qualifies as an ache. An ache is something dull and throbbing and uncomfortable. It is primarily sore muscles. It can be swollen ankles, a general overall feeling as though you'd tackled a runaway garbage truck and lost. Aches are common to any sport or physical activity. Ideally, they will lessen as the body becomes more accustomed to the demands being placed upon it. Some occasional aches in running are to be expected, like the arrival of tax forms every year. Even the most experienced and most accomplished runners suffer aches, sometimes during training, sometimes during a race and sometimes during just jogs around the block.

Learn to distinguish an ache from a pain. A pain usually needs treatment—an ache usually needs time.

Something else an ache needs in order to be rid of it is *more* of the same activity that caused it. The more common form of ache is that caused by the deposit of lactic acid in the muscles. The body produces lactic acid during activities of a strenuous nature. For the person not used to imposing strenuous activity upon his or her body, the lactic acid is pumped out in tremendous amounts, and it sort of clots the muscle tissue, making the muscles feel as though someone has poured quick-setting cement in them by some mysterious osmotic process.

The best way of minimizing the lactic acid buildup is to make sure that there is what is called a "warmdown" period after exercising. I personally think that's a pretty damned awkward term when what you're trying to do is to bring your body temperatures down, to cool them off. Warm things rise. In our discussions of it, we'll call a "cooldown" this period following your exercise in which you keep moving in order to keep your muscles moving lactic acid around your body so that it doesn't all settle in one place. You're bringing your body machine down to a lower operating temperature, back to normal, like a car that was straining to pull a travel trailer up a steep hill, finally reaching the top and going down the other side of the hill where the engine compression begins relaxing the strain that had been put on the car and where the engine begins to cool down.

It is equally valuable to do some type of a *warmup* before engaging in your strenuous exercise, much as you allow your car's engine a few moments to warm up in the morning, but warmups can vary in their benefits and effectiveness between any two people. I do the bare minimum in pre-running warmup exercises, substituting a slow jog for the first 5-10 minutes of my run. That is warming up the body for what I am planning to do as my activity, thereby acclimating myself in advance of the activity. Some people do elaborate stretching rituals. I find that stretching often tightens up the muscles I'm trying desperately to relax before a run. Some runners swear by extensive stretching activity. I suspect that as I run more, I may need them to add strength and flexibility to the muscles that work against the muscles I'm developing in running. By that, I mean that for every muscle that lifts your leg, there is one that lowers it. If you lift your leg all the time, you're going to have to strengthen the muscle that lowers the leg at some point or you'll be walking funny. For a beginning runner, I'd think that stretching extensively is not needed. Later along, it would seem to be more necessary.

Since achiness seems to go along with the first few weeks of running, let's dwell on it a while, because you're going to react to it in one of two ways: the aches are going to discourage you from getting up out of bed to run the next morning, or you're going to want to get rid of them as quickly as possible so you can get down to some ache-free running.

Different people have different reactions to aches. Some people use them as an excuse to avoid doing the activity that caused them. This is understandable. It is not, however, excusable. Aches should be approached in the proper light. They should be telling you something positive about your body—specifically that you do have muscles there somewhere and that they have apparently been under-used. Aches point out where your weak points are and give you directions toward which muscles to develop. Aches also serve as a yardstick for measuring how well you are ridding yourself of years of inactivity.

The best way to control aches is to have the force of will to crawl out of bed the day following your first workout and pull your trunks and sweatshirt on again (this is where not having them washed from the day before works, because the salts deposited in the sweatshirt act like smelling salts and really spur you on to activity), try to bend over to tie your shoelaces or, failing that, have someone else tie them for you, limp out of the house and begin your day's workout at a very slow shuffle. Within a few minutes, the aches will change texture and you'll feel better about the whole thing. The main obstacle is getting out from between the covers on the bed and getting out the door. Each day, the discomfort should lessen, until aches only come occasionally—and then primarily when you add new activities to your running or when you race.

To recuperate best from the first day's aches, though, warmth is the most comforting agent. Take a nice, hot bath before going to bed, maybe get a rubdown from a kind person, or use a light layer of Atomic Balm (Do they still make that stuff?) or Ben Gay on the legs and sore muscles to keep them from cramping.

If you develop a pain instead of an ache, study it thoroughly, localize it, prepare to describe it accurately, and then go see a doctor who knows something about sports medicine. Don't run with a pain, because it will only get worse. Running with an ache will usually wear away the ache as the muscles involved become stronger. It's not a sin to baby yourself a little to make the ache more tolerable, but don't regress from the activity because of an ache—get out there and work it out by the best means possible, and that's more of the same activity that caused it in the first place.

July 10—Ran the 3.4-mile course at Rose Hill, which included running the loop of the two-mile course twice, taking the hill both times. It did hurt a bit, especially on the second loop. Ended with a kick but not a very dramatic one. Injured the second toe of right foot, and it looks as though it will lose the nail as it is all bluish. The toe itself is becoming more bruised than it had been. The toe is longer than the same toe on the left foot, and much longer than the great toe, very obviously a case of uneven Morton's foot. Should cut a hole or a slit in the front of the shoe to relieve it from hard contact when the foot slides forward while going downhill.

G-New Goals

Earlier, we talked about the advisability of setting goals in your running program, of putting down on paper what you're striving for and then making great efforts to realize those goals. Before running your first few days and gaining a knowledge of exactly what kind of shape you were in, your goals might have been different than they are after an honest evaluation of your strengths and weaknesses as they've quickly brought themselves to the surface by some honest pavement-pounding.

Within a few days of starting to run, you should have an idea of how you'll fit into the grand plan of running.

You've learned whether you're a morning, noon or evening runner; whether you need some type of stretching exercises to loosen you up before you run or whether the act of running itself provides its own loosening up. You've found that there are realistic limits to what you can do at this point. You've probably also found that there are other people out on the streets and highways doing the same thing you are, and that you are not really an oddball or a nut, or a candidate for the bug-bin. You've kept your feelings and thoughts and performances—or failures—in your journal and maybe, after your first week, it's time to sit down with your scribblings and put them into some kind of perspective.

There are as many different kinds of runnings as there are runners. Each runner looks for something individual in running—and usually finds it. Some "morning" runners are content to have the heat of their bodies building a shield around them in the pre-dawn chilliness, running at a steady pace down suburban streets with names like Orchard Avenue or Picadilly Lane or Apple Blossom Drive, waiting for that one special moment in a day's millions of moments when the sun squeezes itself above the horizon and brings day to night.

Other runners are constantly in quest of a run that will better their PR (personal record) for a certain distance, while others work toward running a little bit farther on each week's long run, even if it's merely a tenth-mile, hoping to reach numbers like 18 miles, 21 miles, that will, afterward, astound them and cast them momentarily speechless at their accomplishment. Other runners run to become fast enough and good enough to run faster and better than other runners.

Some runners run to lose weight or to build muscle tone or to get fresh air or to develop a feeling that they are not suffocating in a daily routine that has no place for the extraordinary.

One runner I know, a very dedicated runner who runs at least an hour every day, spent an entire year training for one race, a 50-miler, while the man that won the race runs 50 miles or more every Sunday so that the actual races are little more than normal training sessions for him.

Some runners work toward being able to run around the block without being winded, while others run across the country in less than two months. Some runners run to be alone, while others run to find a way to socialize with other people who are like them. Some runners train on hills, while others train on tracks. Some train on roads, while others train on sidewalks.

And despite the incredible number of runners in America today, there are no two alike, even if they train at the same time, over the same distances, with each other—even if they are Siamese twins. Because they each want something slightly different from running, whether it be something aesthetic, something spiritual, some type of psychological therapy, weight reduction, an almost-certain preventive against heart failure, or an excuse to get out of the house and away from the responsibilities that are associated with it.

Do not be surprised or stupified or disappointed if your goals and your view of running change the more you run. They can change from day to day; may well change from week to week; should change with each new month, and must change each year. Running should never be allowed to become a stagnant, purely regimented thing. That's one of the reasons a journal is kept—so that a runner can periodically go back over his record or where he's been in order to map out some new routes for where he's going.

Bruce Dern, the rather accomplished actor, began his running career by running 1320s around a city block, because that's where his high school ran their 1320s. He progressed to regular quarter-mile tracks where he concentrated on the 880. Out of school, he began doing ultra-distance events—marathons, ultra-marathons, the 72-mile run around Lake Tahoe. Now, he's back to doing training that will make him competitive in seniors' track in the 880. His running career has ranged from runs that take 60 seconds to runs that take nearly 12 hours. A runner must be flexible enough to rearrange his running to fit the need and the desires of the moment. Running can be just as flexible as the runner, even more so.

Don't be afraid to set some new goals at this point.

If you've got a course set out that you can run every day, and if you're happy covering the same territory, and if you want to fool with a stopwatch because you like numbers and because numbers are very finite things that you can jot down in your journal every day, go right ahead. I personally don't think it's the kind of running I'd like to do daily, but some people love to skim off a second or two on their two-mile runs through the neighborhood every day. The problem arrives on the day they are slower than they were the day before or when they lower the time to the point where it's just plain impossible to get it down any farther. What's the next step for them then?

Friend Joe Henderson, for eight years the editor of *Runner's World* and the author of numerous books on running, feels it's best to go in the opposite direction. He feels it's to the runner's advantage to use a clock rather than a stopwatch. He urges runners to set goals of half-hours and hours of running, rather than to worry about distances and seconds. He feels that the pace is of little importance, and that the time spent running is all-important.

I guess I fall somewhere between the extremes. I like to play some numbers (because it acts, at least for me, as a motivating factor), but I don't like to become a prisoner of numbers and schedules. I early-on established certain courses that began and ended at my front door. I measured the courses rather roughly with the odometer of my car and then I gave them numbers—i.e., Course Number One, Course Number Two, etc.

The first few weeks of my return to running, I stayed on my initial two-mile course because I felt a sort of security there. By staying on the same course, I found that I could judge (without a stopwatch) how I was doing that particular day— whether I felt better, faster, more confident on my run than I had the day before. I had already been a runner, so I was prepared to deal with the built-in monotony of running the same course every day at the same time of day.

During my runs, I'd write books and travel to exotic places and solve problems by the bushel-basket. I'd smell odors along the road, anticipate which people coming out of their houses were either early or late for their drive to work that morning, figure which houses had dogs that would likely begin yapping when I went by. I even watched the steady, day-by-day decay of a squirrel that had been hit by a car and thrown on the side of the pavements I traversed. Every day along my two-mile course became an adventure.

I knew up front that it was an adventure that would eventually lose its excitement, so on weekends, even though I was scarcely capable of rolling my 200-pound bulk the two miles, I took Saturday off to rest and then on Sunday ran a slightly longer run—like 3.2 miles, usually on a different course, in a different direction, but again ending at my front door, which led to the shower.

The fact that the two-mile run was in the Alexandria, Virginia area *did* help, because there are quite a few runners ambling about there. Even though I never joined any running clubs or organizations in the area, I felt a bit of kinship with other runners I met at 6 a.m. along the suburban roads. We'd exchange a wave or a "hello" or just smile at each other, trying to look as though we were motating along jauntily even if we'd just labored up a particularly difficult hill.

The same runners were usually encountered, although not every day and not at exactly the same time. It became interesting to hypothesize what they were doing on those mornings when I'd be on time on my route and they wouldn't be there. Were they oversleeping? Were they giving up on running? Had they gotten up early to take their run? I never knew, because I never wanted to intrude on their 6 a.m. shell, because when you're running at 6 a.m. there is almost something holy about it. All four of them, however, became fast friends and I looked forward to seeing them along the way, although we never talked or exchanged names.

One old man walked half a block and then jogged the next half-block, going on at a curious pace that was marked by humming during his walking phase. He carried a car antenna to protect himself agains the packs of dogs that got together to terrorize paperboys and runners and cats and garbage cans. He wore slip-on canvas shoes and was always bundled up as though it were eternally December.

The other elderly gentleman was more serious about his image. He wore a regulation high-dollar dark blue sweatshirt with yellow piping. He had gray hair, was very anti-social, and he puffed very hard when he ran, but he ran very well.

A guy in his early 20s wore yellow shorts and a plain, white

T-shirt, and he ran as though doing a 440 when he came down Rose Hill Drive every morning.

The fourth cohort on the 6 a.m. shift was a girl about 17 or 18 who wore a dark blue shirt, white shorts, white knee socks with blue stripes at the top, white running flats, and a ponytail about three feet long that whipped around behind her when she ran. She was the closest of any of us to being a real runner, because she always ran with a smile, she ran with great style, and she looked as though she'd been born running.

With the company of four other runners in a two-mile course, so many dogs, paperboys, people going to work, dead squirrels and an old fellow who drank his morning coffee on his side patio and always waved as I went by, the same course was never dull. It's just that, running it often enough, it became confining, and I began doing two circuits of the course every morning, which came to 3.2 miles, since the loop started in a bit more than a quarter-mile from my front door.

With the move to California, I began setting up courses that ran past my front door and that always came past in the same direction so that, like a kid with an electric train set and lots of track, I could make up any of a thousand combinations. My Number One course was 1.4 miles, my Number Two was 2.35 miles, and my Number Three was 4.2 miles. They were set up so as to avoid crossing intersections whenever possible—which can become a problem in a suburban area, because stopping for "Don't Walk" lights can really throw you off your pace.

I began playing games with the courses, combining them for different distances, trying to eventually top my 18-mile Saturday runs from college. During the week I might combine my Number One and Number Two courses for a spirited 3.75-mile run or for a slow 3.75-mile run if it came the day after a major crack at the elusive 18 miles. By doing my courses 1-2-3-3-2-1, I could get in 16.1 miles, a healthy effort for a Sunday morning.

Even with the variety of courses I began setting up, and with the almost endless variations it provided, I also set aside a day each week when I'd just run, whether I had to stop at intersections or not. It didn't matter much what the mileage was, just so I kept going until I was tired and ready to head back. I also set aside one day for a 1.5-mile run to a schoolyard, where

I'd do intervals, and then run the 1.5-mile route back home. I always took Saturdays off.

Each week, the goals would shift as I'd take a few minutes Sunday afternoon to sit down after my long run to review my week's running in the journal and assess my aches. At that point, I'd set new goals for the coming week. The goals, though, were an ongoing thing, something kept flexible yet moving forward, since I did want to see some improvements but had no illusions about outrunning Bill Rodgers or Frank Shorter in a marathon.

Goals are important to a runner because they give him a horizon he can sight in on. But flexibility is just as important if the runner is ever going to reach the horizon.

July 15—Arose (what an awkward word) at 6:30 a.m. in JT (Jim Thorpe, Pa.) during my last visit home before my move to the West Coast. Ran to the reservoir above town, took a dump amidst some laurel bushes and ran back through the upper portion of east JT. Felt real good. Had some apprehensions before running the distance, because I thought it would be much too far. It always seemed like quite a trip as a child, out South Street to Germantown, up through the reservoirs and then back down the alleys to home. But either the town got smaller or I got bigger, because the distance was not a great problem. It was really one of the most enjoyable runs in a long time because of the quiet and the damp morning, and because it was a chance, before the town awoke, to see what's changed in the years I've been gone. Little has changed really.

H-Going Fast

There is a lot that can be said about running fast, even though what we are generally speaking of is running long. Many people seem to feel that, except in the ranks of the "pros," the two concepts are incompatible.

Maybe it all starts in the mind of the runner himself. There's a curious fallacy there. Here's how it works:

A person is primed to learn early in our society that there are only 25 spots open on the high school football team, nine spots on the local sandlot baseball team, seven spots on the cheerleader squad, maybe 10 spots on the college basketball team. Schools promote intramural teams in an attempt to provide *something* for those not quite talented or motivated enough to make the *real* teams. In most schools, though, the intramural programs are haphazard, disorganized and often pretty useless. Most people realize early on that they can't whack out a good double from an inside curve, that they can't stuff a basketball through the loop or dribble the damned thing through their legs, that they can't high jump their own height or more, that they can't crazy-legs a pigskin around some would-be tacklers and that once the tacklers caught them they wouldn't really enjoy getting creamed, even if it's for the ole school colors.

Most people are pretty inept at the majority of sports, even if they are enthusiastic at them. Part of the blame lies in the fact that there is little grade-school-level development of skills; that when there are programs (such as Little League), parents drive their children to the point of hating the sport because it's *too* serious and *overly*-organized; and there is that damned horrible attitude on the part of some parents that if the child wants to go up to the local park to play ball with the other kids that he or she shouldn't be allowed to if it isn't supervised "because you might get hurt." Kids are supposed to get hurt; it's a part of the growing-up process. A kid who gets through high school and out into the world without at least a few minor scars on the body (and this includes girls) has missed the most important lessons of kid-dom.

In any case, the American kid isn't given enough opportunity to develop the body. The kid is kind of on his own. Sneak some stickball in here, do some tag when the recess teacher isn't watching, get a bruised knee playing basketball, and then keep your jeans on for three days until it heals so you won't get yelled at for being hurt. Schools in less-enlightened towns even fence in the ball field so that a group of kids can't play ball on a Saturday, because it isn't part of the school's physical education or team sport program. (It happened in my hometown. They fixed the ball field up after years of letting it deteriorate, and then they put a fence around it to keep out the kids who should be using it. The fence cost as much as it would have cost to put together a second ball field for after-school-hours play.)

Athletics aren't really encouraged in childhood, and when they are they're encouraged in a less-than-healthy way, with *competition* being more important than participation. The school athletic budgets, although contributed to by everyone's parents, benefit only a very small portion of the kids. For the rest of the kids who can't be shoehorned into baseball, basketball or football, especially in a small town, it's just tough apples.

As a result, most kids grow up having taken very little part in the rather wide and varied world of athletics. Kids grow into adults who find it easier to become spectators than participants. Thus develops the armchair quarterback, someone who maybe played a little ball in school or maybe played none at all, who feels capable of analyzing every move made on the field on the glowing TV screen while no one really cares what the hell he says about that third-and-four play that the Redskins just blew. As the footballer got older, the teams he could join became fewer and only the best survived. If you weren't the best, you're sitting on your ass with a six-pack and bleary eyes, telling those who made it how they are going wrong.

For that person, it would be great if he could get up and telephone 10 other guys and get together with them to meet another group of 11 footballers who'd never made the cut so that they could once again take part in it all. It would be good for them psychologically and physically. But it's expensive providing uniforms, a rather large playing field is needed, officials would help, it would be nice to have a few thousand fans. Well, it's just too awkward to even consider.

With basketball, it's a little easier, because it can be played at the local "Y" after work even if there are only two guys per side. Softball continues to hold an interest for some baseball vets who like to keep in the swing. But again, it involves some talent and some organization and a dependence on other people showing up to take part in it.

Running is entirely different.

Almost everyone can run—some fast, some slow, some gracefully, some not, some for long distances, some for short, but almost everyone can run. In fact, some of the kids who were terrible at regular sports are great at running. I know we had a bully on our street who was three years older than we were. In order to survive, we developed an ability to be as agile as gazelles, sprinting blocks at a time and vaulting walls and shrubbery to avoid being caught and getting creamed.

The universality of running is its strongest appeal these days. Years ago, no one seemed to be interested very much in running. But years ago we were a nation with more of a spectator mentality than a participant mentality. And, with running, it's easy to be a participant—and any sport takes on more of a meaning when you can physically take part in it. Running also has the appeal of being extremely flexible. If a person is shy about putting his running in front of the eyes of spectators, he need not bother. There are numerous back roads and more than enough dark streets at 6 a.m. on which anonynimity is assured. Or, if the spirit moves the runner, there are any number of races and social runs available. It is, in that sense, the perfect sport. The runner is his run; the runner needs nothing else.

Ah, you say, but what has all this got to do with running fast one day a week? I guess it has to do with pride in performance and also what we will be dealing with in the next section (jogger vs. runner vs. racer). A runner, no matter how shy, does find a tendency to want to improve performances. If he doesn't, he will remain forever a jogger—but this is getting ahead of ourselves.

They say that in regard to drugs and automobiles, speed kills. In running, speed—judiciously used—improves performance. Brooks Johnson, 1976 U.S. Olympic sprint coach, has a very good point when he says that long, slow distance running is great if you want to be a long, slow distance runner. This is not to downgrade long, slow distance running (known as LSD), promoted heavily by Joe Henderson. LSD has helped more people accomplish more miles than any other single factor one can point at during the last 10 years. It has also provided many excellent health benefits for people who've been devotees of LSD. Joe has modified his opinion of LSD within the last few years, though, and he and Brooks Johnson are very close in their thinking on using some speed work to improve a runner's performance—whether the runner is training toward the Olympics or training toward running a better two-mile course at 6 a.m.

And, at least for runners just getting started in the sport or just returning to it, there's no need to become fancy about building speed. Once you've got a base built, there are good books available on sharpening it. It is essential to build a base, though, in order to help improve your stride, your endurance and to provide a little extra for those times when you get the urge to stride out.

Even if you're just starting to run, set aside one day per week to do speedwork, just as you should set aside at least one day for rest and one day for a longer-than-usual run. The speed work can take one of several forms. It can be intervals at a track, fartlek-type running or hill-work. The speed-work's purpose is primarily to build your muscles that are used in sprints in order to complement the muscles you'll be building while doing longer, slower runs.

Interval training is best practiced at a school track. Interval training is not difficult but, done strenuously (which I don't advise at first) it can be pretty rough. In interval training, a runner sets up a goal of doing a certain number of repetitions at a certain distance. The ideal place for intervals is the standard quarter-mile (440-yard) track. For the beginner, maybe six intervals down the track's straightaways with a jog through the turns would be enough. *Never run intervals at 100 percent effort.*

I hadn't run intervals since college, and the first night I decided to put them into my workout I forgot that they aren't supposed to be run at full speed. After doing 10 x 110 with roughly a 30-yard jog between, I couldn't walk a straight line and I could hardly make the 1½-mile jog back home. The next day, my legs felt as though it was the day after the first day I'd ever run in my life; the lactic acid was backing up in my legs in buckets.

Run intervals between 60 and 70 percent effort. Save 100 percent efforts for actual races at the distance, at which point you'll only be doing it once and you won't cramp yourself up to the point of being an invalid for two days. As you progress and get your body in better condition, you can add other intervals to your speed day.

If you hold a conversation with someone who's a running veteran, the proper way to speak of intervals is like this: "I did 10 by 220 first and then added 15 by 100 with a 30-yard jog between." When you write it, substitute "x" for the word "by" such as: 10 x 220.

Always schedule a warmup period before doing intervals— usually about 10 or 15 minutes of slow jogging. Likewise, schedule a cooldown run afterwards. As you become stronger, you can spend a good deal of time doing intervals, but don't overdo it at the beginning.

If you are fortunate enough to have hills where you live, you can do hill-work with little problem; maybe you are doing it now in your normal runs. Simply stated, hills develop muscles that aren't developed running on a flat surface. Also, those muscles provide for a great deal of strength when you come down off the hill and hit the flat surfaces. The hills require a higher leg-lift, which corresponds closely to the muscles used in strictly speed running. Don't run too many hills, however. Schedule hill-work on that one day a week either as a substitute for interval work or as an alternate to interval training, doing hills one week and intervals the next. Don't start doing hills with enough vigor that it lays you up in bed for several days. Again, 60-70% effort is fine. As you develop more, you'll be able to do additional repetitions. Use the descent of the hill as your recovery jog. Then, turn around and go back up the hill.

If hills and intervals seem pretty boring to you—and, to be honest, they can get that way if they aren't approached properly—try fartlek. Fartlek can be simple or it can be very scientific. Keep it simple for the time being. Fartlek involves a regular run, preferably off the roads, using trails and running away from traffic and interferences. With fartlek, make sure you schedule some hills on your course and try to use a course that is scenic and fun to run.

The theory behind fartlek is that it's a combination of intervals and hill-work without the boredom. Begin running gently. When you're properly warmed up, pick an object up ahead, maybe a tree or a rock, and pick your pace up until you reach the object. Then, slow back down to a jog. When you're breathing is pretty much back to normal, pick another object and stride out toward it at a nice clip. Drop back to a jog and let your breathing come back down. Run up a hill at a jog. Jog over the top, and give yourself time to recover coming down the other side.

Fartlek is a series of strains and recuperations, stress and redress. It is especially fun as your one-day-a-week speed workout if you have a companion. It will give both of you a little taste of competition racing toward the rock up the road, and running fartlek with a companion gives one a feeling that the stress and strain portions of the workout are being shared by someone else. It is important to run with a companion of approximately equal ability, however.

Whichever of the three methods of building speed you incorporate into your week's schedule is not so important as is the fact that you are doing something to build upon your own natural speed. The speed will be of great assistance once you begin putting in many more miles, because the muscles along the tops of the legs are usually the first to tire on a long run, thereby breaking a smooth stride. Intervals, hill-work and fartlek build up those front-leg muscles and also improve the power of your stride. In this case, speed certainly does not kill—it develops skill.

July 27—Did the 3.4-mile course today. Didn't kill myself at the start, so I felt pretty good at the end of the run. Air was surprisingly cool and clear after the sweltering heat we've been having. It must be the accumulation of all the hot air from the Washington politicos.

I-Jog, Run, Race

Almost as much energy—verbal and the mysterious kind that goes into written tracts—has gone into discussions of the topic jogger vs. runner vs. racer as to the discussions of whether or not there is a God and, if so, of what nature is He?

Dr. George Sheehan, the medical advisor of a whole generation of runners, speaks eloquently of the differences in nuances between a jogger and a runner, and then goes on to define the subtle advantages that racing brings to the runner. Dr. Sheehan's philosophical approach to the question is an inspiration to read, delving into the far reaches of the mind as it does.

Joe Henderson's approach is much more direct. "The difference between a jogger and a runner," Joe contends, "is that a runner has both feet off the ground more than they are on the ground."

Look at either a still picture or a slow-motion film of someone like Frank Shorter or Bill Rodgers or Garry Bjorklund or Brian Maxwell, and you'll see that they aren't really running—they're flying. Their feet are in the air more than they're in contact with the ground. A jogger, then, is a step beyond a fast walker, but the jogger certainly isn't flying. By Joe Henderson's very direct approach to running, a racer (by extension) would be someone who runs in a race. Joe takes his running simple because, to Joe, simple is best.

In their way, of course, both George Sheehan and Joe Henderson are correct. They just approach the question from different angles: George Sheehan from the head and Joe Henderson from the feet.

I guess I approach it from midway between the two—from somewhere in the guts.

What's the difference between a jogger and a runner? A jogger is a plodder who is perhaps working toward being a runner, or perhaps is not and will therefore be a plodder all his or her life. A runner is a jogger who's learned to fly and who never wants to land again. Since nothing on this earth is entirely perfect, though, the runner often finds himself jogging, whether or not he likes to admit it. And a runner doesn't like to admit it. To a runner, the very word "jog" is distasteful.

Longtime runner Bruce Dern thinks that being referred to by the general public as a jogger is a step up from when he was running 20 years ago and pedestrians would chant an army cadence—"Hup, two, three, four"—as he went running past. "Hell," Dern contends, "they don't know the difference. I could be running down the street with Frank Shorter on one side and Alberto Juantorena on the other, and we'd go by a group of people and they'd still look and say, 'Hey, Mable, there go some joggers.' It doesn't bother me anymore. At least they aren't throwing things at us as much these days."

For the average runner, though, the word jogger holds great distaste. It's like mistakenly calling a major a sergeant. Or like using the wrong fork to eat your salad at a fancy restaurant. Most runners take umbrage at the term jogger. Actually, though, most runners still practice a form of jogging on their long runs; I know I do. It'll be a long time until I develop enough stamina to practice a Shorter stride (no pun) while doing a 16-mile run. I drop back to a sort of jog. Doing intervals, where there's a lot of stretching out of the legs, will hopefully build up my stride and endurance enough to allow me to "run" through 16- or 20-mile runs. Ultra-marathoners, those brazen guys who do 50-milers and the 72-mile Lake Tahoe Run and the 100-milers and the 24-hour runs and those things, don't run. They don't even jog. They sort of shuffle.

But they don't much concern themselves about the philosophical or biomechanical differences between jogger and runner. They're too interested in going where few men have gone before. They're a special breed and deserve a book to themselves, people like Ted Corbitt and Dr. Tom Osler and Nick Marshall and Abe Underwood and others. They run until it becomes more than running—it becomes a ritual of endurance, a contest of the human spirit against the road or the track, a battle where their mind's dedication to carrying them on becomes all-important.

For the rest of us, what is the difference between the jogger and the runner and the racer that is fashioned in the guts and that is measured there?

Well, it's a rather curious thing. Although, on level ground, a jogger and a runner are both—according to the dictates of style—supposed to be running with their body trunks perpendicular to the ground (in other words, in a totally upright manner, like a person on a unicycle), there is a difference inside that trunk. It's easiest, perhaps, to use the analogy of the Concorde airliner. In order to help the plane's *lift*—and therefore to assist in slowing the plane on a landing as well as allowing it to rise into the air over a shorter strip of land on takeoff—the front section of the plane tilts downward, like a preying mantis bowing. In the guts of the jogger/runner, this is the jogging phase. There is more an up-and-down sensation to the steps, more a shuffling of the feet, more a tentativeness to the step, as though the man or woman is not entirely sure of what lies at the edge of the earth that might be approached if they broke into a certified run and they are too unsure of their abilities to find out.

When the Concorde becomes airborne, the front, sleek tip section of the plane slowly rises into a horizontal attitude and the plane is like a streamlined dart—a thing that would be out of place on the ground, something that is incomplete flying slowly. Likewise, when the jogger tentatively pushes the release button every once in a while in his gut, there is a shift in attitude within the body, a changing of gears, a more challenging beat to the heart, a bit more noticeable pressure on the abdomen, some stretching in the muscles along the fronts of the legs, a streamlining in the entire body machine.

The gut knows it's become a runner, even if it is only a momentary thing, only a thing that lasts for a half-block. It is a push beyond the comfortable feeling jogging gives, that feeling of blissful body boredom. It is a little push into uncertainty for the jogger, into the necessary gear for the runner who's long since passed the threshold. There's a gut feeling that even the most insensitive can feel—a sliding away of the jog and a streamlining into a run. It needn't be a fast run, but it does have to tell the gut that something more than mere movement is happening. The first few times it happens, it can be disconcerting, but after realizing what it is, the jogger's face usually breaks into a smile, there is a new tilt to the head. If it wasn't too much of a shock to the system, it becomes something that insidiously creeps into the daily workouts more and more until the jogger begins to become unbearable to his jogging friends because a condescending attitude develops. It eventually is replaced by a sense of feeling sorry for the poor jogger because he is missing so much.

I'm afraid my definition of a racer is pretty much parallel to Joe Henderson's: a runner who runs against other runners or a clock, either for position or to advance his own personal times, or to test himself against expectations. That sounds awfully scientific and laboriously wrought, but we've got to make some part of this book sound a little more than a casual conversation, don't we?

Aug. 1—The 3.4-mile course went very well today. It's probably the last time I'll ever do this course. We leave for California in eight hours. Will make entries as the trip progresses. The airline guide indicated that the flight was direct from Dulles to San Jose, but apparently they made some changes, because we had a stop-off in Denver. Arrived at the San Jose Airport and the Budget Rent-A-Car people didn't have my car waiting, although I called yesterday to confirm it. Ended up with a tired, white American Motors Sportabout which is just as well, as we've got enough baggage to fill it. Finally got to Bob Anderson's at 11:30 p.m., which means that, according to our East Coast body clocks, it's 2:30 a.m.

Aug. 2—My first run in California is up Moody Road in Los Altos Hills in the early morning. Did about 2½ miles. The vegetation is very refreshing, the air is great, and there were some large blue birds that kept jumping out of the way as I ran. Hal Higdon was on the "Today" show pitching *Fitness After Forty*. He did a real fine job, ending with the story of Senator Cranston mooning the crowd at a Master's track meet. California seems like an ideal place to run if today is any indication.

J-Alone

I've never quite been able to understand it, but some people can't seem to stand being alone. For some, it is probably a phobia. For others, it is a learned aversion to being with themselves—a dread, perhaps, of meeting someone they won't be comfortable with.

Personally, I think that people should be required to be alone with themselves for at least one hour a day. And I don't mean while you're watching television or in some other artificial way being entertained.

Unfortunately, just as the art of letter-writing has fallen by the wayside in the presence of the telephone, so the art of aloneness—not loneliness—has fallen into disuse.

It is a symptom of the younger generatiion that they've hated to be alone, usually because since they were born they've been entertained or in some manner accounted for. Parents some-how seem to feel it's their duty to nursemaid children to ma-turity.

Not to date myself, but parents didn't feel themselves duty-bound to entertain their children when I was a kid. We didn't have the mass of guaranteed breakable toys that were bought to keep us from becoming bored, either. This isn't meant as a pro-nouncement that our generation was better than the modern generation—just that our generation was different. We were experts at entertaining ourselves, whether alone or in small groups. We were seldom if ever bored. And when we were, we had enough smarts to keep it to ourselves.

Of course, the fallout of our generation's self-inflicted enter-tainment is beginning to be felt. It's not difficult, for instance, to see where George Lucas' mind was during childhood while he was left alone to entertain himself—he'd begun laying the imaginative foundations for what would become *Star Wars*, while his mother vacuumed the living room rug.

It would be paradoxical to apply the term aloneness to some people. The aloneness state of some people is populated by more interesting people and places and things than the middle of a New Year's Eve celebration is for those who dread the spec-ter of being alone. To some, aloneness causes the walls to close in, while for others, it makes them vanish.

For the runner, it would help immensely if he liked to be alone—at least occasionally—because the best running comes either when you're alone or when you're running with only one other person. Unfortunately, it isn't always possible to be run-ning with someone else, either because of scheduling problems or because the other person's ability at running is either holding you back or you are holding him back. Besides which, one of the great drawing cards of the running movement is that it is a sport, an occupation, an avocation, a lifestyle that can be prac-ticed alone, virtually anywhere, from the beach to the mountaintops.

Until the recent increase in the popularity of running, it was easy to categorically state that most runners were essentially solitary creatures—people who weren't afraid of the dark or of being alone or of facing their own thoughts which, on a long, long run is basically all you've got, other than the countryside.

It automatically comes as part of the definition of "popularity," though, that there are crowds involved. For some of the new runners, running can be and often is a social event. For the purist, though, running is never really a social function. Rather, it is a solitary function occasionally infected by the social germ.

W. B. Yeats, the greatest lyric poet of the century, claimed that it is impossible to separate the dancer from the dance, thereby claiming that dancing is the purest form of art. In like manner, it is impossible to separate the runner from the run, making running the purest form of sport. Like great planets in different orbits, however, no other runner can ultimately intrude upon the runner's run. He is alone in the run even if it is in the middle of the Bay-to-Breakers race, where there are 12,000 or more bodies pressing up against each other. The runner, even in a crowd of other runners, is still alone. It is merely less apparent because there are distractions.

Some observers have stated flatly that running and jogging is boring, indicating that they've never seen a jogger other than when he is infected with a pained expression on the face and a boredom in the eyes. To that, it's easy to say, "Bullshit!"

I've seen yoga adepts in trances who look exquisitely bored but who are no doubt vaulting the cosmos. I've seen concert-goers who seem asleep and bored but who are soaring with the music. I've seen learned men wrinkle their brows in seeming boredom, only to be computing quadratic equations on a paper napkin. I've seen the bored look on the faces of runners—I've had it often enough myself—but what is written on the face is often a disguise to what is going on inside the head.

On a good run, it is extremely possible—and, in fact, desirable—to slip into a sort of reverie, the extraneous person making all the necessary turns in the road, performing all the necessary functions to keep the physical body mobile, while the mind attends to solving problems, writing books, evaluating career plans, balancing the checkbook, writing poetry, redecorating the living room, etc., etc., etc. The motion of running, besides its great physical benefits, provides a mobile thinking tank for the runner's mind. It rushes past the common things of life that anchor the mind to mundane functions during the day, and it shakes the mind loose so that it can function almost in a vacuum as though able to program for itself any topic it likes at any time during that portion of the run given over to reverie.

For those who've never really been alone with themselves and with their own thoughts, running can conceivably be a good therapy but a bad deal for them. It may open doors to themselves they'd have preferred left closed—doors that laying-down-on-the-couch-and-paying-$60-an-hour therapy might have creaked open eventually but that running can open on the first slip into the reverie gear.

Running's saving grace in that regard comes with the realization that if the person continues to run, and continues to allow the doors to open, positive therapeutic returns come about. The act of running provides a unique connection between the mobile body and the questing mind that has been too often overlooked, because it has been too long felt that on the college campus the department of psychology is at one end and the physical education department is at the other.

Strenuous physical activity, like running—especially like running—can serve as a perfect valve or spigot for releasing built-up frustrations and hostilities. At the same time, perhaps with a struggle at first but certainly given time, running can allow a person to meet the person who is going to play more of a role in their life than any other human being in the cosmos—and that's the person himself. The person who is hidden, along with his faults and attributes, all day long by the myriad details of life is allowed to come out of the body closet during a long run. We are allowed to meet ourselves, for better or for worse, so that we can come to grips with the person we really are, rather than dealing with the person we either thought or hoped we were. Sometimes, there are pleasant surprises, sides of ourselves we didn't even suspect existed. Other times, there are revelations that are unpleasant but that allow us to reform, in the midst of a run, the direction of one or another part of our lives.

But the revelations and the problem-solving aspects come only to the runner alone. It's nice to run occasionally with someone else, and to run at a comfortable enough speed so that a conversation can be carried on. The practice serves to eat up the miles while allowing the runners to cover topics that are difficult to get into with a television blaring or with other distractions. But the ultimate run is the run alone, the run where the runner is in no way compromised in actually *being* his run. It is a venture into an existence where there is no boredom. It is the venture where, should the runner fail to bring forth topics that need discussion within himself, there is always the run itself.

For the runner not yet in shape to the point where an extremely long run is possible, perhaps the aches of arriving there provide enough company. Even at those moments, though, the run reaches a point where the aches become dulled and the mind becomes sharp, and all things are put into their perspective. Not every day, not on every run, but often enough so the realization that it has happened makes that run something no one who could have shared it would have found boring.

Aug. 7—Went to my first Fun-Run. Tried the half-mile, which I haven't run since gym class in high school. Made the mistake of not taking a warmup jog. Faded badly in the second 440 as legs turned to rubber. Time was 2:57. Tried the five-miler then, and it's the longest I've run in years. Did it in 42:46, and it hurt. Was nice to be running with other people, though. Adds a different perspective.

K-Together

Down the other end of the alley from running's position as a sport that is ultimately aloneness for a participant during most of its practice, there is the fact that more and more streets and highways and mountain trails and park paths are being populated by runners. Running clubs are enjoying tremendous growth, and some runners are finding it a nice change of pace to run with others when the opportunity permits.

As already stated, running is essentially a loner sport, one in which a man or a woman moves against his or her own limitations. It is a sport that can develop a very real sense of self-reliance. And it is a lifestyle that begets acute functioning of the thought and reasoning process.

For those runners unable to accept running as an aloneness participant sport, the very numbers that are now involved have made it possible to run socially, although running soon becomes more a social event than a run after a while if it is not tempered with the uplifting, solitary runs.

It also opens running to the syndromes other "sports" suffer. I know hunters, for instance, who hunt only as an excuse to get out of the house. They leave at 5 a.m. to go in search of the wily white-tailed deer, taking along enough warm clothing to keep the chill off, drive miles and miles into the mountains. Then, they plop themselves down under a tree and drink coffee from a Thermos and, when that's gone, pull out the brandy bottle and sit around shooting the shit until the sun goes down. They come home with cheery-red noses which the wives chalk up to all that time spent trudging around in the cold woods. But they seldom have any game with them, which the wife is usually just as glad of, since she has to end up cleaning it and finding some way to serve the big kill.

Running already has its own variations. A local runner was taking hour-long runs. He'd come home from work in the evening, dash into the bedroom, change into his running togs and shoes, and he'd dash out the door, make a turn at the front lawn and be gone, calling to his wife that he'd make it back by the time she had the table set. Sure enough, an hour later the guy would be back, perspiring and puffing. He'd be smiling a big smile like he'd just set a new personal record, he'd dash into the shower, come out whistling and sit down to eat. A half-hour after eating, he'd be asleep in his chair. His wife took all of this in stride for several weeks. But, upon talking to friends about it, she confirmed her suspicion that her husband should have been losing some pounds doing an hour-long run every day. When she got home, she also checked the bottom of his shoes; they were barely worn.

"Either he's running on marshmallows or he's twinkletoes," she muttered to herself. Slipping her tennis shoes on before her husband got home, the good wife went through the motions of making supper. Hubby came home, rushed to the bedroom, changed and rushed out. The wife followed half a block behind. Hubby took a right turn and went down the block, and then another right turn and, as she peeked around the corner, she saw him dash into the arms of a redhead who was waiting for him at the side door of a house halfway down the block. The guy hasn't been doing much social running lately.

For those who need it, though, social running can be fun as a change of pace or as a regular once-in-a-while thing. Joe Henderson, for instance, runs alone all week. Every Saturday morning, though, he meets a small group of friends at the same place each week and they go on a group run. The group run makes everything move more effortlessly, certainly. At a pace that is not so fast that it makes talking impossible, the miles can be eaten up very quickly and painlessly.

The drawback is that no two persons are exactly the same in abilities and level of training, so it is necessary to run at a speed that's comfortable to the slowest person in the group, which might not be a speed that is comfortable to everyone else. Additionally, when a fork in the road comes, a vote must be taken on which turn to take. It's also necessary, before the run begins, to wait until everyone arrives. All of these factors are not overpoweringly against running with friends. They just make it more inconvenient, and running shouldn't start off on that foot—which is why Joe Henderson usually keeps the rest of the week to himself. In the ultimate sense, running is something done best alone—especially if you're approaching it for aesthetic benefits: the benefits to the soul as well as the body.

Probably the best time to run with other people is when you're entered in a race, which is something we'll talk about later, but even then the socializing should come afterward.

Groups tend to make rules, and running in its purest form should know no such boundaries.

Aug. 10—Right lower leg, front and back, has been extremely stiff from moving a thousand boxes around in the garage and from running the five-miler on Sunday. It is reluctant to loosen up. Ran about 1½ miles today, very slowly. Jill ran a bit last night but is having difficulty starting her program. She might be pretty good if she can get into it, because she certainly has good speed.

L-Dogs and Drivers

*I*n the old days, which weren't so long ago, running was something that was done on a track—usually a quarter-mile track that was arbitrarily put in, like a fence, around the high school football field. Years ago, there were very, very few runners who ran along roads. It just wasn't done. Running was a stopwatch sport, something to be done under certain pre-established conditions, in a certain arena, at a certain time of the year and by certain people. Running was not something that was meant to allow a man, woman or child just to go running about wheresoever he or she pleased. Running, in those days, had more form, ritual, common sense—and was much more stilted and boring than it is today.

Today, running is as close as it's possible to get to the true free spirit. Running has taken to the roads, the paths, the game trails, everywhere it's possible to place one foot in front of the other. Runners today have the audacity to run just about anywhere they damned well please.

Of course, all of this is well and good. It makes the sport more attractive, allows it to give to its participants something other than health and fitness. It adds the element of psychological well-being.

As a new or returned runner, this is one of the things that was probably most attractive about running—this feeling that one can run anywhere one damned well pleases. Once the runner is fit enough that his elementary courses become boring, it is logical—and advisable—that he begin going on runs with no set direction in mind, that he or she give in to the deep-seated wanderlust within the soul. This adds certain new elements to the running that confining oneself to a track never brings.

There are, however, hazards in running about as the spirit moves you.

Already, in your running confined to the area close to home, you may have gotten intimations of some of the possible problems. There are dogs that attack anything that moves, and who feel that a runner's legs are being pounded along the pavement in an attempt to get them more tender for the mutt's teeth. Of course, the dog is supposed to be restrained and kept under control by its owner, but some dog-owners feel that dogs own the streets and that people on foot should stay off the streets.

Be prepared to meet dogs that will challenge your right to be running. Many runners take elaborate detours just to avoid such dogs, while others spend hours on the phone trying to get the authorities to do something about restraining certain dogs that have seemingly been specifically trained to attack runners. Many runners carry something along with them when they run that can be used to ward off the vicious buggers, but carrying something when you run can imbalance your stride. I've seen runners doing roadwork with everything from lead pipes to rawhide whips to protect themselves.

And don't kid yourself into believing that just because you live in the suburbs you are pretty safe from a mauling. In the suburb where I used to live near Alexandria, Va., I ran at 6 a.m. and soon learned that dogs left to run loose by their masters at night usually revert to the instincts of the wild and form roving packs that prowl the neighborhood looking for fire hydrants to congregate around, female dogs who are foolish enough to wander into their territory, automobile tires that have not been properly christened, and runners. One of the shortcomings of running early in the morning is that the masters of those roving pack dogs have not yet hauled their asses out of bed to call the individual dogs into the house, so run prepared to intimidate the mutts.

Usually, a tough stance on your part will frighten off the dogs, because it is usually the stance the dog's real master takes. The alternative is to carry an aluminum car antenna, since it is light and can be telescoped out to a neat whip when dogs approach. The sting from a car antenna usually teaches a misguided dog that mailmen are easier targets than runners. The best protection, though, is to use the telephone to call the pound to come and round up the dogs that are not being properly restrained.

The biggest danger to a road runner, though, is from cars. I know I've had some very close calls from cars going too fast with drivers paying too little attention to the road. Some runners have had serious injuries from run-ins with cars because the car, whether in the right or the wrong, usually weighs 10-20 times as much as the runner and is therefore a formidible object with which to argue the rights of the road.

It is a rule of the road always to run on the side of the road, facing traffic. This allows you to see traffic approaching you so that you have ample time to take evasion maneuvers if a car decides it wants to take the edge of the road you're running on.

Running facing traffic can cause problems, however, since roads are built with crowns in the center portion so that when it rains the water will run off the side of the road and not pool. The runner, therefore, is always running with his left leg lower than the right. This practice can cause lower back problems and leg problems. However, running on the wrong side of the road can cause death if you don't anticipate perfectly the approach of a car from the rear.

The best rule to remember when running a road that cars use is simply that there are no rules. Treat every car as though it is out to kill you, because it just may be. You'll soon develop a sense of what type of driver is going to give you a wide berth and which driver is going to see if he can nip you as he goes past. However, no categorizing is 100% perfect, and the one driver who fools you may be the one that kills you.

And don't assume that, because you qualify as a pedestrian, that you have any rights. In certain states, the driver who hits you will face a huge fine and jail, but that's doing you little good after you've been knocked into the middle of next week. Never trust any driver you encounter. Always be extremely cautious when dealing with cars. Wear light-colored clothing, especially if you're running in the early morning, early evening or after dark. Don't expect the local police to be on your side in a dispute with a car, either. Although the police are becoming more enlightened about running, and although many police officers are becoming runners themselves, and although runners aren't considered quite the nut cases that they once were, running is still not the universal means of travel in America. Therefore, the cars have the upper hand.

Additionally, many drivers feel that *anything* on the road that interferes with their driving, even if they aren't very good drivers, should be removed from the road, and that includes runners. They'll often take great pains to go to city councils to get ordinances passed to get runners off the roads—because runners are, apparently, littering up the highway and causing a traffic nuisance. They may be right. The way our roads and highways were built, they were designed for cars and trucks and not for runners. Unfortunately, as citizens of the borough, city, state and country, the runner helped pay to build the roads and he should have an option on how to use them—as long as the use is within the law and does not endanger the lives or safety of anyone else.

It may be a useless admonition, but runners should be extremely careful when using *any* road. I've seen runners using the middle of the road and then refusing to yield when a car comes along. Sure, idiot runners like that are in a minority, but all it takes is a few of them to turn the whole road-use thing into a war between traffic and foot-soldiers. Make an attempt to find roads that are infrequently used. Also, keep in mind that just because speed limit signs indicate 25 m.p.h. on a lonely road, most motorists have never driven for more than a hundred yards at 25 m.p.h. in their life.

Find trails and paths that are closed to vehicular traffic if you can, cross intersectioins as though your life depended on it, and run facing traffic if you're going to use a well-traveled road, staying off as far as possible to the side. A book could be written on this topic alone. Hopefully, runners will have enough common sense to practice some of the rules passed on to kids when they learn to cross streets.

The other road danger is simple overuse. Get off the road when you can and run in fields, on dirt roads, along pathways or on any softer-than-asphalt surface whenever you can. Constant pounding along black-topped roads can severely injure the proper growth of young legs, can wear out young adult legs and can completely destroy the proper use of aging legs. (And remember that concrete is approximately 10 times harder than asphalt.) Your legs aren't built to accept all that pounding on a hard surface without offering some protest. Give your legs and feet a treat once in a while and find nice, soft places to run. Don't wear racing flats for doing road work. Stick with the heavier but more protective training flats. And don't overdo it with too much running too soon. It's fun to take to the roads when you're more able to run longer and longer distances. But do it cautiously so that you'll be able to continue doing it over the long run.

Aug. 21—Jill and I have begun running the Parcourse at Foothill College on Tuesdays and Thursdays, and as a warmup to the Fun-Run on Sunday mornings. My Fun-Run half-mile time is stalled at 2:53; Jill did 4:58. On the three-mile run, I did okay going out, but on the return I faded badly, realizing along El Monte Road that one of the reasons I've been doing so badly is because I'm carrying along an extra 25 pounds. My weight is down to 186, but I've still got a long way to go; I'd like to get to 155-160. Maybe then I can contemplate trying a marathon or two next year. Vaulted dreams after blowing a three-miler.

M-When and What

*I*f running is a part of your life like it is with me—I mean it really is a part of my life—I don't have to make time for running. It is harder for me to make time for this, that and the other thing, at times even my wife, than it is for running."

The words belong to Bruce Dern, the movie actor, but much longer than a movie actor a hard runner who has competed in everything from the 100-yard dash to the 72-mile Lake Tahoe Run. The words indicate an advanced form of dedication to running so that running has become as natural as going to the bathroom—to the extent that the running is no longer something of dedication, but rather of habit and need.

Bruce Dern has the wherewithal to work his schedule around his running—in fact, at this point in his career, just about to work his schedule around *anything* he wants to do. He doesn't think it consciously, but Bruce Dern may have arrived at this point in his career just so that he would have the option of modifying his schedule to accommodate his running.

Most of us are not as fortunate unless we are independently wealthy, retired, in school or our own boss—and therefore the master of our own schedules. Most of us have jobs and careers and wives and families, and that's certainly all well and good. But it sometimes makes it difficult, but not impossible, to fit in our running.

This observation, admittedly, is a device to set us up for talking about when you run and how much you run. You're already out there 4-6 days a week running, right? You're taking that one mandatory day off, right? When should you be doing your running, then?

That depends on the person. Running should not become an irritant on your schedule, but rather something that is looked forward to, anticipated and that is a very integral part of your whole lifestyle. It won't fit in right away, of course. At first, it's like a new pair of shoes: it needs some breaking in, it needs some time to allow the pain of working out after all those years on your butt to subside, for your body to become acclimated to the new activity and for your mind to explore the possibilities.

You've probably already established some sort of schedule for yourself. You may have also fallen into the trap of believing that the specific time you've found for your running is the only time to do it, when actually any time of the day *can* be a good time for running—even at night if you're running on a smooth surface and there is some adequate lighting nearby.

The story of people includes a chapter about there being two kinds: the "owls" and the "larks." The owls are the night people, those folks who come alive when the sun goes down. The larks, of course, are those who are up with the sun and who do their best work first thing in the morning, whose motors then seem to just run down toward the end of the day so that they are into bed relatively early. It seems logical, then, that the larks find themselves running early in the morning, because the running helps them further open their senses and get their faculties working to maximum as early as possible. The owls, on the other hand, like to get the stimulation of running as a sort of springboard to the night-life they love so much.

There are good and bad points for both types of runners.

Running first thing in the morning can be an exhilarating experience. The world seems new, you can run in the dew, you can do what you want to without being bothered. For urban or suburban runners, it's a wonderful time to run, because the pollution from the day before has pretty well been washed from the air by the night and there is a certain shiny-penny quality about the morning, where your footfalls upon the sidewalk or road serve as a herald to the new day. You run with the morning paperboy, the milkman, the garbageman and the drunk left over from the night before. In the country, it's the moment in the day when the roads belong to you, when the sun peeking above the eastern horizon sparkles off the damp grass, when certain early-morning birds—like the lark—are surprised to see someone sharing their private moments. It's an almost poetic time to run.

Except when it's winter. I probably shouldn't put it quite like that, because if you're properly dressed, early-winter mornings can be nice times to run, too, if you've got chains on the soles of your shoes. For some runners, a blast of cold air as they move out the door first thing in the morning is the worst possible thing that could happen to them, whether they're larks or snow-shoe rabbits. Cold air—especially cold, *damp* air—can cramp the legs, make breathing uncomfortable and cause a general feeling similar to the old Dodge sitting in the driveway that seems reluctant to turn over under those circumstances.

I know I don't like running in the morning when it's especially cold—even though the body machine, like a car, begins to warm up as it shakes off the night's cold with some heat-producing activity. (For those who do like to run in winter morning air, have no fear that the cold air will freeze your lungs; it is warmed by the mouth and throat on its way to the lungs. You can wrap a scarf around your mouth and nose to offer some protection against the formation of icicles on your nose, though.)

Other shortcomings of early-morning runs include the packs of dogs not yet dispersed by the coming of traffic to the streets, and drivers who may be few in number but who are almost invariably driving their cars while still sleeping—plus that necessity to overcome the initial cold.

At the other end of the day, late-afternoon running can be a treat because it is usually pleasantly warm—or at least as pleasantly warm as it's going to get that day—and the body's had all day to get its moving parts working. The body has also had all day to build up tensions and aggravations that the run in the afternoon is going to wring out. For the party person who likes company, the roads are filled with other people doing things.

On the negative side of afternoon running, one of the things that the people are doing is trying to run you down if you're running on the road—or pollute you to death with a great deal of pollution that's been building up all day from the roads being used by cars and trucks, and that is being added to greatly by the fact that it's rush hour (there are rush hours even in small towns). The pollution along the road in the afternoon can be frightening in its way, because the runner has few places to do long runs except along the side of the road.

Unless there is a brisk wind to disperse it, pollution hangs in the air above the road and beside the road, and the runner is moving through what amounts to a stream of pollution materials while he is breathing in unusually large amounts of air. The runner may develop one of the most impressive and unyielding hearts in the world, only to be killed from cancer of the lungs from breathing automobile exhaust fumes. And don't believe that the government has solved the problem, either. The government has merely mandated different pollutants. In order to rid the world of nitrous oxides in exhausts, sulfuric acid gasses have been exchanged. You can't win. The road runner should be aware that the late afternoon is not a good time to run along the roads if he wants to breathe.

I've run both times of the day, and although I'm a lark person, I still prefer the afternoons, simply because I seem to suffer from chronic leg problems and I feel more comfortable having those several extra degrees of warmth on my legs that the afternoon brings. Of course, I'll probably develop cancer of the lungs, but at least my legs won't hurt as much.

From my own experiments with differing times for running, then, my perfect time would be 3:30-5:00 p.m. on a grassy path around the palatial estates of some potentate hidden away in foothills of the Rocky Mountains, an estate on which no cars are allowed and where the grass is kept shag-carpet smooth so I could give my asphalted legs a rest from the pounding. I sometimes think of fantasy places like that while I'm striding along the Central Expressway in Mountain View and Palo Alto doing the last mile of an eight-miler, trying to "blow the carbon out" during the last few blocks. In the meantime though, it's running as usual, although there are good signs on the horizon.

Most of the guys at the office run, at least most of the guys in the editorial module. They do so at noon instead of eating lunch. They change into their running clothes in the men's room and hit the roads, having something very light to eat when they return or nothing at all. Many companies are encouraging their employees to take up running during their lunch-hour and after working hours. Some larger firms have even built tracks behind their plants so that employees can have a handy place to do their running. It's certainly good business, because the employees come back from their lunch break refreshed and ready for a productive afternoon, there is an increase in morale and teamwork among the workers, and the incidence of employees using sick days and health insurance drops drastically. Some companies organize their employees into teams and compete in track and field meets and road races with other companies, much as bowling teams did—and still do—in factory towns.

The great thing is that with running, the interest in the sport—and therefore the interest in having its benefits felt in the company—works its way from the management on down, since it seems that running is a sport that began, at least in corporate structures, among the management. If you work for a company with enough insight into its employees' needs and its own well-being to encourage running during the lunch-hour, you're several steps ahead. If your company is large enough to have such a program and now doesn't, might be time to suggest it. Our current push is to get a shower-room installed in our building so that even those of us who sweat profusely when we run can do our workouts over the lunch-hour.

What it amounts to, though, is that any time is a good time to run if you really want to run badly enough. Some people even run at midnight—but that's another story, to be told later on in this saga.

Sept. 4—Read Joe Henderson's juvenile novel about a young high school miler. Joe tried to put as much good information relative to running in as he could, and it has been helpful in its way. It made me realize that I'm racing too much against the clock and therefore suffering the results of stress—i.e., incredibly sore legs and lackluster workouts. The proportion Joe suggests is 95% LSD (long, slow distance) against 5% racing. Lately, I've been doing 50-50, which is way too much. Have to come back to some LSD and get off the clock-watching.

N-Drinks

*T*here seems to be no middle ground on the topic of running and alcohol. It is almost as though we were back in another era deciding on Prohibition. With cigarette smoking there is very little problem. Although there are some people who both smoke and run (not necessarily simultaneously, although I'm prepared to believe anything), the numbers are few and most everyone agrees that smoking is counter-productive to running—as well as to extended life. Booze and running is another matter entirely.

The fact is—and let's put it up front here so we can get the argument going right away—that many, many *exceptional* runners consume alcohol. There is really no argument about that fact at all, because the runners have been seen doing just that in public watering holes. The furor at this point will come from the fact, as it always seems to, that someone put it into print. There seems to be a rather warped impression on the part of some people that because someone puts into print the fact that many runners enjoy a beer now and again, some of them enjoying more than one beer now and again, it is an endorsement of drinking alcohol beverages and it should be edited out of any periodical or book because it might influence young runners to drink.

In most cases, the young runner is probably like any other young person and has probably already tried some booze, so the ostrich-head-in-the-sand approach is probably too late. Parents really concerned about alcohol and their children should have already done the educating at home regarding booze and other sinful delights. To mention that many runners drink when they aren't running, and to mention further that some runners drink *while they are running*, is not an encouragement to youngsters to become Bowery bums. It is merely a statement of fact—much like stating that runners often go to the bathroom in the bushes before a race because there's no other place to go.

Everyone has heard the story of how Frank Shorter, the night before his gold medal marathon at Munich, consumed two liters of German beer. Big deal. Where's the crime? The beer probably gave Shorter his best night's sleep in a very tense week and certainly put enough liquid into his system to get him successfully through at least the first 18 miles of the 1972 Olympic Marathon.

Dr. George Sheehan, one of the best-loved and most respected runners in the country, has long been a beer-drinker and contends that beer is one of the best replacement drinks that can be taken during a long, hot race. Dr. Sheehen mentions Dr. Tom Bassler, editor for the American Medical Joggers' Association, who runs 25 miles on Sundays, taking a beer every few miles. Bassler's comment on his Sunday runs: "I jog a six-pack."

Dick Walsh of Las Vegas, who'd run 25 marathons in the 3:40 range, took up some serious beer-drinking before the 1977 Boston Marathon. He drank six beers and ate a pizza the night before the big race and additionally had two more beers during the race. Despite stopping off along the way to shake hands and hug children and chat with people, he finished the Boston in

3:17, accompanied by a feeling of euphoria. Walsh is 54 years old.

I do know that I'm not the only runner who, after a long, tiring run, looks forward to walking out the aches in my legs while downing a cold beer. At races I've attended—especially at marathons—about 85% of the finishers look for a can of beer as they finish. The beer, as Dr. Sheehan states, is an excellent replacement drink, probably not as good as Body Punch or ERG, but likely better than Gatorade, because it gets into the bloodstream and distributes the electrolytes faster.

To become fanatic about the mere mention of alcohol in the same breath with running is ridiculous. Some runners have never touched a drop of alcohol and never will. That doesn't make them better runners, however, and anyone who either states outright or infers that alcohol and running don't mix is running at the mouth. On the other side of the road, our argument is not that beer or other alcohol will necessarily make you a better runner, although most of the top runners have definitely allowed alcohol to pass their lips at some time in their lives.

It seems silly, however, for people to complain that until it is proven to be either harmless or helpful to a runner, the word alcohol should not be mentioned in conjunction with running. This is like saying the theory that the world is flat should be held until someone falls off the end and then comes back to tell us that the world is, indeed, flat.

Alcohol is, like anything else, dangerous if taken in excess. For a few people, it is dangerous if taken at all, because there seems to be, in some people, a chemical flaw that, stimulated by the least bit of alcohol, turns them into alcoholics. Gatorade or milk, if taken in excess, is also dangerous to your health.

Some of us, perhaps rather radically, feel that at least beer may be beneficial to a runner—if taken under certain conditions and at certain times. Dick Walsh and Frank Shorter apparently find that drinking it the night before a race helps them load up with carbohydrates and liquid that will assist their bodies in getting through at least the early stages of a marathon. It also enduces a good night's sleep which, especially the night before an Olympic marathon, is a commodity that is at a premium because of the natural nervousness that accompanies it.

Walsh and Dr. Sheehan and Dr. Bassler drink it during long runs. It quickly replaces some of the lost fluids, and its soothing effect can possibly serve as a light shield against the common aches that develop during a long run, making the runner more euphoric and less of a hypochondriac about every little muscle twinge that comes along while he's running.

After a race, a beer gets the body started on refilling the reservoirs where necessary liquids and electrolytes are stored.

My own experiments to this point with beer during a run indicates that it does have a beneficial effect as far as ridding the body of an awareness of aches and pains. I tried some beer in my first 16-mile run in 10 years. My legs were sore and bothered me at the 11-mile point and, after drinking approximately 12 ounces of beer over a 1½-mile period, I found that the aches were, if not gone, at least faded considerably. I also found, however, that because I was sore and was trying for my first 16-miler in 10 years, it was necessary to encourage a sort of killer instinct, a dogged determination to force myself to keep going. Once I drank the beer, my killer instinct, my desire to force my body to keep up the pace, was dulled and consequently my pace dropped off a bit.

The entire subject of beer-drinking and running needs more serious investigation by that large percentage of runners who see it as an ally in their running.

Sept. 5—Felt a bit restless this afternoon and, even though I was sore, I decided it was warm enough to sweat off some weight. Ran my course number one (1.4 miles) twice, which was a first. I went easy, and although I was a little stiff in the legs from yesterday's running against the clock, I had no breathing problems. There was a slight hint of a pain in the right side, but I was apparently going too slow to aggravate it. I think I should investigate shoes a little closer. Some of the leg problems might be coming from that direction, as my shoes always wear out on the outside heels, and wearing new shoes without pre-worn heels might be partially to blame. Even though they're getting ragged around the edges, maybe I should revert to my old Countries.

O-Boredom

*T*he feature of running that makes it so enticing and available to so many people is the fact that it can be done virtually anywhere. Anywhere a person can walk, he can run. Besides giving the sport universal appeal, it also contributes to making running a sport with as many variations as the imagination of a runner can invent.

Running in Denver, Colo., is very dissimilar to running in Phoenix, Ariz., which has little in common with running in New York City or in Weatherly, Pa.—yet it is all joined by the common thread that it is still running: whether it is up and down hills, or up and down mountains, or along miles of incredibly level desert.

The fact that the earth is not monotonously the same along every square inch of its land mass provides the basis for keeping running extremely interesting.

There is the theory that the jogger clings to the monotony of a single course day after day while the runner ranges far and wide over the countryside. This does not necessarily hold true. If it did, during the 1960s all track runners would have been joggers, even if they were capable of a 4:06 mile. It is only of recent vintage that runners have taken to the roads, and joggers as well as runners like to see what there is to see while putting in their miles. They do, in fact, get more of a chance to see the scenery than the runner, because they are usually moving past it slower. At the other extreme, there are runners who, in order to improve their speed and stamina, like to measure their efforts by running measured courses for time.

Whether a jogger or a runner, a new runner or an old, returned runner, the daily running does not have to be more boring than the runner wants it to be. There are thousands of variations and changes in the local landscape that can be taken advantage of in order to make running an interesting experience. There is one suburban runner we've heard about who has, by studying a map of his housing development, come up with 57 different courses within an area of less than a square mile. He has each of the courses numbered and he keeps personal records (*personal records* are referred to by runners as PRs, and the term is not to be confused with *public relations*) for each, which would seem to be rather a monumental task in itself.

Parks and wooded areas are excellent places to run without boredom, because they are usually criss-crossed with trails and paths, there is little traffic (except the occasional bike rider) to worry about, and the surface is a nice change from the unyielding concrete and asphalt that characterizes most road racing and running.

Many colleges and parks and businesses are adding a Parcourse to their facilities, which makes an excellent running course. A Parcourse is, like a golf course, a series of stations (greens), usually 18 on a full course, that follows the lay of the land and that directs participants to follow a series of arrows from one station to another. Various exercises are prescribed— everything from sit-ups to leg-lifts. During the early stations, the participant is instructed to walk between stations. This serves as a warm-up session. Farther into the course, the participant is instructed to jog between stations. Toward the end of the course, the participant is again instructed to walk, thus painlessly being given a cooling-off period as the exercise course comes to an end.

The full Parcourse is usually two miles long, but it can vary, depending on the terrain available at the college or park where the course is built. The course offers a pretty complete exercise program while changing the scenery with each exercise station. There are instructions on boards at each station, and the participant can modify the number of repetitions on each exercise to match his current physical development. The days I accomplish one pull-up, I feel like I've licked the world, while getting over the vaulting bar without touching is a major accomplishment, since I'm literally that inept at anything requiring coordination.

The Parcourse also offers a great cross-country course for runners to use on days they feel the rest of their body is in good enough shape that it does not need additional building and toning. Of course, a cross-country course can be set up almost anywhere there is a hill and some untraveled roads.

Other runner variations are to buy a bicycle, pump it the several miles to a good running area, do your running and then pump back home. You manage to get in two different forms of exercise in one session, the bicycling contributing to your leg development.

On weekends, either alone or with some runner friends, pack a light lunch in light knapsacks and take a running hike. Even if it develops into a walk-jog session, you'll be covering miles painlessly and combining some touring with your running.

For those who like to stick close to home and who don't want to venture into anything too far removed from the normal, a simple and effective variation even if you have only one course, is simply to run it in the opposite direction on alternating days. The scenery appears to be completely different, much like a trip to the far side of the moon, because you are seeing sides of houses you didn't see on your original running of the course.

The important thing to keep in mind about running—even with a limited number of courses—is that it need be no more boring than the runner makes it. Some runners aren't bored as quickly with the same scenery as others, and in fact feel more comfortable with familiar surroundings. The important thing is that the runner know when a session of boring running is coming up and that he be prepared to fight it off with a little imaginative running. Variety, as they say, is the spice of life— it's also the spice of running.

Sept. 13—Took two days off to let the legs heal a bit and then ran at the Fun-Run, taking the next day off to recuperate from that. Hope that changing back to my old, trusty Countries will help my leg problem. Tonight, went to Bob Anderson's to run with him, but he got held up at the office so I ran by myself up Moody Road. Started slowly and built up speed. The wind was pretty heavy in the trees, like a locomotive moving through them. Felt pretty good by the turn at the top end of the road, although my breathing was a little ragged. On the return, my breathing dropped back, the pace picked up and everything felt good—much like it used to 10 years ago. Picked up the pace, ignored a blister that was beginning to form. Felt very good, ending up at Foothill College, jogging back slowly.

142

P-Racing

One of my first assignments upon arriving at *Runner's World* Magazine was to write the main feature for our special "Beginning Racing section (*RW*, December 1977). I was logically a good choice, because I hadn't raced in years. Since arriving in California, I'd run (badly) a few Fun-Runs at Foothill College. Everyone else on the staff had been running—and racing—for years. Joe Henderson, for instance, had been racing for 20 years and he was only 34 years old. The thinking was that my perspectives on racing would more logically approximate the perspectives of new runners. They were correct. For those contemplating racing as an adjunct to running, the "Beginning Racing" guide is presented. I'm not of the opinion that every runner should race. I do think, however, that every runner should at least give racing a try—at least on the Fun-Run level.

There were 12,000 entrants in the Bay-to-Breakers race in San Francisco. At the Atlanta Peachtree race, there were 6000 racers. There were 5000 entered in the New York Marathon and in the First Chicago Distance Classic. Amateur Athletic Union and Road Runners Club races are sprouting up like mushrooms on a warm night. There are more than 200 Fun-Run sites with more being added each month.

The bulk of the record entry fields at San Francisco, Atlanta, New York and Chicago is made up of novice racers—people who've seemingly come out of nowhere, gone into training and entered major racing events. The spectacular influx of new faces at the established races has prompted a huge demand for new local events.

The jogging and running explosion that is evident along every quiet street and busy highway very obviously has a racing counterpart. The running and the racing are forming a dual boom, thanks in large part to the refreshing attitude toward racing that the new runners have brought to the sport. Racing is no longer considered the exclusive preserve of the elite. The average runner has suddenly realized that he is part of a huge mass of runners and that races are as much open to him as they are to anyone else.

Everyone who's running seriously seems to be considering racing, if not doing it in one form or another already. The overwhelming entry lists at major races asks the questions: Is there room at races for every runner? Should every runner want to be a racer?

The first question is the easier of the two to answer. Yes, there is room for everyone who wants to race. Some organizational and logistical changes will be made in major races in order to accommodate the vast numbers of racers and their varying degrees of skill and preparation. At the same time, there are new races being established to keep the racer within the runner satisfied.

Racing is not something to fear. It is a logical progression in a body that is suddenly more willing and able to run faster. Racing is a sort of acid test that can be applied to all the miles that have been run as a solitary avocation to test if they were run properly. Has my training put me in good shape considering what I had to start with? Is my pace reaching competitive standards? Can I handle the tension and anticipation of pitting myself against other runners? All of these questions can be answered by racing. Or can they?

Is racing for everyone who runs? Isn't racing giving up the solitary enducements of running that drew you toward it in the first place? Isn't racing getting you back into the very rat race you have been running to escape?

No matter what the veterans may say, racing is not necessary for everyone. For those who run to escape the arena of competition they face every day on the freeways or on the job or at home, racing could very easily be one more tension situation. Running for those people is an escape and a rejuvenation ritual that would be violated by racing.

For most runners who find themselves becoming more and more serious about jealously guarding their half-hour or hour per day when they commute the back roads and the byways in order to commune with their own bodies and minds through running, and who are finding that running is a necessity for their psychological well-being, racing may hold some unexpected peaks of heightened sensation in the overall running experience.

Racing for most runners is also a good measure of their accomplishments—a measuring stick that makes the weekday training sessions more meaningful. And, for most runners, racing is an opportunity to give in to that urge that is present to at least some degree in every person—the urge to compete.

With the tremendous growth in running during the past few years, it has been impossible for most runners to have a coach. This fact needn't disturb a runner. Be assured that most running veterans have trained with no other coach but their instincts and what they've read on the topic of running. For better than a decade, many runners have used *Runner's World Magazine* as their first-string coach, because the magazine has been the only national forum addressing itself to the runner's needs in such detail. The magazine has also been responsible for the publication of many fine books on the subject of running which, combined with other available books, have provided the runner's basic library. These days, there is a vast book shelf of material on running.

Before we get into the serious matters of racing, like any coach worth his salt tablets, we'll give runners who really don't want to go any further one last chance to jump ship. For those runners who are dead-set against racing, our advice would be that it is in your best interest to avoid it. Going into a race with apprehensions greater than can be naturally expected might well destroy the good things you've found about running at your own speed, on your own courses, under your own program and in your own style.

For those coming along to their first race, let's put up front the fact that the material rewards of racing are pretty damned meager compared to other fields of competition. There are trophies for the best racers, sometimes plaques (again, for the best of the best), often there are T-shirts and ribbons and almost always certificates for everyone who can make it back to the finish line before the supply is exhausted.

The rewards, however, often are intangible and can't be displayed on the den wall or placed on a bookshelf like the neighbor's bowling team trophy. The rewards more often come as do the rewards of daily running—in subtle and pleasantly insidious ways, in the feeling of having placed one's training and preparation on the line, of having tested oneself against the clock and against other runners.

Racing is the vaulted roof that tops the foundations of training. Racing is the test of the daily training. But racing has even more valuable rewards.

Begun in a logical manner, properly prepared for and entered as a learning experience, the first races can become tremendous motivators to one's personal running program, as well as providing a balancing factor to the daily training diet. Competition for many runners is the little special edge that the whole running experience was lacking.

The only caution for the beginning racer we'll make at this point is the same caution that is extended to beginning runners: don't overdo it at first. As you wouldn't jump into a bathtub of ice water and then calmly stay submerged, we must caution you to ease into racing. Don't start with anything that's too difficult or complicated or overpopulated. The word "marathon" is not magic and you shouldn't gear yourself to breaking into racing by trying to suffer through a marathon.

Enter a *convenient* race, a race close to home. Enter a race where the psychological rewards will outweigh what the race demands of your body, pick a race that you *know* you can finish in a respectable manner. Start, then, at either an organized Fun-Run or at a run that will be fun. The more casual the race, the better.

Racing can very definitely develop a new level of psychological involvement in the sport for the serious runner, it can provide a mental and physical climax to all the training and work that has led up to it, and it can provide good, playful fun if entered as a learning experience and not as a race with the devil.

Racing is readily available to any runner on almost every weekend of the year within comfortable driving (and sometimes biking) distance. Each issue of *Runner's World* carries a directory of Fun-Run locations, and the Amateur Athletic Union has quite a comprehensive listing of races that run the entire spectrum from Fun-Run type contests to races featuring world-class competitors.

It is logical at this point to ask the question: "Just what is a Fun-Run, anyway?"

Besides being a very euphonious phrase, a Fun-Run is a very euphoric experience. Perhaps you'll excuse a slight digression to describe a typical Fun-Run, in this case Fun-Run Site Number 001 at Foothill College in Los Altos Hills, Calif.

Picture, if you will, the peace and serenity of a Sunday morning. The streets and roads are only sparsely populated with automobiles, and there are hardly any trucks. Nestled in the foothills just off Interstate 280 is a well-manicured and well-maintained two-year college. Since it is Sunday, the parking lots are deserted, and there is a distinct feeling of the pastoral about the setting.

From our observation point atop a nearby hill (we are still shy about racing) where the warming sun is beginning to spread a pleasant nectar through our veins, we can see several cars pulling into the parking lot. There are also several bicycle riders converging on one corner of the previously deserted lot. The people who are arriving are dressed casually, several of them wearing warmup outfits. Some of the people converge into a loose group and begin talking while others begin taking loose jogs around the parking lot, obviously doing limbering-up exercises.

More cars arrive, as do some people on motorbikes. The sun is becoming warmer, and the little assemblage below is beginning to become the size of a small crowd—but still exhibiting very casual and unhurried characteristics. A man is setting up a card table, and placing various colored papers and books and magazines upon it. The texture of the crowd is a typical cross-section of the community: there are young children, old people, male and female, an occasional dog running from one group to another, trim people and medium-build people, with a few obviously overweight people sprinkled in. Their unifying characteristics seem to be their running shoes and the fact that they are all moving and milling about, if only a few steps at a time, as though the entire crowd is waiting for the arrival of someone important.

Almost as casually as the whole thing has fallen together, an elderly man of trim build walks to the road fronting the parking lot. Most—but not all—of the crowd follows him. We're too far away to hear his words, but he's speaking to them for a moment. He raises his hand with a stopwatch in his free hand, says a few words. Some of the people in the crowd are crouched down, ready to run, others are standing casually in the group as though there wasn't a stopwatch within a thousand miles. He drops his hand and the crowd breaks into a run along the road.

There are a lot of stragglers, and many of the children seem to be running along just to be running in a group. Some of the hardier runners race each other up front, but more than half of the people seem to be running just to run and be with others. Many of them seem to be talking as they run. It takes a long time to get the race finished, because most of the people would definitely be called stragglers in a sanctioned race. But they don't really seem to care.

Some of them move to the table and they are handed colored certificates, while the elderly man beckons the crowd to join him at another starting point. No one seems to be hurrying and there's no pushing or shoving. The warm sun and the fun everyone seems to be having down below is enough to make the observer wander down and join them. There doesn't seem to be any registration table, and it looks as though no one would mind if there was one more runner in the starting field for the next race.

That, of course, is the typical Fun-Run, a nationwide gathering of local runners at a predetermined spot, on a predetermined day, at a predetermined time, to run predetermined distances with seemingly no predetermined expectations. Fun-Runs are socialized versions of running alone—the middle ground, as it were, between pleasure running and sanctioned racing.

There are, of course, people at a Fun-Run who are as dead-serious about their running as they are about everything they do in life, for whom walking across a crowded intersection is a competition to see who gets to the other side first. In a sanctioned race, it is difficult to ignore a runner who is out to win no matter what the cost. At a Fun-Run, it's very easy simply to ignore the occasional runner who feels every move must be made in deadly earnest. A runner can race at his or her own pace, completely with his or her own goals in mind, and let the life-or-death competitor race against his fondest dreams.

There are some times, of course, when a runner should avoid even a Fun-Run, and those times are as important to know as it is to know when you *are* ready to run competitively. Consider not running when it's either too hot or too cold, or when the distance or terrain is either too hard or too long for your present state of conditioning.

A runner should not race, either, if he or she does not come prepared with the requisite number of aches and pains and pat excuses ready for dragging out and exhibiting if things do not go according to plan. These excuses are the sign of a veteran, and if you don't know them going into your first race, you'll most likely have heard most of them by the time you line up for your second race.

A runner who races is expected to come to the starting line brimming over with stories of sore Achilles tendons, lack of sleep, tight muscles, gout, a death in the family—anything that will explain why he may not do well on a particular day. When you line up, have some tales of woe ready to relate with proper embellishments in order to put yourself in the middle of the fraternity of racers. Be suspicious of other racers who have a litany of health problems that makes you question why they've come from their sick-bed without an ambulance to pick them up five yards down the road. These rambling wrecks are, indeed, the veterans.

If you want to enter your first race like a veteran, then, be prepared to talk about how badly you'll likely do in the race, and have enough excuses ready to follow up with a good tear-jerker. (Unfortunately, the best excuse- makers are usually cooled down and showered and on their way home by the time the average runner reaches the finish line, and most people don't get to hear the excuses first-hand.)

Don't, naturally, race if you *actually* are sick or injured where a race would further aggravate the ailment.

Don't enter a race arbitrarily because it seems like a good idea. All comments directed toward racing that we're making assume that you, as a runner, have decided to race after putting a proper amount of time in training. We would not encourage a beginning *runner* to become a beginning *racer* until he is confident that the training phase needed to become a good runner has been passed. Entering a race unprepared can inspire a runner to go back and put in that extra tarining needed to make him a better racer after a disappointing initial try at competition, but it will more often turn a runner off because of his inadequacies. Any comments we make on racing, then, assume that a proper level of training in a non-racing capacity has already been reached.

Our emphasis will be on aspects of the first race that are usually taken for granted—until the new racer finds, halfway through the event, that a last- minute pitstop should have been made at the local rest room, or that he has already expended all available energy on keeping up with the hard-core racers during the first half of the event.

The easiest way to find out about what is involved in racing is to ask someone who has raced or to join a local club where there is a free and frequent interchange of information. For the convenience of the new racer who has no inclination to be a joiner, or who forgets to ask some of the simplest questions that may become monumental problems when they are overlooked, let's get started.

Let us make two important points at this juncture where you've decided that you do want to try a race and that you'll begin with a Fun-Run because you are dutifully cautious about entering upon dark and uncertain seas.

First of all, consult the literature on the sport on building up and tapering off for your first race of various lengths. Your training runs by this time should have given you some indication of where you are physically and what you can expect of yourself. Take an easy training run the day before entering a race so that your body is ready for a top performance.

Secondly, and probably most important for your training at this point, please heed our caution and do not prepare yourself to run your *first* Fun-Run or sanctioned race as an all-out campaign on the world record. Plan on running your first race at a cautious pace so that you will enjoy it and so that you will be the master of your pace. Do not allow the race to become your master, dictating an unrealistic pace or unrealistic ambitions. You may ultimately be bound for glory, but you needn't set fire to the roadside grass by the friction of your passing at breakneck speed. Do not trust your instincts in your first race; trust your cautious half and work not to exhaust yourself, but to enjoy the experience.

As the first step in preparing for the race, a stop at the

doctor's office or the hospital for a thorough checkup might be in order. There are a lot of pros and cons to this advice. The detractors say that a non-sympathetic doctor can read your body analysis in such a way that his advice will have you sitting on your butt for the rest of your life. On the other hand, it is better to have a good idea of what kind of shape the body machine is in before putting it to the chore of racing. After all, you have the family car checked over before taking a long trip, right? And your body's worth more than a 4000-pound hunk of metal and rubber, isn't it? So get a checkup. Just be prepared to get a second opinion on the findings. Ideally, have the tests administered (and interpreted) by a doctor who is familiar with the unique profiles of a runner or who runs himself.

Since society judges people too often by the clothes they wear, clothing may be a good place to begin. Let's extend our coverage to "clothes and comfort considerations":

As far as the topics of clothing and shoes go, the rule of thumb is that you never wear anything in a race that has not been tested previously in training. As far as specifics go in the clothing you'll be wearing for your first Fun-Run, comfort and practicality are the key words. Ignore the top-shelf warmup outfits; plain old gray sweatsuits are just fine. Don't get sucked into buying the fancy Pierre Cardin-type running uniforms for your first race; a T-shirt and comfortable pair of shorts will do. You'll probably run better the less concerned you are about the clothes you are wearing.

Bear in mind, however, that the shorts that are comfortable for training may begin to chafe during a race, because they will be asked to undergo more strenuous use. The material may begin to irritate the inside of the legs, because the legs will be moving faster and longer than usual. Use of a soft pair of shorts (usually nylon), or the application of a thin layer of petroleum jelly to the inside of the legs may prevent the chafing that can result from racing or from running distances farther than you are used to.

Remember that your body heat will build up as you move farther into the race. Therefore, wear a combination of clothes that can be shed in layers as your body becomes warmer. In most Fun-Runs, it is not improper for a male to remove his shirt entirely if it becomes hot. Female runners often run with a tank-top shirt that is either cut or torn off at the midriff as the last layer of clothing next to the skin so that, should it become hot during the run, the clothing down to that shirt can be discarded while the shirt allows the passage of air over as much of the body as possible within the limits of modesty.

The use of an athletic supporter for males or a bra for females is completely optional. Some men will feel more comfortable running in a simple pair of jockey shorts under their running shorts, while small-breasted women may feel comfortable running without a bra (whereas big-breasted women may prefer a bra in order to avoid discomfort and soreness after the race). Women should keep in mind that if they go braless, they may want to wear a dark-colored shirt because perspiration is likely to make a light-colored shirt comparable to a second skin midway through the race. This, again, depends on the woman's individual attention to old-fashioned modesty as opposed to modern concern with comfort. Bear in mind that dark-colored clothing, although providing more modesty, also absorbs rather than reflects the heat of the sun's rays.

For cold-weather competition, a racer needn't overdress, since the running body works like a furnace, generating tremendous amounts of heat. Make sure that the ears and hands are warm. A stocking cap and mittens (which allow a runner to bunch up the fingers) or sweat socks over the hands should pretty well take care of the sensitive body parts. It is also permissible to wear long-johns, tights, or pantyhose if temperatures are extremely low. Stay comfortable and loose. A turtleneck sweater of light material is a good cold-weather modification to a racer's attire, because it holds in the heat contained in the blood moving up through the arteries to the head.

For female runners who want to look good at a race, go lightly on the make-up, both because your exertion will add color to your face naturally and because application of too much make-up may cause it to run once you begin perspiring.

The matter of whether or not to wear socks is something of an individual preference. Again, experiment in training sessions and not in actual races. Some runners find a pair of socks confining and refuse to run in anything but bare feet inside their shoes, while other runners would feel naked and unprotected without a pair of socks. As though to emphasize the individuality, some runners find that they get blisters from running without socks, while others find they suffer the pains and discomfort of blisters from wearing socks. Novice runners who are suffering blisters might try switching their preference in wearing or not wearing socks. Sometimes, such a simple matter can completely eradicate the blister problem. Never try to solve a blister problem by ganging up socks—i.e., putting on more than one pair. If you find yourself doing that, either try running without socks, take a good, hard look at the shoes you're wearing or consult a good foot doctor.

Socks also help cushion the foot, although many runners find that modern training or racing flats are so well-cushioned that they make the use of socks superfluous.

Still on socks, keep in mind that if your feet are getting numb while running, but that the numbness leaves when you stop running, you may be wearing socks that are too thick or shoes tied too tight. When running, the feet expand and shoes should not be pressuring your feet into discomfort and numbness. Even though tight-fitting shoes may feel nice and snug, you could use some space for expansion of the foot a half-mile into the race.

The most important piece of hardware, of course, is the shoe. Even though we've covered the topic previously, the shoe is so important we'll make a few more points about running shoes, even if we repeat what's already been said:

Good running shoes are the runner's biggest investment and his dearest friend—or direst enemy. Don't buy cheap or junk shoes or bargain imitations of running shoes! Buy one good pair of training flats; it will be your single best investment. The training flats can and should be used for racing at this point in your running career. In fact, for the beginner, it's best to use the training flats you've been doing your roadwork in, because your feet will already be comfortable in them and will not be in for a shock on race day when you force them into a new pair of shoes that are not already familiar friends.

When you go to an athletic shoe store to buy your running shoes, go to a store that stocks several brands, and then, if it takes hours, try different shoes until you come across a pair that will make your feet feel as though there are no shoes on them. For a first-timer, almost all the running shoes you try on will feel much more comfortable than the shoes you're used to. Just keep trying them on until you find the best shoe in the whole store for your feet. Your feet will communicate to you when the perfect fit has been made. They'll feel closer to bedroom slippers than shoes. Once the soles begin wearing down, don't go rushing out to pay $30 or $40 for a new pair. You've already worked hard to get your original pair broken in, so go to a resoling place and have new soles put on your shoes. Don't be afraid to ask for some type of sole the shoe did not originally have on it as standard equipment.

(When I get my Countries resoled, I have Jeff Sink put waffle soles on to replace the herringbone soles because I need more shock absorption than the herringbone pattern gives me. Have the shoes modified to your needs; never modify your feet to accommodate the shoes.)

The race, though, how about the race? Let's get back to that now. We'll call it the pre-race rituals: rituals that will soon become very familiar to you, but that may be confusing at first. Following are some cautions and some information that will seem obvious tomorrow but that may not seem so today:

Once you have training shoes on your feet and are ready for a race, take care to do two things with the laces: (1) tie your car key to one of your shoe laces near the top so that you won't have to carry a whole chain of keys along with you, and (2) double-knot your laces, both so that you do not lose your key if they become untied and so that you do not have to stop along the route to re-tie your shoes, as Bill Rodgers once had to during the Boston Marathon.

Now, the most important aspect of pre-race preparation: jettisoning waste matter. Although in most cases the human body will take care of itself by becoming nervous before a race and will therefore force a runner to go to the rest room, take the precaution of going even if you feel you don't have to. Whether or not you realize it at the moment, *you really do have to use a rest room.* You may even have to use a rest room several times before a race. It is not unnatural.

Take the simple precaution of stashing a handful of tissues inside the elastic band of your running shorts in case a little spot of woods has to become your rest room or in case a band of other runners used up all the tissue paper before you arrive.

A race is a form of competition, but it is also a social event. Some racers are extremely nervous before a race and they will become incredibly gregarious, while others become close-mouthed and anti-social. As a new racer, it is usually advisable to play the social aspect before a race by ear. Don't interrupt anyone who looks as though he doesn't want to be interrupted. Conversely, don't be afraid to walk calmly away from another runner who wants to talk your ear off when you want a moment or two of quiet repose in which to decide whether or not to make one last pitstop or whatever. A race is a race until it is over; then it can become a social event. Use the time before the race to go down a mental checklist of little things that you may have overlooked in the excitement.

Whether it's your first race or your 500th, there will be some degree of apprehension that you will feel very real or psychological pain in the race. There will undoubtedly be some very physical aches, because a race is run in physical territory beyond the usual limits of your training. The physical aches are often easier to deal with than the psychological ache of realizing that you might embarrass yourself by a bad performance.

As for the physical aches, disregard what some people have told you or have said in the last five minutes before the race starts: Do *not* always run through physical pain like some wild-eyed monk intent on fanaticism. Run through aches, but don't run through severe pains. Analyze aches and pains through your training sessions to learn which is which. An ache is a dull pain that arrives because you are exerting your body beyond its normal capacities; a pain is something sharp and shocking like the passing of a kidney stone. Do not run through a severe pain, because doing something stupid like that to be a hero to yourself could put you out of running for a goodly while. Listen to your body and learn to understand its signals that differentiate an ache from a downright pain. Be assured that you are not the only person who started the race suffering from aches. The aches are a necessary part of racing. Be prepared to put up with some degree of ache, braced with the knowledge that as you race more your aches will become less common.

The psychological pains are something else entirely. They are harder to deal with, and they *should* be run through.

Everyone who's lined up for the race is worrying about embarrassing himself. It is natural and it is nothing to fear. Take a deep breath before the gun, and push the fears of embarrassing yourself down into your legs where they can be wrung out as you run.

The milling masses of runners at the start of even a Fun-Run can present a problem of logistics for the new racer. Where should you place yourself? The best advice for a novice is to line up the back of the pack, for two reasons. First, if something goes wrong at the front of the pack—i.e., someone trips at the start—you will not be that person and you will not end up being stepped upon. Secondly, if you begin at the back of the pack you'll likely pass more people at different portions of the course, thereby giving yourself more of a needed psychological lift, than if you'd started more toward the front and spent most of the race being passed by people coming up from behind. If you are somehow maneuvered into the front line, simply get out of line and walk to the back. If you find yourself in the middle of the pack, try to ease your way over to one side so that you have an escape route if something in front of you or around you begins to go wrong.

Before you get anywhere near the starting line, get information on the course and the race site. Give yourself plenty of time on race day to get to the site, and take a walk around at least part of the course in order to see just what kind of terrain you'll have to traverse.

Your best companion at your first race might well be a stopwatch. As much of an enemy as a stopwatch can become when followed too closely and when used as a taskmaster on training routines, so it can be a companion on the first race, acting as a governor with split-second reliability for the anxious new racer who needs unbiased pacing. From practice runs with the watch, it will be easy for the new racer to establish a pace that will guarantee his success in completing the race instead of allowing pace in the race to be set by things as capricious as the front-runner's pace or by the mid-race panics. The stopwatch can be a faithful friend that will keep whispering to your eye whether you are overexerting yourself or whether you can afford to pick up the pace.

Make sure to keep a record of your training pace for several days in advance of your first race, and then set yourself up with the stopwatch to just slightly out perform your training pace. For instance, if you run a 7:30 mile in training, attempt to set your race pace at 7:15. The extra adrenalin pumped into your system during a race situation can usually be milked for the extra 15 seconds of speed per mile.

As far as the pre-race butterflies are concerned, be assured that many people who race have them. The butterflies are an indication that there's activity going on in the mind and the body to prepare you for the race. The best DDT for those butterflies is the shot from the starter's gun—or if the starter is giving vocal commands, his order to "Go!" Experience as a racer also contributes to decreasing the butterfly sensation. The butterflies will soon be replaced by that old hornet, the competitive urge, which your stopwatch will keep under control.

Once the race has begun and you've cleared the starting line, stay flexible and watch what's happened around you. Arthur Lydiard's advice on pacing is simple: Treat the race as two separate events, and divide it right down the middle. Stay fresh and relaxed in the first half, with the feeling that you're holding something in reserve; be confident, strong and in control of yourself when you reach midpoint. Then, begin to push. This modifies the natural tendency to start too fast (there's little danger of starting too slowly) and in reality produces an evenly-paced race.

The pacing should be on your mind during the entire race. You've done everything that's necessary before the race, now all that's left is the race itself. Keep your pace steady; do not make any sudden spurts or slow-downs, but make every change in your pace gradual and smooth. Run from one competitor to the next; key on the competitor in front of you.

When you do pass, pass on the outside (i.e., on the open side, farthest away from any obstructions on the roadway). Be careful of traffic if you are passing on a road. Avoid making contact with the other runner. If you are being passed by a faster runner, give him or her plenty of space to get around you; anticipate the runner (by listening for the sound of breathing or footsteps).

At about the midpoint of the race, even if you have closely

followed your stopwatch and the race is going as you've planned, take a reading of your body's instrument panel. Is your breathing regular? If it's becoming ragged and labored a momentary drop back to a slightly slower pace might be called for in order to get you to the finish in good shape. Are you feeling fatigue? You should be feeling some signs of fatigue, especially in your legs. If they aren't sending any signals to your brain indicating that they are working diligently, and that they are tiring a mite, you'd do well to pick up your pace. Your second wind (and there is such a thing) should have come either during your warm up or during the early portion of the race. Your pace should have noticeably shifted into that overdrive gear where you are running easier than you could have if you'd started cold. If there's been no second wind, you may have started the race too fast and gone right past it, like missing a shift in an automobile. This will be evident if you find your breathing at this point ragged and uneven.

If you're experiencing ragged breathing and fatigue, it's against the rule to throw yourself under the wheels of an oncoming truck. Slow your pace a bit, and try to get your breathing into some semblance of a rhythm. You can battle against the fatigue by relaxing and by concentrating on other aspects of the race. You can sometimes do it by slowing your pace, sometimes by picking up the pace until your body finds a more comfortable niche in the conditioning you brought into the race.

Some aches and discomfort at the midpoint of the race can be expected, even for the experienced racer. It is merely an indication that there is exertion over and above training exertion going on; body fuel is being used and the engine is being run at a higher r.p.m. than usual. Some fatigue is natural and to be expected; an excessive amount of fatigue would indicate either that you are still too uptight about the race, or you are cheating your pace up above what your stopwatch is telling you.

The body at this point should begin to exhibit a few aches that you didn't know you had. A caution: be careful to keep your stride smooth, or the fatigue that's creeping into it will begin taking its toll on ankles and knees and legs and shoulders that will be running out of sync with your perfect running machine. Make every effort to remain smooth; like a tire out of round, a stride that deteriorates at this point will feed its bad alignment back to other parts of your chassis.

As the finish line comes into view on the far horizon, your body should be hurting pleasantly from the strain. It's time to grit the teeth and see if you can dredge up any more energy that's been hidden in remote crannies of your body. Dig down into the guts and into the sinews, and come up with as much loose energy as you can find to put into an increased stride for the last half-mile. Not a sprint—a slight increase in your stride. The hurt will increase a bit, but you can grit your teeth and run through that kind of ache.

Finishing with a speed superior to the speed you had at midpoint will leave you with a feeling for the race that is more positive than the impression you'd be left with if you remembered the midpoint. And besides, it'll make you feel good as a finisher, and the finish is where the crowd—no matter how meager—is located.

With more races under your elastic band, you'll enter that delicious territory of the racer, where it becomes a pleasure to let the body have its head so that it can increase its stride and send a feeling of being on top of your position in the race through your body like a physical climax. This sensation often occurs for a veteran racing during the last stretch of a race; for other racers, it begins as far back into the competiton as the midpoint. There are very few sensations that can compare to riding your body toward the finish line at a racing pace.

A good finish will help psychologically to carry you into a good start in your next race. You can draw upon that reserved energy. You wanted to try a race; here's where the runner really becomes a racer. This is where it counts; this is what the practices all week are about. Wallow in the aches if you have to, because the finish line is the only Band-Aid in the world big enough to cover properly the hurts and make you smile as you cross the line. Good. Let yourself slow down gradually if you can.

If you've just literally used up every ounce of energy you had left in every pocket of your body, stand in one spot (but out of the way of incoming runners), put your hands on your knees and fill yourself with air that your legs aren't going to steal away from your lungs. Walk as soon as it's possible so that you don't tighten up. If there's water available, take a little sip and pour a few handfuls over your head. Take some deep breaths and observe that other runners are in the same state of achiness as you are.

You've joined the growing fraternity of runners who race, and the other racers feel pretty much like you do. If you heard your time as you crossed the line, savor it for a moment and then forget it. If you were too centered on your efforts to push yourself across the line and didn't hear your time, you needn't worry about it. The time you ran the race in isn't as important as the fact that you've successfully finished it.

If it's available (and you might want to get in the habit from the first race of carrying it in your car), drink your fill, slowly, of Body Punch or ERG or some other fluid replacement solution. There are direct beneficial effects from the habit of using replacement fluids, the most apparent being the ability to head off drowsiness later in the day and to prevent some of the aches the day following a race.

Get your sweats on so you don't take a chill, and go into a warmdown routine. At this moment, while parts of your body still hurt and before your breathing comes down to normal, is the best time to evaluate your race and to pick out points that need improving, because later in the day, once all the heavy breathing and sore muscles have dulled, you'll see the race in a completely different light.

How adequate was your preparation for this race? Did you stick to your strategy of pacing? Did you let yourself get carried away? Is there anything on your pre-race checklist you forgot to include in your preparations? Did you control your breathing, or did your body's need for air take control of your breathing? Did you pass other runners smoothly? Did you allow faster runners to pass you without it becoming either a big chore or an obstacle for the other runner? Do you feel elated or depressed? Did you have strength left for an honest-to-goodness kick at the end? Does that mean you didn't expend your available energy at an even metering throughout the race? Or did some other runners have to help you across the finish line? Is the blood-taste in your throat an indication that you're still a bit out of shape, or does it mean that you are

160

bleeding to death and that you'll shortly drown in your own
vital body fluids?

How long should you walk off the stiffness in your legs?
Until you can walk without fearing that you'll fall down if you
don't keep your arms out to balance yourself.

How do you get rid of this overall crappy feeling? It'll go
away on its own as your body comes back down from a racing
machine to a limping pawn-shop reject.

Does that guy over there throwing up feel as bad as you do,
or is he just putting on a good show for the fans? Most of the
other runners (er, racers) feel the same as you do; they've just
learned the secrets of mind-over-matter and are hiding the
pain until they get home and can moan in privacy.

How come, with all the miles you've put in during the last
two weeks, you're being beaten by people older than you? This
is a good point at which to assure yourself that you are not a
superman and that a bit more training or a different approach
to training may be called for. It is also a good juncture at
which to realize that there are some people in the race today
who've been running 10 or 15 or 20 years, and who therefore
have quite a start on you. It's also a good point at which to
realize that you have two paths to choose from: you can either
give up and go back into your shell, thereby staying away from
the races, or you can re-evaluate your training program and
keep with your workouts and use the people who were faster
today than you were as examples on which to key.

If you did better than you expected to do, how come you're
feeling a letdown? The race is the thing. Once the race is over,
the levels of adrenalin that you've managed to push through
your body begin to drop, and there is a natural depression that
sets in as the body emergency equipment goes back into its
normal mode. Don't worry, you'll see the race in a positive
light again once you've gotten home and get a refreshing
shower and get some of the stiffness out of yourself.

Now that you're properly recovered to the point that you've
put your sweatsuit on all by yourself and are walking in
straight lines instead of in circles, where do you go to collect
your time and place and award (if any)? In a sanctioned meet,
the officials will direct you to the proper table. Wait until
they've had a chance to figure up the results before bugging

them for information. If the race was a Fun-Run, your time was probably shouted to you as you crossed the line, and in your excitement at finishing you forgot what it was. That's good, actually. This first race should not count for much of anything other than to acquaint you with the process of racing and to familiarize your body with the agonies it can bring on.

Q-Marathons

Although racing is not for every runner, it can become an excellent weekend diversion for many runners. Since races are not overly long, many runners make the races a family affair, using the occasion as an excuse to get the family to some part of the state for the weekend where they haven't been before. In that way, the runner in the family has his fun, and there's still plenty of time left for the rest of the family. Races are usually held at sites that are attractive and that have some interesting things to see and do within easy distance.

Too much running and racing can become addictive, however. Not that it's necessarily bad—if it's prepared for properly.

The current rage is the marathon. The marathon is a run that is 26 miles, 385 yards long, commemorating an Athenian courier's run from the Plain of Marathon to Athens to announce the news of victory, at which point the courier reputedly fell dead. At one marathon that wasn't going especially well for Frank Shorter, he commented that he wished the courier had died at 20 miles. The marathon is tradition-ridden and attainable. It is a race that is almost preposterously long but that is still within the range of most seasoned runners.

(The Athenian who feel dead at the gates of Athens bearing the good news could not have been a veteran courier. Athenian couriers were used to running almost as far as the Tarahumara Indians, hundreds of miles in a few days. They were the communications link between armies and cities. The messenger who arrived at Athens was likely romantically killed by some poet in an age several thousand years later who didn't read his history books. Death at a young age is very romantic now, just as it surely was then.)

Accept your first race as an experience meant for learning and not as something that will go down in the annals of racing. Remember, you were supposed to be running against yourself and your stopwatch more than against your fellow competitors. (If you did hear your time, or if you remembered to click the time on your stopwatch as you crossed the finish line, give the Fun-Run coordinator your time and your age and he'll fill the time in on a color-coded certificate for you to take home as your reward.) After this experience, you are now more able to approach your next Fun-Run or sanctioned race as a veteran. You know what it's all about, how it feels, whether it is worth it to your own personal program or not.

Now, all you have to do is figure out a way to transmit the excitement of the race—and of your completing it—to your friends and family without sounding like some barroom braggart. Is it normal, now that you're in your car, in your sweats, cooled down from the excitement, to feel a little cocky about having run a race and lived to tell about it—if there's anyone willing to listen?

Why shouldn't you feel a little bit of exhilaration and accomplishment? This is a big moment in your life. You've done your last training session as a mere runner. From this moment on, you're officially a racer. And at the moment, except for the advancing charley horses in your right calf, that's a stride in the right direction.

Sept. 25—Tried my first long run today. It went tolerably well, I suppose. Jill rode along on her bicycle and zoomed ahead every few miles to get a soda at a garage. Ran down Middlefield to Stierlin/Bailey/Miramonte, then along Foothill Expressway and home along San Antonio Road. About 11 miles. By the last mile, I was barely putting one foot in front of the other. Spent the rest of the day drinking a good deal of beer and some diet sodas mixed with liberal amounts of Body Punch mixed with lemonade. Maybe I should be put out to pasture.

The unfortunate thing about the influx of new runners is that most of them come into the fold with little background in running and without a coach to guide them sensibly through the steps of running. I ran some 100-mile weeks in college, but although I began running again in June 1977, I've no plans to enter a marathon until May 1978—and then very carefully building toward it. Yet, there are many instances of people, who wouldn't think of trying to dive off a cliff in Acapulco before they know how to swim, jumping into marathons before their training flats are broken in. It's kind of frightening to me. I doubt that those poor people will ever find any of the joys inherent in running; they won't have time to feel any joys through the constant pain.

The marathon is there as a goal. There are better than 200 of them in the United States in a year—anywhere in size from a guy we know who gets together a dozen of his friends on his birthday to run a marathon to the New York City Marathon with 5200 entrants in 1977. No matter what the size though, the distance is still almost four football fields beyond 26 miles. There are enough excellent races at five and 10 miles to start at without becoming the dead Athenian at the end of 26 grueling miles. If the marathon is your goal, and there's no good coach handy, read *The Complete Marathoner* and *The Marathoner* magazine, as well as the annual February marathon issue of *Runner's World* magazine, study the training schedules, and be prepared to go into your first marathon with enough training miles behind you and a good race before you.

The marathon can be a great, uplifting experience. It can also be the downer that chased you away from a sport you may have enjoyed greatly.

Oct. 2—Tried to do a 16-mile run today and failed badly. After the Fun-Run, Jill and I came home and set out at 11:30 to do last week's course backwards with the Fun-Run 4¾-mile course thrown in to add extra miles. I should have kept at last week's 11-mile distance. I made it to El Monte Road, and when I turned onto it, knowing that I'd still have to come back that way to pick up my course on Foothill Expressway, it was like a psychological concrete slab falling on me. I took my first walking break at the second block of El Monte then continued on to the college, where I again walked partially up the first hill. Realized that I'd done two things wrong: (1) I'd started too fast, and (2) I'd made grand plans for the day without consulting my body to see if it shared my aspirations. On the way back, my running was even more ragged and then, back in downtown Los Altos, Jill's bike developed a flat tire. We pushed it home under a cloud of disappointment.

R-Ultra-Distances

With the marathon becoming such a popular distance, it raises the question in the minds of many competitive runners: *Is there life beyond 26 miles?*

In the running world, there are two regular columns I read intently, even if I have to take time from running to do it. They are Joe Henderson's "Running Commentary" in *Runner's World* and Ted Corbitt's "The Ultra-Marathon Scene" in *The Road Runners Club N.Y. Association Newsletter.* In Joe Henderson's column, I find inspiration and companionship for my daily running. Ted Corbitt's column, on the other hand, is like dream-shopping through a catalog of the bizarre. I am fascinated by that small group of runners who are ultra-marathoners. I have a tremendous respect for them, knowing full well that they are not in possession of all their vital mental equipment. I feel a kinship—if not in accomplishment, at least in spirit—with them. They are the astronauts of the running world, those who have gone where men have never gone before.

They are Max Telford running from Anchorage, Alaska, across North America, to Halifax, Nova Scotia, a distance of 5166 miles. They are wonderfully crazy people like marine Frank Bozanich who won the 100-kilometer race in Hawaii in seven hours, 14 minutes and 46 seconds during 1977; like Jo Schroeder who, in the same race, was the first woman finishing—in 19:58:57; like Nick Marshall of Camp Hill, Pa., who came to California at the end of the summer of 1977 to run in the AAU 50-mile championship, finished third there, and heard that they were holding the annual Lake Tahoe 72-mile Run two weekends later and who, running in that race (at an altitude of 7200 feet for the first time in his life) won the race, only to return home to Pennsylvania and enter a marathon near Pittsburgh before the memory of Tahoe had even begun to fade.

It's people like Dr. Tom Osler who, on Dec. 9, 1976, at Glassboro State College in New Jersey, went to the track at 4 a.m. to attempt to break 100 miles in 24 hours. Osler is a 36-

year-old math teacher at the college. At 5 a.m., wearing two sweatshirts, sweatpants, black trunks, gloves and a cap, he began his insane circling of the quarter-mile cinder track. He was reputedly looking forward to the sensations a runner gets beyond the 12-hour mark; he'd once run 10 hours straight. Fueling on highly-sugared tea and dates, Osler started at an eight-minute mile pace and slowed to 11-minute miles by the 17-hour mark. Students and faculty and the curious dropped by during the 24 hours to cheer Osler on and to run with him, Neil Weigandt running 54 miles with Osler. After 18 hours, 20 minutes and 13 seconds, Osler cracked the 100-mile barrier. He made a pitstop at the fieldhouse, where he ate spaghetti and took a quick nap. He returned to the track and walked/ran the remaining five hours left in his bizarre day. The temperature at the end of his run was 29 degrees. To quote Ted Corbitt's description of the post-race scene:

"Afterward, he could walk, and he had no stiffness. He had suffered no pain while running. While running, his main problem had been the track. It thawed out during the day and at one point was flooded, forcing Osler to run in the outside lane. The track softened up so that footsteps froze at night, producing a lumpy running surface. Osler said later, 'It was like running on concrete with ruts.' Other problems included cinders getting into his shoes, meeting the challenge of a stiff wind during the day, and a cut toe later in the evening. He got no blisters during the run. He went home and fell asleep while talking to his wife and some friends." Jeeze, and people say the age of heroes is over.

Oct. 12—Suffering from sore legs. I still think it's the shoes, and I'm going to have to do something about that very quickly, before it puts me down for good. Also have developed a sore throat. Miserable. Went running with Jill tonight, but the legs were so sore after a half-mile that I had to walk home. Hope things improve soon. Must go to Anaheim tomorrow for sporting goods trade show and to interview Bruce Dern on Thursday and Friday in Beverly Hills.

S-Clothes and Heroes

Wherever heroes walk, there too walk the plastic peacocks. Glancing back this sentence sounds slightly Oriental; or perhaps it sounds like a password from some James Bond thriller. Actually, it's neither.

I spent a good deal of my free time in college going to sports car races—hillclimbs and Sports Car Club of America club meets and national championship events. I liked sports cars, and I liked to see them race. Along the circuit, there were some very good "amateur" racers. The majority of the field, however, was made up of people who found in sports car racing a hobby that gave them a certain image that they liked to see in themselves. They purchased a sports car modified to competition specs and they went racing with it on weekends, always being careful not to hurt it, always being careful to spend a lot of time polishing it before the races, and always being sure to have the requisite number of car and race patches sewn onto their jackets.

They often wore scarves and affected a slightly foreign accent. Some of them even smoked cigarettes at the end of cigarette holders. Even going to the store in the family sports car (often an Opel Kadett), they wore patent leather driving gloves. Many of them had cars that couldn't get out of the way of a 10-year-old Plymouth with mismatched tires. But they always made sure they had cars obscure enough that they ran in a class that was ill-populated so that no matter how badly they drove (and they always drove over-conservatively but with the mad glint in their eyes as though they were right on the edge of disaster), they were sure to take home a trophy that they could show to the neighbors—who couldn't understand what all this was about when, on a test run down the alley behind their house, the riding mower had gotten to the corner faster than the D Sports Racer. None of them ever really raced as far as I was concerned.

I recently had business in Beverly Hills, and I happened to drop by a local drug store to grab a bite to eat at noon. Most of the counter was taken up with middle-aged women. Most of them wore sunglasses even though the smog was so thick the sun was obscured, flashy high-heel lounging sandals even though it was well into the mid-portion of the day, and they crossed their legs and smoked their cigarettes like a bad imitation of Joan Crawford. None of them had ever starred in a film, of course.

They were plastic peacocks, strutting through the life they'd never really know. The real racers I met at the sports car races had grease under their fingernails, and while they walked around the pits it would have been hard for a newcomer to pick them out as drivers. The movie star I'd gone to Beverly Hills to interview wore clothes more fitting to a logging camp than to a rerun of "Dinner At Eight."

In the running world, the heroes and the increasing glamor of the big prestige circuits are drawing the plastic peacocks. The $80 sweatsuits that have never been sweated in and the Adidas TRXs that have never been run in are popping up at the country club and at the races and at the receptions accompanying the races. The beautiful people are buying extravagant sweatsuits that the manufacturers don't even put price tags on in advertising, and the plastic peacocks walk about spreading their feathers and sniffing at each other.

Controversy rages over whether a 5200-runner field at the New York City Marathon is good or bad for the sport. Yes, it's good, some say, because it brings that much more awareness of running's new status as a sport to be reckoned with. No, others say, it's taking the essential element that made running what it is—the individual—and relegating him to a small speck of sand along a huge beach. The truth probably lies somewhere in between.

But the sign that the sport has arrived is the plastic peacock. Be careful to sidestep its droppings on your daily runs.

Oct 18.—Bought a new pair of Adidas Countries today and ordered a pair of Tiger Montreal IIs. My current feeling is that I need simple shoes, basic shoes and not the modern shoes with all the frills for people who think something is wrong with their feet before they take a running step—when, in reality, there is probably nothing drastically wrong with them. It would seem best to start with simple running flats

168

and then, if problems develop that simple inserts or modifications
don't help, check into the shoes made with special features for special
problems. Simple is often best. (In subsequent days, I would find this
holds true; going back to simple shoes began clearing up my leg problems almost immediately.)

T-Therapy

Something about running that the plastic peacocks and
other assorted fringe people miss is the fact that it has a
great therapeutic benefit. There are, in fact, little pockets in
the psychiatric community that are experimenting with using
running as a therapeutic tool for treatment of seriously mentally ill patients. Although the number is not great enough at
this time to have a sample of results large enough to satisfy the
body of cautious medical men, the several doctors using running as therapy are extremely excited about what they've
found.

The use of running as therapy follows the belief that the
mind and body are not quite as separated as some people
would have made us think—that in mankind there is a very
real jointure between mind and body; that when the savage is
comfortable in front of a warm fire the sensation stirs his mind
to certain activities; that when he's freezing his butt off waiting in the weeds for some game to come by, his mind is pushed
into a certain gear; that a man running is coming to some
understanding of himself.

This is not a realization that should shock or surprise us.
Anyone who grew up in a small town or a big town or the
country and spent lazy summers just laying around waiting for
things to happen was less likely to be someone people would
like to be around than someone who'd been out playing ball or
swimming or doing something. The active summer rushed by
too quickly and was fun, while the lazy summer slithered by on
snail's toes and became frustrating enough so that going back
to school was almost a treat.

The body immobile seems to have too much time to fester

on itself, to dredge up things that are unhealthy, to invent difficulties and to wallow in misfortunes. Running offers a therapy that combines "running away from problems" with "running into problems" headlong. It does that by clearing the mind of all the garbage that clutters the thinking. The first few steps begin shaking loose the tattered cloth of personal difficulty. Something of the savage running free emerges; like the rolling stone gathering no moss, the body leaves the signs of its difficulties behind. The complications fall away, and there is just the runner and his run. At that point (and it doesn't come to the first-week jogger), the mind clears itself to deal with problems one at a time or in any combination it chooses without encumbrances. There is no blaring television, no irate driver behind honking his horn in a mile-long traffic jam, no children, nothing. There is only the runner and the rhythmic slap of his shoe against the road. It is almost hypnotic in its simplicity. It is also difficult to describe.

It is as though the runner moves to a slightly different plane of existence than the rest of the world. He does not smile maniacally like some moron who's just enjoyed the benefits of a frontal lobotomy. Inside the runner's head, a certain order develops. Camouflage that may have swathed the real problems in a thousand different diversions is pulled aside. A certain knowledge of oneself begins to emerge.

For the person unprepared, it can be a rather disrupting influence. It can open doors to the person that have never been creaked open before. It can slowly, day after day, mile after mile, reveal the person to himself. They are not always pleasant revelations, but the very act of running makes it somehow easier to deal with what is dredged up—because what is being dredged up is being exposed in a sort of vacuum where other influences aren't present to make something of it that is not there.

Looking back on the last few paragraphs, I find that they are very abstract and very insubstantial. They are paragraphs that I'm not especially comfortable with, because they seem to be saying things that are confusing and that mean nothing to a person who has not had similar experiences. It seems unnecessarily arcane, almost as though I'm purposely trying to confuse the issue. Perhaps I am. Perhaps the topic of running as a therapeutic tool is something too personal, something that each runner must experience for himself. Perhaps it can't be talked about in concrete terms.

What I do know is that on a day when I've had too many phone calls, too much pressure from deadlines, too many unexpected complications, a quick change into my smelly T-shirt and my running shorts and my shoes makes me feel better. Once onto the road, the frustrations of the day are washed away like the sweat that runs down my body. There is a certain mystic quality to the run, a certain feeling of being complete with the body, and for the extent of the run a feeling that there is no problem too large to solve. The glow that is established along the run carries over sometimes for hours after I've stopped running, as though it were intertwined with the slight ache in my muscles. Eventually, though, the feeling is gone, and the effects of the run have worn off, and the problems creep back into life. But the very fact that there is a place, out along the road where problems can be solved and where the inevitable wearing away of the psyche by everyday frustrations can be stopped makes a person better able to handle the ruts in the rest of the day.

One does begin to find, however, that the addictive peace and serenity of the run are more and more necessary, that it becomes more and more important, that it becomes like a fix to a drug addict, that it becomes a necessary part of every day. For some, it goes beyond that.

Oct. 23—The NYC Marathon. Geeze, what a mess. Too many people and too little thorough organization. Helicopters over Narrows bridge at start almost crashed into bridge and each other. We had a truck full of photographers, though, who could have covered the accident magnificently. Second photo truck (a pickup) kept getting between us and the runners, though, as the race wound through the various boroughs of New York City. Taking good pictures was out of the question. The problems were complicated by our truck's need for shock absorbers and NYC's need for asphalt in its potholes. Truck driver was either a half-mile ahead of runners or on top of them. Crowd was so tight on First Avenue while the cops stood around with their hands behind their backs that the photo truck got held up and Jerome Drayton just about ran up our tailpipes. He looked up at us through his sunglasses and said, "You fuckin' assholes!" He was right. Rodgers was magnificent in his win; he says he tightened up toward the end, but he looked smooth and confident which is incredible, since they did everything they could to tire and overtax the runners with social affairs day and night leading up to the race. New York is still very much high-pressure. The crowds of runners were still coming in three hours after Rodgers. They covered the survivors with silver foil, making them look like corpses on "Star Trek." I still can't get into New York. It gets more dirty and depressing every time I see it.

U-Addiction

*A*nything that cures the body and uplifts the mind, gives a rise to the spirit and clears the psyche must be either illegal or otherworldly—i.e., it's either a drug or a religion. Running, I fear, is both.

There is a decided addictiveness to anything that a person likes very much but doesn't get in the daily flow of events. Hobbies can be very addictive and all-consuming, for instance. I know a guy who doesn't work to support a traditional wife and a hutch filled with squalling kids. He works to corner the market on Lionel trains and accessories. He has his attic half-filled with a marvelous train layout that runs all year long and that would make any Christmas tree proud to be part of the set-up. The other half of his attic is filled with boxes—yes, boxes!—of Lionel locomotives and cabooses and flatcars and tankcars and track—all of them unopened. He has more rolling stock than the Amtrak system—and it's in better condition. I'm sure it was one of the reasons for his divorce. He spent more time fondling his livestock car than his wife. The one time that I visited his layout (it's decidedly not a house; it's a layout), he sat behind a huge control panel like a madman, switching Erie-Lackawanna boxcars, moving Penn Central passenger trains back and forth, just generally being consumed by the thing. I could picture, on his gravestone, a huge letter *L* with a circle around it. I was surprised that he didn't wear a Superman-like outfit when he played with his layout, displaying a huge *L* on his chest.

He was really addicted. I know other people who are equally addicted to collecting old records (myself included), going hunting (and housing enough munitions in the house to invade any of the emerging nations), adding dingleberries to the inside of their cars, saving Popsicle sticks, collecting jewelry, having kids, and on and on and on.

Running is perhaps more addictive than all those things. With Lionel trains, it can be said that besides playing with them, they are increasing in value, because they just don't make Lionel trains like they used to. Same for collecting records. As for hunting, it can be said that, "With the price of meat like it is these days, I'll just hop in my $8000 Land Rover and go git us some meat off the hoof." Adding dingleberries to the inside of the car increases its value—if you can find someone to buy it who is a dingleberry freak, too. Popsicle sticks... well, maybe you're making sure they don't litter sidewalks by turning them into ashtrays and doll houses and stuff. Jewelry has its own rewards. And kids, well, they're a mania and not an addiction, and not very easy to rationalize when all the emotion's stripped away.

Running, though, has its immediate rewards. If you're doing it you can point to immediate rewards:

"I lost 20 pounds in the last six months and I feel great."

"I can scale great mountains now where six months ago I couldn't make it to the corner 7-Eleven."

"My heart rate has fallen right down there to the point where I'm only finding it necessary to pump blood on every other day."

"I feel so great when I come back from running, it's such a relief from the cares of the world that daily batter me, that my ulcer's going away and I can even put up with my mother-in-law this weekend."

Running is the great, legal escape from problems—escape heart disease, escape fat, escape being winded, escape that run down feeling, escape sleepless nights, escape the turmoil of your household for an hour of blissful peace along the country's back roads. It is, almost literally, a natural drug. There is, in fact, research being conducted to determine if there is a chemical that the body secretes into the system when it's running that actually acts as a drug to give the runner a "high" and to contribute to his feeling of well-being.

In the big drug movement of the 1960s, marijuana and other drugs were treated, by some people, as a religion. Dr. Timothy Leary led his flocks of drug-users into the desert to experience the uplifting effect of artificial stimulants and depressants. Anything that delivers one from the mundane problems of the day must be divine. Drugs became the great religion of the 1960s, and Timothy Leary became the savior. Unfortunately, there was no one to save poor Timothy Leary, who wasn't then and certainly isn't now all that stable.

As we exit the 1970s and head valiantly for the 1980s, exercise, and specifically running, seems to be taking over as the next great religion. Oh, it isn't running rampant at the moment, but it is growing. Anything that does what running does must be divine, worthy of its followers developing religious fervor about it and certainly worthy of being spread to other needy people. Runners are, I'm afraid, some of the world's most ardent missionaries.

And running (I hate to call it a sport, because it's gone beyond that) *lifestyles* have taken on an almost religious fanaticism. Unfortunately, this tends to cause problems in some households—at least in households where all members are not equally fanatical. There can be great schisms in households between the runners and the non-runners. It ultimately becomes a battle between which is a more powerful force—inertia or movement. Since the universe exists because it moves (referring to chapter one; see, this book somehow managed to have some method to it after all), the runners usually win in the end.

Running has, therefore, become something of a family service in many households. At the local Fun-Run, which is held at 9:30 Sunday mornings, there is a certain church-like atmosphere. Whole families come to the Foothill College parking lot, socialize a little with friends and acquaintances, do stretching exercises, follow the set instructions of the group leader, go about their run, come back and shake hands with the group leader on the way out and discuss with each other what an uplifting experience it was. And, quite frankly, it is.

Running first thing in the morning, along country roads, probably puts a person closer to God than does comparing new hats or listening to sermons that become a dull hum in the ears in a stuffy church.

Running breeds religious fanatics because running allows virtually anyone to become a participant, something that is denied in most sports...er, lifestyles. Much like religion encourages people to become participants, even if they become passive participants, running becomes something people can believe in, and they are very anxious to share the feelings with other people. As with any other fanaticism, it was the "now" runners who laughed at and ridiculed runners in the 1960s. People who had thrown beer cans at passing runners 10 years ago are the staunchest supporters of running now—and its greatest missionaries. And so, like a religion, it spreads. It spreads into hearts and minds no religious missionary would have dared plumb. It is almost frightening. Fortunately, it doesn't show any signs of putting together an Inquisition.

Nov. 1—Ran over to a park along Middlefield Road in order to begin doing intervals one night week. Haven't done intervals since college. Goofed up, though. Did 10 per 120 with 50-yard jogs between at 100%. Dern just went over all this a few weeks ago, reinforcing the theory of doing intervals at 60-70%. Guess I wasn't listening too good. My legs are killing me, and I heard and felt every weak point in my legs giving out in succession. Will have a hell of a time running at all tomorrow. Too much too soon is too much.

V-Exploring

As a child, I was fascinated by Western movies. My grandfather was equally fascinated by them, and he used to read huge mounds of paperback Westerns. On Saturdays, I'd go up to his house to watch Westerns on television with him because we didn't have a television set at the time and because my grandfather never hassled us when we watched television with him. He'd read through the channel guide between shows, and I'd jump up and turn the channels for him so we could watch Westerns all day long. Neither of us wanted to be a cowboy or anything like that. I know I never asked for a horse for Christmas like some kids did. Maybe we liked Westerns because they were pretty basic, while being a form of escapism that took us, for a Saturday, outside our small town.

When we watched the Westerns, I always found myself fascinated by the Indian scouts, those phantoms that would appear and disappear along the landscape at will, utter a few profound words on what they'd found up ahead or say something about a waterhole within a half-day's ride, and then vanish. They struck me as being people who everyone else thought to be extremely lonely, but who weren't really lonely at all because they knew exactly where everything in the West was. They knew the secret way out of a box-canyon, they knew how to get into and out of a rowdy town without being seen, they could sneak up in the middle of the night to a bad-guy's camp and take dollar bills out of the bad-guy's billfold while leaving change in his pocket without even being suspected of existing. They were kind of the supermen of the Old West, a combination of the invisible man and Spiderman. I always wondered where they went for vacation. I always wanted to be an Indian scout. Unfortunately, I had some things working against me, the prime items being that I wasn't Indian and that the era of the Great Television Western was fading like a pair of blue jeans.

For years, I entertained a certain sadness whenever another Western was cancelled from television: "Maverick," "Bronco Lane," "Yancy Derringer," "Have Gun, Will Travel," "Rawhide," "Wagon Train," "Sugarfoot" (I wasn't too sad when he left the West, actually), "Wanted Dead or Alive," "The Rifleman," "Cisco Kid," "Lone Ranger," "Roy Rogers," and finally "Gunsmoke." There was no more employment for the cowbody hero—and somewhere in Hollywood there was a long unemployment line of Indian scouts kind of shuffling their feet and being unable to sniff out their next job. It was all rather tragic.

When I got back into running in June 1977, though, I found

that I suffered from one of the same problems I'd encountered when doing great hunks of training for cross-country in college: I had the wanderlusts. Running the same courses five days out of the week seemed okay, but on the weekends I had a bit of extra time and the urge to go somewhere I hadn't been before. It's like getting a new car; it must be driven *somewhere*. As the body becomes more acclimated to running longer distances, the spirit moves the body and the body wants to just keep going for as long as it can. The sensation started in about the third week of my training. I knew that I still was not capable of running great distances effortlessly. But I knew I could probably find a greater enjoyment in my several miles if I'd take them somewhere off the beaten path. (I'd grown somewhat tired of seeing the same people waiting for the same bus each morning, I suppose.)

In a suburban environment, there aren't exactly a thousand unexplored paths to run. Fortunately, about a block away from our apartment there was a Virginia Electric Power Company right-of-way. Since the power company had its huge steel towers erected along that stretch of earth, I knew there weren't going to be any homes built upon it and certainly no streets for cars to use. So one Saturday morning I turned down the path and within 200 yards found that within the tightest stranglehold of civilization there is still a certain wilderness.

To properly have access to their lines, the power company had constructed a very rough dirt road that matched the contour of the land—which meant that in order to drive the road, you'd have to own a four-wheel-drive vehicle. I soon discovered that the runner is the Renaissance Man of the 20th century. In one left turn, I found myself becoming an Indian scout, first and foremost, because I realized that except for the occasional car or dog or squirrel I discovered, no one knew I was back there. I was invisible to the rest of the world, because who takes a power line right-of-way into their consciousness? They're there, but no one ever notices them.

I also found that I was a sort of mapmaker, trying to figure the winding road's relation to the suburban streets I knew and traveled every day; an ecologist, noting how certain plant life was reclaiming its place among the right-of-way once it was left alone; a game preserve inspector, finding a deer one morning right there in the middle of suburbia and coming upon rabbits at almost every step; a sanitation inspector, finding that some other people knew about the right-of-way but seldom cleaned up after themselves; and sort of a spy, in that I was getting a view of the back of people's houses along the edges of the right-of-way—the back ends that no one ever sees. Some homes were kept up spotlessly in the back, while others were depositories for every piece of junk imaginable. As I made my way farther along the winding, hilly road, I came upon homes that I hadn't even suspected of existing, some of them with swimming pools hidden away in the rear of their properties, one with an old Edsel half-hidden under a tarp.

I felt no embarrassment for having discovered their rear ends. I wasn't trespassing onto their property; I was merely catching them unexpectedly with their guard down, and they never knew it because I knew I was invisible, because when a runner isn't along the side of a well-traveled roadway to have taunts and beer cans thrown at him, he's pretty much not there. As I topped a rise and was hit by the full blast of the sun coming up over the hill in front of me, making that little singing sound start in the high-tension wires high above me, I wondered if my grandfather had ever suspected that he had an Indian scout in the family.

Nov. 6—Got up at 9:30, out the door at 10:00 to do a long run. Legs hurt, but after the first few miles they loosened up a bit. Learned that I'm either draining too much of my mental psyche at work or in some other way, because I have little of it left for running. My mental half sometimes fails me, and I become bored and discouraged along the long run. At one point near the middle of the run, I felt the separation for a little bit—maybe two miles. Felt tired most of the way, though, noticing little aches and pains that began to crop up. The whole run became more of a plod than a run. My euphoria near the halfway point quickly gave way to soreness in the legs. I need more psyching; should explore what goes on with the mind during a long run. Some surges of power, especially along the Central Expressway where I run on asphalt (which is reputedly 10 time less hard than concrete pavements) and where there's a cool breeze that dries up the sweat and makes me feel momentarily better. I should also explore the damage to the psyche of the run when you fail to make the traffic light at the few intersections. On the second-to-last lap of the run, I was joined by a typically California girl (blonde hair, sun tan, etc.) who went along for the circuit. She plays tennis and likes to run about three mile to keep in shape, she says. Visiting from San Diego. She came in fresh and forced me to pick up my pace. As a result, the last lap was a killer. Had hoped to be able to do 18 miles, but did only 16.1. Didn't bother to time myself, which was probably just as well.

W-Mountains

Coming from a town where the only way out is to travel up-hill, perhaps my fascination with hills is prejudiced. Having talked with other runners and with people who take part in other outdoor sports, I think that perhaps it is not. In most of these people, there is seemingly primitive feeling that arises when they stand before a foreboding hill or a frowning mountain. The feeling seems to flow, like a swift, underground river, through parts and regions of the body that are still un-fathomed by the great probing tools of science. There is some mysterious closing of certain organic valves, a building of pressure within the system—a kind of nervous energy that builds like a closet filled with steam, wanting to break down the door and explode up the hill or into the clutches of the mountain, not so much to conquer it, for what man can con-quer a mountain that is still there when he is gone, but to join it in some primordial feast of feet against rough stone.

As a child, I used to stand or sit in our family's backyard and watch the mountain behind our house in Jim Thorpe. It had personality and it had feelings; it changed like people did; its features altered with the seasons, and its hues with the time of day or the weather. Perhaps I took extraordinary pains to hear it speak to me, but it did in its telepathic way that seemed to span eons with a great sigh of understanding. It wanted me to join it, and I wanted to comply.

As I grew marginally older, I found paths that went down from our backyard into the valley between our house and the mountain. I found myself anxious to get beyond the homes that were perched precariously on the lower portions of that mountain—one of them in which my father had been born one long-ago September—because I wanted to go beyond civilization and sit atop the mountain. There was no challenge to conquer it like mountain-climbers feel; there was simply a challenge from its wrinkled face to come and share the world with it, to sit atop its head for a while and look about at miles and miles of other mountains. Beyond the line of homes, there were rough paths that confirmed my feelings that other people gazing upon the mountain's face had used to scale it. I ran up the rough path, leaping from rock to turf of hard grass, puffing and sweating. Closer to the top, the path vanished because the surface became huge conglomerate boulders older than the imagination of man, tumbled upon one another and left there to be worn slowly away by rain and snow and heat and determined feet.

Upon the top of the mountain (and it was a long mountain), there was again a path that ran along it lengthwise, like a path along a snake's backbone. Like an Indian just freshly broken loose from jail, I ran down the path toward the head of the mountain, where hundreds of feet below the Lehigh River made a wide swing around the mountain's nose. There were ruins of canal locks far below from 75 years before when the coal had been transported down the river to Philadelphia and New York. On both sides of the river there were railroad tracks, Lehigh Valley on one side and Jersey Central on the other. And on the opposite mountain, the road leading out of Jim Thorpe (nee Mauch Chunk) had been carved.

But my mountain, except for the scars along its lower sides from the insatiable railroad builders, was untouched. It was not as high as the mountain opposite, upon whose top the Flagstaff Park perched, where the Dorsey Brothers and other big bands had played in the now-decaying ballroom during other eras. But it was *my* mountain, sort of like a pet dog, a friend I'd never really know and one that would seem to know my innermost secrets each time we looked at each other.

During my childhood, my brother and I ran up that poor mountain's face and down the back of it sometimes twice a day. Against orders from our parents, and perhaps as a way of getting back at their trespassing on *our* mountain, we played among the railroad's empty coalcars that were parked along a siding on the backside of the mountain—often as not throwing rocks at them like you would at a mangy dog, trying to chase them away. Enough rocks fell off the side of the mountain to give us plenty of ammunition, as though it were a conspiracy between we three against the railroads.

Even today, when I return and sit on my brother's back porch and look toward the mountain, there is a subtle pull. The railroads are all but gone, much of the track in the yard down by the river already removed. Someday, it will probably all be gone and the mountain will be able to begin repairing its scars—if they don't build the highway along the old railroad right-of-way like they've been talking about for 20 years.

I've been reluctant to give in to the mountain's subtle invitation to run back up it, though. I suspect I'm afraid that I'll find that it, like everything else, has changed and that we don't feel the same respect for each other that we once did.

Yet, the more I run the more I know its primitiveness, its roots in a mysterious age millions of years ago when to run to the top of a mountain was a cooperative venture with the mountain, not a destructive urge to conquer and enslave and kill that mountain. Maybe there has been a complete return to the savage primitiveness of childhood by getting back onto the roads and the trails and the hills with just the feet to move the body in search of the mind's origins.

Maybe the mountain will more easily recognize me the next time I sit gazing at it from a Jim Thorpe backyard. And maybe now I'll be able to return to it refreshed and renewed and free of the idiotic iron filings of civilization that began to cling to a modern man as he moves through his life. Maybe the mountain still waits.

Chapter Six

Making the Return Trip

Running's career as a bashful sport and as a closet life-style is over. It is, perhaps, a sign of the age we are in—an age where we are currently engaged in no massive, energy-sapping war; where the recession that pinched us several years ago is over; where Americans are feeling that it's time to pay a little less time to their television and their car, and to invest that time in doing something for their own bodies.

Television, after all, has hit an all-time low in mediocrity, and the American automobile has been legislated into an item less exciting than a damp firecracker. But the American body—despite daily reports of possible cancer creeping into it from everything from soda pop to just plain air, and a million other possible maladies ready to jump upon it and bear it to the ground and its grave—is incredibly elastic. Americans in unprecedented numbers are suddenly trying to pay attention to their body's needs. They are polishing the body machinery, tuning it, trying to make it last longer and run better. They are suddenly changing their angle of attack. Where before they were likely to buy expensive or stylish clothing to drape over their bodies in order to hide expanding waistlines and flabby thighs, they are now getting to the source of the problem.

And running (or, as most people refer to it, jogging) is becoming the first answer to the problem that confronts the American striving to do something positive with a failing body.

A Gallup poll released on Oct. 6, 1977, indicates that there is definitely a startling change in the American lifestyles. In 1961, a mere 24% of the people in this country admitted to exercising daily. Today, the percentage is up to 47, a massive change in priorities for any group of people.

Gallup indicates that as with many "behavioral and attitudinal trends in America," this exercise phenomenon started in the affluent and higher-educated groups, and then trickled down to the other groups of Americans. The interest in exercising began with the college-educated, those in the upper and upper-middle income brackets, and in the professions, according to Gallup. It is also common among the younger people (those under 30), with the largest increases coming among people in the northeastern and western United States.

In response to the attention given to "jogging" by the media during the last year or two, the Gallup people sought to get some firm answers on the number of Americans engaged in the running boom.

"The results indicate 11% of adults (24% of those who exercise regularly) jog. And most joggers, 74%, are traveling at least one mile during their routine," the Gallup people report.

The demographic profile of the American jogger is pretty much as expected: young, college-educated, living in the northeast or far west, single and in the upper-middle income brackets.

Of course, as with all polls, this one is a mite behind. The running boom is spreading into all socio-economic groups. On a social run or at a race, the man or woman you're running next to is likely to be from any walk of life, any part of the country, a pauper or a philanthropist, single, divorced or married.

My own feeling about the whole upsurge in running is that we are embarked upon a time in America not unlike the 1920s. People are interested in having a good time in their spare time, they have more spare time to have a good time in and more resources to have that good time. They are exploring ways to do things for themselves. They are becoming more hedonistic in a healthy way. The by-product is the statistic that for the first time in almost two decades, the country as a whole has seen a *decrease* in the number of people dying from heart-related diseases.

But, like the 1920s, it seems to go beyond common sense. People aren't running merely to ward off dreaded heart disease. Yes, they are becoming more conscious that it can have a very beneficial effect in that direction, but Americans are notorious for taking the long way around things that they know are good for them.

I see the increase in interest in running because running presents an individual challenge to the American wanting to challenge himself. He finds the avenues to challenging corporations and establishments in this country just too frustrating. Challenging Ma Bell or the United States Government is a frustrating, uncertain affair; you never know when you've drawn blood, because the beast is too big and unwieldy to cooperate by bleeding where the wound's been made.

Instead, America is seemingly on the verge of a great, crazy era, where incredible and outrageous challenges to individuals are sought and accepted—whether it be along public highways or along quiet, suburban lanes with cute names.

During 1977, two foreigners seemed to set the stage for the days that are dawning in America, and their accomplishments seemed to come right out of the 1920s.

Tom McGrath, an Irish bartender, spent his honeymoon running across the United States, from New York to San Francisco, traveling 3046 miles in 53 days. That averaged out to 57 miles per day, breaking the existing record for the cross-America run.

At the same time, farther to the north, New Zealander Max Telford was on what is believed to be the longest ultra-distance run in history—traveling 5166 miles from Anchorage, Alaska, to Halifax, Nova Scotia, averaging 50 miles per day.

That refreshing craziness struck much of America during 1977, with great numbers of first-year runners challenging the distance of 26 miles, 385 yards in marathons that were swollen to seas of people washing over city streets and country roads in a kind of fitness love-fest. The country seems to be turning into a mass of people trying to make their diaries into their own *Guiness Book of World Records*. After struggling along the roads and streets for nearly four hours, sometimes five hours, sometimes six, in the company of other human beings enduring the same tremendous hardships, the most common comment heard at the recovery area was: "It was the most wonderful experience of my life. I can't wait to do it again."

For Americans cast into the mold of the faceless masses, running races at seemingly ridiculous distances sets them apart even in the midst of more masses. The fact that running away from being a mere number in the computer puts a new number on their chest and again makes them a part of the pack seems to not bother them at all. What seems to be important is what is happening within them while they are within the mass. There is a wonderful change that goes on somehow chemically, somehow psychologically. The member of the mass becomes a noteworthy individual who challenges the clock that daily assaults and humiliates him. The clock becomes a new kind of taskmaster, almost an ally.

The 1977 New York City Marathon had 5200 entries, a number approaching the total number of marathon entrants for all marathons in this country five years ago. There are nearly 200 marathons in America each year, everything from the venerable Boston to marathons with as few as 27 finishers. And running in them is no longer a diversion of the occasional eccentric or weirdo. During the late 1970s, running is becoming an obsession of the masses, a sort of lemming stampede to good health by the back door.

I say "by the back door" because although most Americans start to jog after they have heard it is good for them physically, they often find themselves becoming runners because it is something very worthwhile psychologically. People find themselves along the roads when they're running and, on the whole, they seem to like what they're finding.

A good barometer of the true growth of running would have to be the publications that chronicle its advances and its proponents. Ten years ago there were a mere handful of publications covering running, most of them very modest and amateurish. Today, there are dozens of regional running publications, and the runner's bible, *Runner's World,* has grown from a circulation of 59,000 at the end of 1976 to better than 200,000 at the beginning of 1978. There is no indication that this growth is going to end, despite the fact that the magazine is still very much an "in" publication among runners. Additionally, the magazine may never again see an issue of less than 100 pages.

Perhaps the greatest single indication of running's growth, however, is the fact that these days hardly anyone even remarks when they see a runner. What at one time only a few years ago was a sight to cause comment from a carload of kids or an elderly couple sitting at a corner waiting for a bus is now ignored. Runners are so common and so numerous that they have become invisible, a part of the landscape. There is among people a feeling of uneasiness, a feeling that something is wrong, when they spend an hour on the streets or roads and don't see a runner plodding on to some phantom destination.

The refreshing aspect of this growth is that if a runner is really open to the sport/lifestyle, it has a way of never growing old. Like certain wines and like great musicians, the longer one allows running to mature and open itself, the more there is to be found.

Veteran runners are very willing to spend hours expounding on the many things they've learned from running at the point when they thought they knew it all. Running is something that always has more to say to the person who keeps pursuing more knowledge. After the great rush of information and wisdom that is imparted within the first few months to a body that has not known it, running continues to drop bits of knowledge on the road in front of the serious runner. It is like a religion that is always renewing itself with new revelations, or like a psychologist who does not confine himself to Freud or Jung but who turns up new revelations and signposts to the mind with each new day.

It is why this chapter is inserted here. I found that running had not yet imparted enough to me to pass on to fellow runners just to stop where chapter five ended. These are not even subtle revelations that have come between the ending of chapter five and the contemplation of the last chapter. They are massive pieces of information from other runners, from speeches heard at clinics and workshops, from running more miles down quiet side roads. They are pieces of information I felt would have been missed had I allowed the book to close sooner—because you, as the reader, might have turned down some of the same side roads and found some of these things and felt you'd been shortchanged by the book.

I've put together the remainder of this chapter as a sort of series of informal essays, again interspersed with items from my running log which may reveal to you something *not* to do in your own running rather than something to do. Looking back on this book, there is probably more to be learned from my mistakes than there is from my accidental runs down correct trails. Perhaps I hope that those runners who read this book are of the same ilk I am, in that they learn more from what they've done wrong than they do from being preached to in order to do the thing that is right.

My only fear is that I will fall into the temptation of drawing this book out forever. But that fear is negated by knowing that editors set deadlines to prevent that very thing from happening. I only hope that they make me adhere to the deadlines, for your good and for mine.

Dec. 26—Still raining. I thought we were in the middle of a drought here. The clinics at National Running Week started today, after open house at the office. Managed to get some running in between the afternoon clinics and going back to Palo Alto for the evening workshop.

Very tight at start because of lack of time to get running in this week. After about four miles, legs began to loosen up. Rain not really bothering me very much, as the shoes keep my feet pretty dry and generally it's just like running in a shower but with clothes on. No time to go much longer than seven miles. Too much to do. Too little time. Wondering how my running has so quickly become non-running during National Running Week. There's something perverse there—something that must be better guarded against.

Undoubtedly, one of the greatest attributes a runner can have is an open mind. Without an open mind, the runner reaches a plateau, and at that point he begins running in circles. Running is a constant learning process; in the process of learning, it is possible to learn that what was learned the first time through on a subject might not have been precisely correct.

Back in the middle of the last chapter, for instance, I mentioned stretching. I indicated that I didn't think it is the most important thing in the locker room for runners, that their warmup of a slow jog would work just as well. I left the option open that stretching might be helpful later on as a runner did a larger volume of running and as he aged, thereby losing some degree of natural flexibility.

I have allowed myself to be convinced by various runners that stretching may, indeed, be important—under certain circumstances. George Sheehan, Joe Henderson and others have convinced me that there are many good things to be had with stretching—as long as it isn't overdone.

Running very effectively builds up certain muscles. As in physics, there is a reaction for every action—so in running there is a muscle *not* being built up for every one that is. The muscles that aren't being built up need some attention so that they can counter the built-up muscles, thereby assuring a runner of good flexibility and good, even strength. Building up the opposing muscles also helps prevent injuries because your strong, running muscles aren't going to imbalance you under certain situations (such as swerving to avoid running over a kid who dashes in front of you) and cause injury.

Stretching can be done before running, during a break in mid-run (especially when you feel yourself tightening up on a long run or in the middle of a marathon) and after a run.

Currently, I do all my stretching before I run in order to avoid injuries. I'll eventually find myself doing stretching after a run, too, so that I'm not going into my next run tighter than need be.

I doubt that I'll ever spend as much time doing stretching as some people I've seen. They go through elaborate stretching rituals and actually spend more time stretching than they do running, putting their legs up on cars, moving trucks, little kids, anything they can find, so that they can stretch their arm toward their toe as flamboyantly as possible.

But George Sheehan and others have a point in telling us how long ballet students do warmups (45 minutes) before they ever get into the real thing. Runners should set aside at least 5-10 minutes for stretching before they begin the actual process of running. It needn't be anything elaborate; there's no need to chase cars so you can put your leg up on them to stretch it out.

Do toe-touches slowly and carefully, avoiding bouncing, just allowing yuour trunk to bend gradually toward the ground until you feel muscles pulling themselves a mite. Never overdo it or you may find it difficult to unwrap yourself.

Do sit-ups by lying on your back, crossing your ankles after pulling your legs up toward your body, and then doing the sit-ups.

Stand at arm's length from a wall or a telephone pole and lean toward the pole, keeping your feet flat on the ground. Feel the stretching in your calves. Again, don't bounce, just lean.

Sit on a tall chair that will allow your legs to dangle. Hang a paint can from your foot and lift the foot, alternating it by rotating the ankle. This prevents shin problems and strengthens the ankles.

Stand three feet from a wall with your side toward the wall; lean into the wall with your shoulder, putting all your support on your wall-ward leg. This stretches the outside of the knee, which is important if you're going to be running on slanted surfaces or rough surfaces. Alternate with the other leg; repeat it twice per leg.

There are many good stretching and limbering-up books and exercises, and just about any yoga class will teach you

189

elaborate but effective stretching techniques. Use some of them and they'll allow you more injury-free running with continued flexibility, which is very important if you want to continue to be able to tie your shoelaces without help 10 years from now. And don't be unnecessarily down on the concept of stretching as I originally was. Doing stretching—especially in the rain and in dampness that sometimes comes through town like a hobo between freights—keeps the legs from cramping up and makes them feel as though they are stronger than the hostile world they're about to run through.

The key is to not overdo it. Start, build it up, and then feel out where the stretching should end and the running begin. It is all a building process. In the beginning, do very little stretching. Do more as you do more running and as you age. But be careful that you don't become obsessed with stretching or you'll begin doing the opposite of what you're trying to do: instead of using stretching to become stronger and more flexible, you'll find you're becoming increasingly stiff and unyielding.

Jan 4—The rain continues in drought-stricken California. The roads are beginning to flood and the ground, which began soaking up the rain water like a desperate sponge two weeks ago, is saturated. Convinced that I should do a marathon at some point farther down the calendar, I am beginning a rather ambitious training program. Ran down Middlefield Road to its intersection with Central Expressway in Sunnyvale, returning by way of Central, adding two laps of the

number one course to get 90 minutes of running in. Roughly 10.1 miles.

National Running Week is a rather elaborate affair that started over the Christmas Holidays of 1975 as a way of celebrating *Runner's World*'s 10th anniversary and of calling national attention to running as an alternate lifestyle. During 1976, the week was not held because the energies of *Runner's World* were directed at coverage of the Olympic Games in Montreal. The National Running Week was again held during the Christmas Holidays of 1977, though.

The week consisted of panel discussions, clinics, workshops, a Runner's Night banquet, the National Fitness Run, Fun-Runs, open house at *Runner's World*, informal discussions, a Runners' Equipment Show—and ended with the Midnight Run in Los Altos on New Year's Eve.

One of the most depressing portions of National Running Week 1977 for someone who has eaten his share of Hostess Twinkies and Pizza Hut pizza was the presentation made by Dr. Nathan Pritikin, the man who co-authored the bestselling *Live Longer Now*. In a world where it is still possible for a talented speaker to make his point with strength and lasting power while still having a little verve, audience involvement and humor, Pritikin is a speaker almost totally devoid of humor.

During the session on diet and nutrition, after hearing presentations on carbohydrate-loading and vegetarianism, Pritikin proceeded to berate listeners for allowing protein, especially in the form of meat, to pass their lips. He took great pains to graphically paint pictures of what was happening to the body when protein is ingested. It was taking calcium from the bones and excreting as much of it as the body could excrete, while depositing the rest of the calcium in the aorta, where it was calcifying the aorta. Additionally, the protein and other fatty things we've been eating were forming build-ups on the inside of the arteries called plaques, ultimately causing blockage of the major arteries and veins. The blockage, Pritikin said, ultimately caused heart attacks. The heart he contended, was strong and remained solid and whole, but the arteries being clogged did the damage.

Pritikin was scheduled to talk for a half-hour; his speech

rolled into 50 minutes, and he was still telling the audience how they were going to die from eating protein. There was a feeling of resentment to all of it because, while we watched Nathan Pritikin tell us how we were going to die for our meat-eating sins, while we felt him paint a depression over a week that had been very upbeat, we noticed that poor Nathan was probably the most unhealthy, sallow-looking person in the room.

He began using examples of non-meat eaters who are exceptional athletes. He made the mistake of using the Tarahumara Indians as an example, citing their substantial running achievements. He stated that they only eat meat about once a month. He never mentioned the incredibly depressing statistics on the poor Tarahumara, a race that no living man would want to be part of. He never indicated that 45 years old was ancient in their crude civilization. He never mentioned that the only reason they don't eat meat regularly is that they can't get meat regularly and that during the one time a month average when they do have it, even if it's a scrawny chicken, they have a celebration and a feast and a huge drunk. They feel that the meat consumption makes them stronger and more virile. (See *Tarahumara Indians* by Jonathon F. Cassell, The Naylor Company, San Antonio, Texas.) The chicken, in fact, is quartered in an elaborate ceremony, the blood and innards being consumed by favored tribe members.

The slightly positive portion of Pritikin's speech came toward the end, when he indicated that his diet had done marvelous things for some people who were in serious trouble with their arteries and that he'd caused some remissions to happen that seemed to defy the normal expectations of medical science by taking people off eggs, meats and other such foods. He never indicated what the saving diet was, apparently figuring that the audience would rush out to buy his book to save their bodies.

Dr. Tom Osler didn't make it to Pritikin's presentation, and when I got together with Tom a little later to discuss his doing some stories on ultra-distance running for *Runner's World*, we began talking about the scare tactics some people use in order to make a point.

Osler has frequently done incredible things—things that people would think the body incapable of. He's done 24-hour runs and things that boggle the layman's mind. He is, except for a few leg problems, a fit, healthy-looking, compact man.

"I think the best philosophy for dieting," Osler said in response to the capsule of Pritikin's speech I'd given him, "is to do things in moderation. I was reading the story on what runners eat before they race in the January 1978 issue of *Runner's World* and those accompanying stories on what Shorter and Rodgers eat. I don't know if they're saying some of those things to psyche the rest of us out, but I think it's conceivable that Shorter likes to eat Ding Dongs and drink Schlitz beer, and that Rodgers loves cheeseburgers and doesn't deprive himself of them because he runs. I've seen too many good runners eating some of the most supposedly atrocious dietary junk without it having an adverse effect on their performances or their health to push health food faddism.

"I think that it's just a matter of being sensible—of not overdoing it. Everything in moderation, I suppose. That seems to be what the athletes are saying. And, in a run, you can throw that out the window. I know that in my 'ultra' runs I drink highly-sugared tea, and I don't eat sugar normally. Some runners drink one can after another of cola because their bodies need it at that time. That doesn't mean they're going to drop dead from it.

"I think that too much effort to eat everything right according to the prevailing 'expert' diet can kill you just as quickly as eating meals at McDonald's or Arby's or Pizza Hut—especially since most of the 'experts' don't agree on their diets and since some of the diets are downright dangerous. It's been shown that most of the nutritional things you need are in a Big Mac, french fries and a milk shake—including greens. Not that I recommend everyone rush out to the corner junk food place and chow down.

"I don't know," he said in conclusion. "It comes down to a personal matter. But if you worry about it too much, the worrying about what's going to happen to your body if you eat all this stuff is going to give you a heart attack from developing bad nerves and high blood pressure and who knows what else."

Tom refrained from taking a stand on cautioning moderation in distance running.

Jan. 10—Bought a pair of Adidas SL-72s, hoping that they would be a refreshing change of pace from my Countries, which once again are beginning to get thin in the sole. Although prejudiced toward Countries because they've been faithful friends over many years, I'm still trying to be open to the possibility that there are training flats available that are just a bit more suited to my feet—especially considering my increasing mileage. The SL-72s don't seem to be the answer, though. They seem hard and tight (even though my narrow feet move about in them laterally) and make my calves stiff. Did a 45-minute run, falling short of the hour I'd have liked to do. Don't want to push the stiff legs to cramping in the dampness. Will go back to the Countries tomorrow after some application of good to the soles.

Jan. 11—Legs still very sore from the SL-72 experiment last night, but they are tolerable—the legs, not the SL-72s. After 20 minutes of running, my right calf feels on the verge of cramping, but it never really does. Trying to get back up to the mileage set down in the schedule. Fell nine minutes short of the prescribed 90 minutes tonight.

During National Running Week, when we weren't discussing the relative merits between a slice of pizza and a health food sandwich, Tom Osler and I were examining his running shoes as one would examine a rare tropical bird or a stolen watch.

Placing them gently on a checked tablecloth, Tom allowed me to watch his shoes sit there before enlightening me about their origins and peculiarities. Somewhere in the ancient past the shoes had begun life as a pair of Tigers. But that was a long way back in murky regions long forgotten. Tom apparently had something against running shoes (perhaps his life as a child had been threatened by a pair of running shoes or something), for the tools he used on his shoes haven't been seen since the days of The Inquisition. What he was trying to get the shoes to admit to, I'm not sure, but they had been scarred, tattered, stretched, wounded, deflowered, cut open in a half-dozen places. Tom had cut holes in the front to relieve pressure on his toes. There were other places on their shanks where he'd made cuts to relieve other pressures. They looked as though he'd stolen them from some garbage can belonging to an old woman with terminal bunions.

But the most shocking things about the shoes were the soles—and heels. Yes, heels. Tom had taken off the original soles and had apparently cut up an automobile tire, fashioning his own soles that still seemed to have some of the original tread on them. They looked like they might originally have been a 750 x 14 from a small sports car. At the back of the soles, he had attached actual heels—not Cat's Paw heels but more rubber seemingly cut from a thicker automobile tire or maybe a truck tire.

Now, Dr. George Sheehan recommends that if you've got certain foot problems, to begin piling in the soft material under your heel even if it lifts your heel out of your shoe. I'm subject to heel bruises and follow Dr. Sheehan's advice to a more conservative degree, adding Dr. Scholl's heel pads in the back-insides of my shoes. Tom Osler, because of his unique problems, adds his heel lift *outside* the shoe, making them like dress shoes. For most runners, the shoes would conjure up all sorts of injuries coming Tom's way, from falling off the damned things and breaking his nose to developing rather acute knee problems. Tom suffers none of those discomforts, though. In fact, he's just peachy comfortable in the ugly things, because he has run enough miles, while being sensitive to his feet and legs, to know what's good for him. The shoe companies don't know what's good for Tom Osler, because the shoe companies don't have Tom Osler's feet. Tom Osler knows what's good for him and Tom modifies his shoes to fit his particular problems.

What Tom did to those Tigers is what I refer to as the Runner's Princess-And-the-Pea syndrome. In the fairy tale, the true princess was tested to see if she was indeed the real princess by having to sleep on 18 mattresses. Under the bottom mattress, the testers placed a single pea. If she were the real princess she'd have the worst sleeplessness in her life because princesses, as everyone knows, are notoriously sensitive to things like a pea in the bed.

Runners must do the same thing. They must be sensitive to things their feet are telling them. If a blister is forming at a certain part of the foot, the runner should explore the corresponding area inside his shoe to see what the problem is. He can often take some measures to make adjustments to the shoe, by either putting a dab of petroleum jelly there before he goes running or by shaving down the offending protrusion or by cutting it off. If he has Morton's foot, he should take a single-edge razor blade and cut an incision in the front of the toe box of the shoe so that the pressure is relieved from the second, longer toe when the foot slides forward in the shoe. That will get rid of black-and-blue toenails very effectively. You don't need to have a solid cave of shoe out front to keep your toes in because your toes drive off the bottom of the forepart of the shoe, not off the tip, unless you run upside down.

Never allow yourself to be convinced by anyone that the company that made the shoes you're running in knows more about your feet than you do. You've lived with them all your life, they haven't. And don't waste time and money by rushing off to a doctor to have every little problem taken care of. Many of the adjustments can be made at home with things in the tool box. In most cases, the alterations to the shoe can be made much simpler than Tom Osler's. And, as you run more and more miles, you'll learn more and more tricks that'll make your feet happier than a princess in a pea-less bed. Running shoes are like automobiles; they usually run better once they've been properly broken in and modified.

Jan 14—It rained steadily again today, the downpour building every hour or so to a waterfall. Cut my run down yesterday because a downpour developed and I was soaked within a block. Even though I couldn't get much more soaked, the rain was making things rub, causing slight chafing and promising blisters if I continued. Newspaper said again today that the drought is definitely not over. Hope I can dry my shoes out by tomorrow. Changed my scheduled runs around a little to accommodate the weather. Rescheduled my 120-minute aerobic run for today, to be followed by an hour aerobic run on Sunday, Monday and Tuesday.

Headed down Middlefield toward Sunnyvale during a break in the rain. Halfway to Sunnyvale, though, the first drops started and a brisk wind began punching me in the face. The wind and rain picked up, and I began getting pelted with lashing rain while my back stayed dry. The rain stings the eyes and batters the body, but it seems to wash away something of the dirt of civilization, and in its way it felt great. Nothing to battle the wind and rain with except one's own legs and body; no car windshield for protection. It's just your run against the earth's elements. With the lack of traffic this early in the morning and the sound of the wind, the run becomes very primitive, very much a wonderful experience. It makes one feel as though part of the whole scheme of things, even if just for an hour or so.

At Central Expressway, the turnaround put the wind at my back and I became uniformly soaked. Glad I wore a turtleneck shirt under my T-shirt, because if I hadn't the wind would have put gallons of water down my neck. The first hour of the run felt good; I felt strong and confident. During the second hour, though, once back through Mountain View and into Palo Alto, fighting the wind early in the run caught up to me and I began to feel weak. Then, with a half-hour to go and two miles from the house I was hit with one of those chills that indicates you'd best get your ass inside as soon as possible or you're courting a cold that'll put you in bed. Headed home and fell 10 minutes short of the planned 120-minute run. It's better to cut 10 minutes off a run than to cut a week out of your running by allowing yourself to get sick.

Running has begun to attract women. Not the groupie-type women that other sports attract, although there are some female groupies who like to hang around the male "name" runners, but the average woman who has, in most cases, never had an interest in sports before. This is a good thing and is in keeping with my earlier-expressed feeling that we are entered upon a period in history where we are *all* becoming more conscious of and concerned with our own health and general well-being.

Sports in America have always discriminated against women. That has not been something unique to America, however. The role of the woman in most societies has precluded her taking part in most sports because, down there at the subliminal level where the guts begin and the primitiveness lies waiting, societies have used sports as an emotional outlet—which has tended to make many sports rather explosive and violent. Women have been expected to handle their emotional problems in other releases: in their child-rearing, in social dickering with other women, in bouts of depression culminating in a good cry, etc.

There were virtually no sports for females in the dark ages of the 1960s. There were maybe field hockey and swimming and sometimes girls' basketball, which is one of the most incredibly complicated and silly games ever invented. Women, because of their alienation from sports, have traditionally done badly at them when going up against males. Because of inexperience, their fielding of a ball is awkward and uncertain, and there is a certain timidity about approaching a clutch of players battling for a soccer ball. There have always been the exceptions, however. But the tomboys of childhood almost always forgot their sports prowess once they discovered that there were other ways to tackle boys than on the football field. I've always had a certain respect for the potential of a female in sports, perhaps because I once had it beaten into me by the tomboy on our block.

Times have, fortunately, changed. And running is one of the prime arenas of sport that women are finding to their liking—which is very understandable, actually. Running does much the same thing for women as it does for men. It offers a sport that can be approached as the individual wishes to approach it. It offers the option of competing against oneself or against others, competing for fun or for prizes. There are virtually no boundaries.

Women who have been very shy on a tennis court find that they can jog around the block a few times after dark with impunity. They also find, often for the first time in their lives, that they are capable of accomplishing something that means something to them and something that paradoxically makes them feel more feminine by breaking a sweat—something that only men were traditionally supposed to do. Running allows them to compete when, where and under whatever conditions they wish; they needn't come into the light to run until they are ready. They find that running is something very much for themselves, just as men have always found it so.

There are incredible strides being made in women's running. Marathoning times for women are falling with a vengeance as they rapidly make up lost time at the 26-mile, 385-yard distance. There is talk of great potential for women at the ultra-distance, although this has yet to be proven conclusively.

It is doubtful that any sport/lifestyle holds more potential for the typical American woman—especially for the housewife who does not necessarily want to join the front ranks of the female militants. Running can be done at any time, almost anywhere, so that a woman can probably more easily work her hour-per-day running program around her schedule since she dictates her schedule much more than her husband, whose schedule is dictated by his job.

There is a backlash within some families where the wife and/or mother had taken up running. The children usually see this action as a threat to their being pampered, and they resent their mother taking an hour a day to squander it on herself. To that attitude, the simple response is that if children run your life that much, you'd do well to demand two hours for yourself a day. You owe yourself the hour or two, and if they don't like it, adopt the typically male gesture of thumbing your nose at them. You've earned the hour or two a day.

The second reaction usually comes from the husband, whether or not the wife has children. He begins to see the wife as a runner and himself as a potential coach. Don't allow it to happen if you want to maintain your marriage and your sanity. You've begun running for yourself and for your own enjoyment, and you should keep it that way or you'll lose it. Don't allow your husband to dictate your schedule. If he's been running longer than you have and he knows something about running, it is nice to ask him for advice when you have questions, although you can just as easily read the books on the subject as he can. Don't allow him to become your coach, however, or you're simply perpetuating the traditional husband/wife relationship. Find a female coach or a coach outside your household if you feel you need one. Then, if things go badly during a day's workout, you won't take it out on each other.

Work to resist the urge to rationalize your running by saying you're doing it for someone else in the family. Don't begin running—and then perhaps competing—to make other people proud of you because of your accomplishments. What they think of your accomplishments can be either a positive or negative aspect of your whole running program, certainly, but build the running program on a foundation of self—because self is what it boils down to. Out there along the road on your hour a day, your family and friends are not there. You are there; do it for yourself first. If adulation comes along as a by-product within your circle of family and friends, fine. But don't push it, and don't expect it. Expect it from yourself. Give yourself your own praise—it will keep you going farther longer.

And don't stop short of breaking a sweat in training because it seems unladylike. Breaking a sweat brings life and color to your cheeks, and pushes your body and your mind to the threshold of new accomplishments and experiences and longer runs that will open whole new worlds.

There is tremendous potential for women to realize themselves through running. Although it can be a rugged, tough sport, running is also a very graceful and classic sport. It is, in fact, the oldest sport known to man—or woman. Ancient civilizations often restricted women from running. Women are no longer restricted, and if they don't take advantage of the opportunities offered by running, they're missing one of the biggest advances possible for them.

The only trends I find disturbing with women's running are the assertion by certain militant feminists who also happen to be runners that there are massive psychological differences between men and women runners, and the tendency for women who have so vocally denounced sexism in running sports to establish now their own exclusive running series.

Certain female "experts" on running tend to make blanket statements that men and women approach running from completely different angles and get completely different things out of running and because of the woman's unique way of looking at things, what they get from running is somehow superior to what men get from running. My feeling is that it would be easier to find a man and a woman who get the same things out of running than it would be to find a group of men and a group of women who get radically different things out of it. I think that the kind of attitude some women are expressing is just as bad as someone saying that women will likely get nothing out of running.

To pigeonhole what a *runner* will get out of running, either psychologically or physiologically, by sex, is absurd. To my way of thinking, running is running and runners are runners. Most men welcome women runners as they are welcomed into no other sport—often because male runners want everyone else in the world, no matter what their sex, to experience the same things they are experiencing from the sport/lifestyle. Running, like anything else both men and women do, offers a common ground on which to meet, talk and experience life. Anyone who tries to pigeonhole the experience of running by the kind of private parts a runner has seems to me to be missing the point.

On the matter of exclusiveness, women runners have fought long and hard to be allowed to run with the men. In the late 1960s, great strides were made in that direction at the Boston Marathon until today many marathons are beginning to have nearly 25% women. If women have fought so hard to have the right to run with men, it seems hypocritical to me to see racing series springing up that are exclusive to women. This is not to criticize Jess Bell and his Bonne Bell mini-marathon series, which has been a greater boon to getting more women into the sport than almost anything one can credit. Jess Bell's motives are sound, and he's put his money where his beliefs are; that's great for the emerging woman runner. It seems that there is a bit of reverse discrimination there, however.

I wonder what kind of outcry would squeal from the feminists if Vitalis V7 were to sponsor a *men only* running series. The Jess Bell people tell me that when men enter their Bonne Bell races they'll be issued a number, but in the results they aren't counted.

Ah, well, discrimination has a place in the human heart that it earned years and years ago, and it probably won't go away no matter how much people say they'd like it to.

Jan 21—Did my long run today since I won't have time tomorrow as I'll be going to the Paul Masson Champagne Marathon. Dan O'Keefe's pitches for it all during National Running week must have gotten to me. We finally got some sunshine today and, after spending the morning at the office, I went home for lunch to take my long run. Naturally, as I walked out of the door the clouds came over.

I didn't quite make the full 120 minutes because the back of my calves began to really tighten up. They seem very anxious to cramp on me, possibly due to the fact that the heels of my shoes are wearing down faster than I can put repair goo on them. The problem was aggravated by the fact that I used a slightly more ambitious stride length today, which puts a little more strain on the calves; will need some stretching exercises to loosen them up after the run. Did the first eight miles in about an hour; nothing spectacular yet, but it's sure an improvement over six months ago.

Running, for some people, becomes very compulsive and addictive. In some ways, this is good. It certainly assures those people of continued health and well-being. It can, however, cause mild traumas when they are prevented from getting out for their daily runs. Joe Henderson sprained his ankle while running and the podiatrist, a runner himself, put a cast on Joe's leg because he knew the mad compulsion that would put Joe back on the roads the next day if he weren't protected from himself. I've known runners who've come down with a flu (and runners are not immune to catching colds and flu and such) who end up on the edge of divorce because they become unbearable when forced to chafe at the bit.

We have a problem around deadline time at the office because all of us run. Although the main priority is to get the current issue to the printer's on time, I find the troops slipping out back doors and crawling out windows so that they can get their runs in rather than face the dubious duty of deadlines. It would be wise to not encourage running as a physical activity in the Marines. In battle, pinned down under fire, the urge to go out and take a run may become too strong to deny, and the officer in charge couldn't even report it as desertion.

It is, indeed, a strange compulsion that drives runners, whether they be world-class marathoners or Fun-Run three-milers. It is something a non-runner wouldn't understand unless he or she were a smoker. To the average American, it seems unnatural to run. To the confirmed runner it seems very unnatural *not* to run.

In some very important ways, this compulsion aspect of running is good. It makes for a dedication to the sport/lifestyle, which is a dedication to the person's self. It makes it easier to face the elements when they aren't favorable. And it allows the runner to maintain the base training necessary to maintain running as a pleasurable joy rather than as a chore.

Running is a renewing experience that can make the rest of

a person's life more valuable both to himself and to those around him. It can be like an eternal spring, where a person can dip in and take from it something valuable every day without emptying it.

Some runners feel a sort of guilt about giving themselves that part of the day. They feel that they are ignoring their responsibilities during that time, ignoring what is traditionally expected of them. In a way, it is ignoring responsibilities while seeing to the primary responsibilities. It is certainly a form of play, a return to primordial pleasures of the body that have long been forgotten in the face of more complex, artificial pleasures. Yet it is fulfilling a responsibility to yourself and to the people around you by taking steps to make yourself a more sound person. Running heals some minor psychological flaws, helps solve minor and major problems by presenting them in an uncluttered version during a long run, and assures physical stamina. The runner instinctively feels all of this happening to him or her and often tries to hoard the feeling, as though if exposed it will vanish or be stolen.

It seems to me that one of the duties of the runner is to take pains to articulate what he or she is getting from running. Talk to the people around you who are being affected by your running in an attempt to verbalize what you are feeling, what is happening to you when you run. This is not to convert them and not to bore them, but at least to have the decency to make an attempt to explain it all to them. Many times the people around you, the people who interact with you on a daily basis, are not trying to persecute you because of your running; they just simply don't understand.

The benefits of running far outweigh of of the inconveniences. But do not assume that because you realize this everyone around you does. Talk about running, try to capture your feelings in your journal, attempt to share it with your family and friends—and if you do a good enough job of it, your family and friends will usually be willing to open that time and space in their day for you to make your run without hassles.

Don't use running, however, to mask personal problems—and don't blame running for personal problems. Running should and can complement one's life if it is done on a regular basis and if it is accepted for what it is. When it begins to take more from your life than it is giving, it is time to back up a little and examine the motives for your running.

Jan. 23—Brian Maxwell won the Paul Masson Champagne Marathon yesterday, looking very strong and confident after a rough midportion of the race in which he felt stiff and overwhelmed. He knocked nine minutes off the old course record of 2:29. As with each race I've attended, this one gave me added inspiration to put a little more effort into my own workouts. Although my schedule does not yet call for time trials, I took on the 8.3-mile course, trying to do it in less than an hour. I felt very strong and the run went smoothly. Although I know it's a long way off Brian Maxwell's pace for thrice the distance, getting to within 17 seconds of breaking an hour gave me a tremendous feeling of elation—perhaps because I'm feeling (at least for the moment) no ill effects. Maybe tomorrow it will catch up to me, but for today it felt great.

There seems to be an infection sweeping the country. It isn't the dreaded Russian flu, however. It's someting called "marathonitis"—the urge to run marathons, even if you aren't exactly sure what a marathon is. People who've never seen a marathon are going into training (often training with no real reasoning or rationale behind it) and running marathons.

I went to New York in October 1977 to cover what was being billed as the largest marathon in the country. I suppose that it was indeed the biggest. There were 5200 entries, and probably half of those people had never run a marathon before. Some had never seen a marathon. As I sat in a room in the Barbizon Plaza overlooking Central Park as the sun was going down, there were still people 18 floors below me staggering in the last mile. To my way of thinking, that isn't running. It's something else I have difficulty describing. If that's what they want to do with their Sunday, that's fine by me, I thought. Taking six or seven hours to cover 26 miles isn't something I'm fond of contemplating. Being laid up for days after a marathon does not sound that enticing, either.

Perhaps I was spoiled, though. I was on the main photographers' truck in front of the lead pack, watching Bill Rodgers and Jerome Drayton and Lasse Viren and Ron Hill and Chris Stewart astound me as they clicked off 26 consecutive miles at a pace I was incapable of holding for one mile.

I don't like crowds to begin with, and I didn't like the crowds at the New York City Marathon. I was probably more impressed by the incredible performances of some of the top marathoners than I was by anything else I've ever seen in my life, though. I swore to myself as I looked down on Central Park, as the sun was falling and as it was changing its texture from a place of relative festivity to a place of muggings and rapes and dejected people, that I would never run a marathon.

Perhaps I was soured by the depressing, cave-like aspects of New York City itself, a place I had years before found fascinating and that I now found depressing. Or perhaps I was soured by the fact that some kid about eight years old had thrown a rock at me from a hilly knoll while I was leaving Central Park after the four-hour point in the marathon. The rock had caught me on the back of the head and had pissed me off; I'd have run after the kid, but I was burdened like a burro with camera equipment and I was afraid of what I'd do to him if I caught him. No marathons for me, I swore.

In December, I drove up to Livermore to see their marathon, which Fritz Watson won. And during December, I was hard at work on putting the finishing touches on the marathon issue of *Runner's World*. Then, there was National Running Week in which every other speaker was talking about marathons. Maybe, I thought, I've been away from running too long and I'm overawed by the distance of a marathon. During December, the marathon was all around me, and I reluctantly found myself giving in to the urge to try one. I told myself that I wanted to do one now, because there was a certain challenge involved and because working toward a marathon would give my training some direction, some inspiration.

Despite the fact that I'd gotten to run only about 10 miles during National Running Week, I felt that the base I'd laid down gradually over the months would give me a good jumping-off point toward a marathon. I kept my head long enough to realize that if I was going to do a second marathon even farther down the road, the first one should be a pleasant experience and not a death march.

So, in the midst of the annual marathon issue, I found I had three longterm schedules I could work with: Joe Henderson's updated schedule for people who wanted to finish a marathon without killing themselves or their enthusiasm; Brian Maxwell's schedule for racing a marathon, which was more ambitious than Joe's and worked on the assumption that the runner had already experienced a marathon, and Arthur Lydiard's schedule for running your first marathon comfortably and well on an 18-week schedule.

I wanted to make my first marathon the Avenue of the Giants Marathon in early May and, if I started on Jan. 2, 1978, it would be a perfect 18 weeks until the race day. I chose Arthur Lydiard's schedule. I also chose it because it seemed to be a little tougher than Joe's and Brian's, and therefore gave me confidence that even if I fell a little behind on one part or another, I'd still be tough enough to make the 26 miles and still be able to walk and talk at the end.

My mileage before National Running Week was about 35 miles per week, during National Running Week about 10 miles, and the first week of January it skyrocketed to 60 miles per week. The understandable problems occurred. The first two weeks went pretty well, but I had to begin modifying the schedule a bit during the third week to allow my body to heal.

I also discovered that it's possible to forget simple things while frantically trying to stay on schedule.

Despite the increased mileage, I forgot to take an occasional salt tablet and increase my intake of liquids; I began cramping up in the calves. The heels of my training flats began to wear away like ice cream on a hot day and I got behind in building them up with repair goo, which also contributed to tightening of the calves. I made the discovery that my left leg is apparently shorter than my right, because when I run facing traffic the crown of the road causes pains in the left outside of my knee. The pains go away when I run with traffic, thereby putting my left leg up a fraction of an inch over the right leg.

In the meantime, I made every attempt to not deviate from Arthur Lydiard's marathon-training schedule. For those who are interested in using the same schedule in case the marathoning insanity strikes, I'm including it below. Do take special care to build the foundation first—and not for merely one week before embarking on the entire schedule. I can testify that it's not the way to make it through the first six weeks.

Foundation and preparation training:
Monday —30-45-minute aerobic run.
Tuesday —60-minute aerobic run.
Wednesday —30-45-minute aerobic run.
Thursday —60-minute aerobic run.
Friday —30-45-minute aerobic run.
Saturday —60-120-minute aerobic run.
Sunday —45-60-minute aerobic run.

From 18 weeks down to 13 weeks before marathon date:
Monday —45-60-minute aerobic run.
Tuesday —60-90-minute aerobic run.
Wednesday —30-45-minute easy fartlek run.
Thursday —60-90-minute aerobic run.
Saturday —90-120-minute aerobic run.
Sunday —45-60-minute aerobic run.

From 12 to seven weeks before the marathon date:
Monday —5000-meter time trial.
Tuesday —60-90-minute aerobic run.
Wednesday —10,000-meter time trial.
Thursday —60-90-minute aerobic run.
Friday —30-45-minute fartlek run.
Saturday —90-150-minute aerobic run.
Sunday —60-minute jog.

From six to three weeks before the marathon date:
Monday —8 x 200 meters fast relaxed running.
Tuesday —60-90-minute aerobic run.
Wednesday —5000-meter time trial
Thursday —30-60-minute fartlek run.
Friday —6 x 200 meters relaxed striding.
Saturday —90-150-minute aerobic run.
Sunday —60-minute jog.

Two weeks before the marathon date:
Monday —30-45-minute fartlek run.
Tuesday —60-minute aerobic run.
Wednesday —3000-meter time trial.
Thursday —30-45-minute fartlek run.
Friday —30-minute jog.
Saturday —60-minute aerobic run.
Sunday —30-minute aerobic run.

The week before the marathon date:
Monday —45-minute jog.

Tuesday —2000-meter time trial.
Wednesday —45-minute jog.
Thursday —30-minute jog.
Friday —30-minute jog or rest day.
Saturday —marathon race!
Sunday —45-60-minute recovery jog.

(Naturally, if the marathon you are aiming for is on a Sunday, slip the entire schedule forward by one day.)

Check back with me directly after your first marathon. Maybe we can get a group rate at the local psychologist's.

Jan 28 —Went out intending to do my 120-minute aerobic run today instead of tomorrow, since we have to go to San Francisco for Jill's Bonne Bell 10,000-meter race. Legs are very stiff. They never seem to recover from the previous day's runs anymore. Will begin again scheduling one day per week off instead of sticking strictly to Arthur Lydiard's schedule. Shoes are starting to wear down, too. Must get my other Countries into Jeff Sink's and back with new soles. Maybe I'll try some other type of shoes, too, to see if I can get broken in to another brand.

Jan. 29—Bonne Bell Mini-Marathon began at 10:06 a.m. in Golden Gate Park, with the fog horns in the Bay sounding regularly. Jill's been practicing for the race for several weeks. At 6.2 miles, it's better than a mile longer than she's ever run. About a thousand women of all shapes and sizes, all ages and abilities turned out for the run. It's great to see so many women doing something like this for themselves. There are some looks of strain on their faces, but the applause from the crowd makes them smile and they almost always mug for the camera. Jill placed something like 692nd, doing the distance in about 68 minutes, not stopping along the entire route. Good steady pace wasn't fast but was efficient. Good start for her.

Feb. 6—Bought a pair of Pony Californias and took a very good run to Palo Alto, in the dark and without my glasses—accidentally going beyond University Avenue, which is where I had planned to turn around and come back. My legs eventually became tired but did not get sore. The shoes are very comfortable except near the end of the run; but that was due to the continued drought, which put water inside the shoes, causing a blister to form on my arch. The only negative thing about the shoes is that they wear awfully fast in the soles. At this point, though, I'll take quick-wearing soles over harder soles that give me leg pains and keep me off the roads. Will run 10 or 15 miles of the West Valley Track Club Marathon next Sunday to get the feel for the marathon race before doing a full one in May.

It is probably unanimous among runners that the greatest moments in their running lives come when they are alone. Joe Henderson speaks eloquently of long runs along mountain-tops; Brian Maxwell remembers vividly a night run that to him was very mystical.

The runner, in communion with his body and with the ribbon of earth he is covering, sets up a sort of divinity among that mind, body and earth, and at some point all three are in perfect relation to each other and there is almost an other-worldliness about the experience. It is a trip without drugs, without artificial stimulation—a sort of trip created by body chemicals reaching the critical stage, mental electricity sparking into those chemicals, the formation of a sort of flying carpet where the legs are so much a part of the earth that they are forgotten.

The often-mystical experiences that come at times like that do not come until the runner has built up a base of training so that the runs are no longer a strain during the first few miles, but merely the warming of the cauldron in which the great experience might be formulated for that day's run. The great experience does not come with every run, and it is not always the same. It plays a sort of game with the runner, surprising the runner during a run that started badly but that has become smooth and effortless and uplifting. It fails to arrive sometimes on beautiful days when the body feels ready for it. But when it does come, it always comes when the runner is alone, when there is solitude so that the great experience is not shy about appearing.

It would be wonderful for running if someone could find the secret key to guarantee the great experience on every run. But if someone did, perhaps it would no longer be the great experience, because it would become as expected as yearly income tax, bellyaches from eating too much ice cream and presidential elections every four years.

I've always favored the solitary run, and still very much do. But my prejudices against running with other people in something other than races are beginning to be worn down.

Several of us now do Saturday morning runs near the Stanford campus in Palo Alto. Typically, we start from downtown Palo Alto, cross the Stanford campus (taking whatever detours happen to catch our fancy, to watch some girls playing field hockey or to take a closer look at an exotic car in a parking lot), climb some fences and do some hillwork near the radio telescope, where there's a great view of the foothills and I-280 off one side and of the red-tile roofs of the campus on the other side. From there we head to Angell Field where we do intervals for 45 minutes or so. The entire routine takes nearly 2½ hours, but there's no great rush. We talk during the easy parts, and we go where the spirit moves us. With the right people on the run, everyone is loose enough that they're agreeable to changing direction on the slightest whim from any member of the group.

I'd resisted the "social run" for a long time, but have found that—with the right people, with a group that doesn't go beyond five runners—it can be the high point of a week's training, making the 2½ hours vanish in seemingly no time.

Additionally, at various portions of the run two or more members often find that there is a particular hill that interests them. Often without communicating it in words, they can jointly depart the group for a side trip up the hill, rejoining the group down the other side. That secret communication comes in like telepathy when two or three runners begin spontaneously to stride out, matching speed perfectly, weaving around ruts in the road, seemingly matched like pearls on a necklace, striding on for a mile or so in perfect unison—not racing, but lightly testing the other's thresholds for a moment, falling back to the pace, almost like sled dogs without restraints. Again, as with the solitary run where the great experience arrives unheralded, the striding out with companion runners either comes very close to mysticism or else goes beyond it into something that only runners who've done it can share.

Chapter Seven

On the Run

*T*he massive little truths that strike a runner on the run are the crushed cherries atop a beautifully-constructed ice cream sundae. The beautifully unexplainable stretches of euphoria are the crushed nuts, for they open to us parts of ourselves that are two left turns past tomorrow's psychology. The documented benefits such as lower pulse rate, stronger heart, better muscle tone, endurance, incredible oxygen uptake constitute the cherry topping the sundae.

But the largest mass of the confectionary construction is the ice cream itself, and in running the largest single factor is probably the body awareness.—The primitiveness of feeling muscles and guts and fleshy parts and bones and joints that sometimes seem at such ends with each other coming together to make something greater than themselves happen. The very act of running is the great benefit of the sport/lifestyle.

There is a feeling of power and jointure with the wind and the elements when running in a storm. When the sun shines and there is a gentle, warming breeze meeting the runner, there is a swelling of the capacity of the body to be part of the world through which it moves. When the body chugs up a steep hill or a mountain, there is a marriage between the runner and the great mass of rock and dirt under him that he instinctively recognizes. A run along an ocean beach is usually accompanied by a friendly tug from the waters from which man originally came, so that the runner finds himself in the trough of the surf that has just sucked itself back to the seas, taking a memory with it.

Every element the runner passes through on this earth exerts a certain familiar tug. And the very act of running heightens this sensation: the ache that comes on early in the run that is deep down in the long muscle of the left leg that leaves mysteriously as the body warms itself; the hint of a stitch in the right side that never comes; the excruciatingly delightful feeling at the midpoint of the run that the legs could go on forever in their easy stride. The body responds to the running as though it has come home to a quiet farm where it spent a summer as a child. It speaks and we listen, ready to learn something of ourselves, of our mysterious past where the elements have attempted to wash away our footprints even as it now tries to reclaim land we allow to sit quietly for a few years.

We have conquered the earth and are now alien to it, but on the run we find that it wants us to come back—if we are willing to come back under its provisions.

More of the earth's offspring are heeding the call of that wild yearly. There are more people mountaineering, taking camping trips, moving back to the country, taking up hiking—and becoming runners—than ever before in the earth's history. The artificial earth man has built has not been perfect, and mankind is trying to do something about leaving it and going back to simpler times and pleasures.

Within recent years, it has become a massive exodus back to the earth, much of the impetus coming from the post-World War II baby boom. The groundswell has risen to a wave. The wave is coming close to reaching a majority.

There will, of course, never be total commitment to such a return. But as the return is made by many, the benefits will begin to be felt.

For even the most misanthropic runner, it is pleasant to venture sometimes into the world of the running masses and take a peek at what's going on.

Runners are a very mixed group, and when it comes to their running they are decidedly individualistic. They know what's right for them, and they intend to see that they get it. Most of them, however, are not fools, and they know that there's more strength of conviction in numbers. It is, therefore, not uncommon to find runners who've never joined anything in their lives—in fact, who took great pains to never join *anything*—being first in line to join running clubs.

Clubs offer advantages that are unavailable to the single runner. Although many of the benefits are of a social sort, the club functions around fielding teams in racing events and/or sponsoring racing events.

Seeing the number of dedicated runners at World Publications and matching that number with an equal number of people at least casually interested in running, we felt, in early December 1977, that we had the makings of a club. Knowing that the local West Valley Track Club was sponsoring its annual 50-mile Christmas Relays on Dec. 18 from Santa Cruz to Half Moon Bay—a scenic stretch along California Route 1 fronting the Pacific Ocean—we rushed our paperwork together and sent for AAU cards for everyone, also submitting our paperwork for a charter to become the *"Runner's World* Road Club."

We had just about enough runners to field two seven-man teams in the relays, so Doug Latimer, our general manager, and I put together an A (competitive) team and a B (fun-run) team. According to the rules of the relay, the B (or *slow*) teams would be leaving the University of California at Santa Cruz at 9 a.m., while the A teams would be leaving at 10 a.m. Theoretically, the A teams would catch the B teams somewhere along the 50-mile stretch. Doug was so sure that his A team of himself (running the first leg of about 10 miles), Joe Henderson (five-mile leg), Lyman Dickson (5½-miles), Lew Patterson (9½-miles), John Bork (five-miles), Bob Anderson (4½-miles) and Dave "The Amazing One" Prokop (10½-miles) could catch our fledgling team of Jim Lilliefors, Ray Hosler, Bill Green, Phil Lenihan, Bill Howard and Keith Holden, that he bet me a case of Heineken they would do just that. Now, for a case of Heineken he should have known that our team would scale mountains—which is exactly what happened.

We started 20 minutes behind schedule under rainy skies in Santa Cruz with Jim Lilliefors, editorial assistant for *Runner's World*, leading off. Jim had run the Livermore Marathon the previous weekend, but being his supervisor I had convinced him he should run again this weekend.

He handed off to Ray Hosler, who had run the Fiesta Bowl Marathon the previous weekend. Our other editorial assistant,

Ray, knew he'd have a lot of Dr. Sheehan's medical advice to edit on Monday if he didn't come through.

Ray handed off to company lawyer, Bill Green, who is more of a sprinter than a distance man. Bill took off as though it were a sprint and eventually slowed a bit as the distance got to him, but he turned in a tremendous effort in the last mile.

He handed off to Phil Lenihan, who was coming off the Honolulu Marathon the previous weekend.

Phil handed off to Bill Howard, a new employee from Florida who'd never run more than five miles in his life.

Bill handed off to me, still well over the ideal running weight, and I ran less than a half-mile before I began chugging up the first mountain. I'd given everyone else the option to pick their own legs, and I'd taken what was left. It was the shortest leg (only about 4½ miles), but I found out why they kept it short. On my way up the second mountain, a female runner came next to me and told me that I should pick it up, that this was the last hill and the exchange point was down the other side. Like a fool I believed her—hell, it *felt* like I'd gone 4½ miles.

I crested the mountain and found she'd told me that just to push me into burning myself out. There were actually two more mountains to run up and down. I was so numb that I could hardly move up the mountains and was having trouble going any faster *down* the other side than I was going up the front sides. I walked three times, finding that when I got too numb I could regain some strength by walking. I was panicked, too, because some of the A team had driven up to my starting point, indicating that they were catching us.

I finally came down the last mountain, numb in every part of my body, and tagged Keith Holden—who indicated at the start that he was out of shape, was doing only very slow distance work and that he was going to try to keep an eight-minute-per-mile pace unless Prokop caught up to him, in which case he was going to try to stay with him.

After handing off to Keith, who had a 1½-mile mountain to climb and then a pretty smooth (but long) run to the finish, I found that my time for leg six had been 32 minutes—despite my walking three times—which, for my conditioning at that point, was incredibly good. Keith moved along at a steady lope and, as all of us gathered in Half Moon Bay waiting for the finishers, the rest of the A team began arriving, so we felt the finish would be close.

Keith came flashing into view and, perspiration dripping from him, rounded the turn and finished, our fun-run team getting to the finish before the competitive team. We handed him a beer and a sandwich, had a celebration, picked up our ribbons and waited for Dave Prokop, the A team's anchorman. Better than a half-hour later he finished, despite the fact that the A team had been started 55 minutes instead of an hour after us. We had, we thought, proved that beer does make runners go faster. Doug delivered the goods.

*P*robably one of the most unique groups of runners assembled meets in the little town of Los Altos, Calif., on New Year's Eve. The runners have been meeting there for nearly 20 years, huddled together in a mass to keep warm and waiting for the stroke of midnight, when they run a five-mile course through the sparsely-illuminated streets as their way of bringing in the new year. Then, true to their penchant for celebrating and imbibing, they'd begin their New Year's partying, going until the sun rises on the new year.

In recent years, *Runner's World* Magazine has gotten together with the town to co-sponsor the Midnight Run. The event is used to close out National Running Week, which the magazine also sponsors. It is fitting that the week be closed with a race. The 1977 week of panel discussions, workshops, equipment shows, etc., began with the National Fitness Run, also a rather unique affair in which five legs of a scenic 15-mile course are run at a 10-minute-per-mile pace, beginning in Sausalito, crossing the Golden Gate Bridge, running through San Francisco, and ending along the Great Highway beside the Pacific Ocean.

A new twist had been added to the 1977-78 Midnight Run by the running magazine. Many of the continent's top distance runners had been brought in for the National Running Week festivities, and those runners would be assembled, along with other top-shelf runners, to compete in a special Invitational Midnight Run that would be held at 11:15 p.m. over the same course as the people's Midnight Run. The

Invitational field included Bill Rodgers, Jerome Drayton, Marty Liquori, Duncan Macdonald, Brian Maxwell, Hal Higdon, Josh Kimeto and 38 others. By running the burners up front, well before the mass run, fun runners would be able to see the running stars; conversely, with their race over, the frontrunners would be able to see the masses make their run, something they seldom see because they are too far in the lead to see the mass of the field.

For California, New Year's Eve 1977 was a fairly nippy evening. Having arrived at 9 p.m. to help get sign-up tables set up, take instructions on being officials and timers for the race and just to satisfy our curiosity as to what goes on behind the scenes, we spent the night looking at breath clouds forming in front of us.

Perhaps as a fitting paradox, or perhaps because everything in the world works in cycles, the headquarters for the run was set up in the corner gas station where I had weeks before abandoned my 18-mile run, where my wife and I had downed some root beer while discovering that her bicycle had developed a flat tire.

I had been prepared to accept the fact that the run into the new year would be very symbolic—as it was supposed to be—but my suspicions were becoming piqued that it would become more symbolic than I would be able to comfortably explain away as coincidence.

At the gas station, there were two guys standing about watching the activity. They were wearing cut-off T-shirts and trying to act very macho while their teeth chattered and their goosebumps got goosebumps. There was talk that it might rain later in the evening, and when the two heard mention of that possibility their smiles around their chattering teeth faded.

Town work crews and police had barricaded the end of Main Street and were setting up other barricades, manned with police officers who had been persuaded to give up their New Year's Eve celebrations just to accommodate a bunch of crazies. It helped, of course, that the town's mayor was one of the crazies bouncing around in an attempt to get warm.

(Los Altos seemed to be one of those strange places where everyone was either very much in favor of running or very much against it. The run, which had originally been held at nearby Foothill College, had grown so quickly and had become so successful that there was talk of changing the run's location the next year from downtown Los Altos. Even the pro-running mayor was giving interviews to that effect. The lovely streets of downtown Los Altos, decorated with tasteful white Christmas lights on the now-barren trees lining both sides of the street, might well be zoned for drunks only by the next New Year's Eve.)

People in various strange costumes began arriving to sign up for the run. They seemed to have pulled whatever they could find from their closets in order to keep warm before taking part in the run.

Complaining about the damp cold that had rolled in, the municipal employees and the *Runner's World* employees and friends got the proper streets blocked off, the crowd controlled, everything organized in time. The excitement, which had been in a state of suspended animation because of the cold and our early arrival time, began to build quickly as the countdown for the invitational run started. World-class runners began warming up by doing stretching exercises and short runs down side streets. Marty Liquori, who was warming up too close to one of the barricades, had to stop every few minutes to sign autographs.

"I'm not really ready for this," Brian Maxwell said. "I'm in training for a marathon and haven't gotten to my speed work yet. Can you schedule a marathon for next year instead of a five-miler?"

"I don't know what I'm going to do," Bill Rodgers said, lining up on the outside edge of the pack along First Street as Joe Henderson walked back and forth in front of them, nervously hefting the starting gun. Hal Higdon and Dave Prokop had taken Rodgers, who had been suffering from jet lag the previous afternoon, in tow at the Runner's Night banquet, making a tour of all the night spots in the area, keeping him out until 3 a.m.

"I'm just goin' to run through it and see what happens," Bill said. "I'm out of shape; I'm on my down period," He smiled weakly. "I don't feel well, either."

Rodgers had, three weeks earlier, set the world's fastest

marathon time for 1977 in the annual Fukuoka run in Japan. He'd suffered through a flu the following weekend on returning home to Boston after attending some activities surrounding the Honolulu Marathon but not taking part in the run itself. It wasn't the flu he was referring to, though.

The excitement mounted and any weariness or depressions left as John Bork, coordinating the run, spoke briefly to the field of competitors, giving them instructions. The course officials urged the crowd to move back onto the sidewalks so that the runners would have space to get past them. The countdown was called off by Phil Lenihan, atop a flatbed truck that was blocking the intersection from unwanted traffic. Joe Henderson still paced back and forth, nervously waving the starting gun. Despite instructions that the count would reach zero, there would be a call of "Set," "Go" and then the gun, the field heard "Go" and took off, rushing Henderson, who fired the starting gun in self-defense and backpedaled out of the way.

A roar went up from the crowd of 2500 spectators as the field vanished down a very dark First Street, led by a police station wagon with flashing lights to keep spectators off the course. From his observation point, Phil Lenihan could keep track of the progress of the leaders by following the flashing police light as it moved through town. The five-mile course was three laps through the downtown area

The excitement built as the first lap neared completion and the leaders rushed up Main Street, the crowds lining the sidewalks surging forward to get a better view. As they came into the light at the intersection, flashbulbs on cameras going off like mortar fire, the large digital display board showing their time above their heads, there was a three-way battle for first among Bill Rodgers, Josh Kimeto and Duncan Macdonald. The rest of the field—Liquori, Drayton, etc. came through on their tails, not yet spread out. Phil Lenihan, his voice beginning to give out from yelling into too many microphones during the too-long week, exhorted the crowd on to even more excitement. The officials, timers, police and municipal employees worked to keep the crowd off the street as they strained to see who would be in the lead for the next lap.

Lenihan kept the crowd at the intersection posted as to the race's progress by watching for the police light and by listening for the shouts of the crowd at various other parts of the course. When the leaders again flashed into the light at the intersection, it was a hard-pitched battle between Duncan Macdonald and Bill Rodgers. Macdonald, a track standout at nearby Stanford University in years past, was still an outstanding road racer and marathoner; he looked strong and confident. Rodgers, a mere wisp of a man at about 128 pounds, looked as though being kept out until 3 a.m. was beginning to get to him.

The rest of the field had broken up quite a bit. Jerome Drayton, who'd been incredibly nervous before such a low-key race, was passing Josh Kimeto and trying to catch Marty Liquori as they came through the intersection. The rest of the field was pretty well spread.

The funnel that would lead the runners down Main Street past Phil Lenihan's position as they passed the finish line after the last lap was set up quickly, officials standing on both sides to keep the crowd back so they would be able to record times and places. The crowd sent up a roar farther down Main Street, and moments later Duncan Macdonald flashed into the illumination of the streetlights, in first place by 20 yards over Bill Rodgers. In a rush, they were through the chutes and their times recorded. In minutes, the other 43 runners were similarly recorded. Liquori placed a distant third and Drayton a threatening fourth.

As the results were being tabulated and read to the crowd by Lenihan, 2000 runners were lining up at Main and First Streets to run the course just warmed by the world-class runners. I turned my stopwatch over to race officials and quickly removed enough clothing to get down to my running clothes. I put my coat and pants and car keys and sweatshirts into the back of Bob Anderson's jeep and walked toward the back of the huge crowd, figuring to run a nice, easy five miles with the stragglers. Incredibly, I found my wife in the mass and arranged to run with her for the first lap. Standing next to us was the man from Los Altos Hills I'd met along Moody Road during one of my first 6 a.m. runs in California back in August.

"You sure look like you did lose some weight," he said.

"Great to see you here," I answered him, bouncing a little to keep warm and to loosen up enough to do some stretching.

Phil Lenihan, still talking away, was now beginning the countdown to midnight. As the moment arrived, everyone in the mass of runners shook hands, embraced and kissed. The fact that the run had started didn't reach our consciousness for at least 45 seconds, because our segment of the crowd just stayed where it was, standing still, exchanging congratulations on making it into another year.

The front of the crowd had begun to move, and the movement eventually got to us. For half a block, though, the very size of the crowd beginning its momentum caused us to walk forward a few steps, stop, then move again, only after several minutes allowing us enough space to run and then only at a slow stagger. Although I had not yet run my first marathon, this was giving me some indication of what the start is like, where precious minutes are lost waiting for the massive crowd to move out of your way enough to take a step.

We finally got moving and took our time, playing it safe, trying to avoid being stopped again, trying to avoid stepping on someone smaller or older than us while avoiding being stepped on ourselves. The moment was exquisitely electric, but somewhere in the back of my mind was a nagging wish that there was a road as lonesome as Moody Road was at 6 a.m. so that we might run together alone.

The sensation of running at night, into block-long shadows and then out into streetlighted intersections, was a bit strange. The fact that we were moving removed some of the chill from our bodies. In fact, it became quite pleasant as the body furnace began being stoked up and the cool air hit it. Far in front of us, many of the local runners were battling for first place while the rest of us treated the run as a just-for-fun event.

Dan O'Keefe from Paul Masson Wineries was giving out wine and champagne to the first 10 finishers; he was still busy gaining exposure for his marathon 22 days away. For some runners, every run is a race to begin with; the further inducement of beating 2000 other runners and getting a bottle of champagne became all the encouragement they needed. By the time we had jogged through half of the first lap, we were already being lapped by the competitive runners.

Unknown to us way in the back of the pack, many of the world-class runners had decided to run in the people's Midnight Run. Brian Maxwell was a little in front of us, Hal Higdon a little behind us, taking his time as we were, running it for fun.

After a lap, my wife found Joe Henderson's wife Janet and they ran together for a while as I picked up my speed to a more comfortable pace, passing some people and wondering how the fast runners were handling all the broken-field running necessary to negotiate the course.

New Year's Eve celebrants lined the streets waving bottles of champagne and calling either encouragements or taunts to us depending, apparently, on whether they were celebrating the end of the old year or damning it.

"Give up, you're never gonna win!" one drunken spectator yelled.

"Just being here is winning!" one of the runners yelled back. The drunk drank to that.

An hour after it had begun, the run began to end as the last of the stragglers came in. They had taken better than twice as long as the world-class runners had to run the same course.

"But we had twice as much fun being out there twice as long," one plodder said.

When I arrived back at the gas station, all sweaty and steaming as my body heat met the cold night, I found that Bob Anderson's jeep had left to go to his house to get things set up there for the party afterwards. My pants, coat and car keys were gone, and my body warmth was beginning to have difficulty fighting the cold. Hal Higdon and I commandeered a ride with Doug Latimer to Bob's house while my wife and her girlfriend stayed at the gas station to keep an eye opened for Brian Maxwell, who was coming to our house to get a shower before going along to the party at the Andersons'.

By the time I returned with the car keys the downtown Los Altos scene had changed dramatically. There were only a few people about, all the barricades were gone, some clumps of people shared a bottle of champagne in a parking lot. The police were gone, the crowd was gone, there was hardly a piece of scrap paper in the gutter. The swarm of locusts had left, and there was little evidence they had ever been there.

I limped over to Phil Lenihan's VW Microbus, idling in the gas station lot. I had inserted Dr. Scholl's arches in my shoes during the afternoon, and one of them had come loose during the run and had given me a mean blister on my left arch. My wife and her girlfriend were inside Phil's van listening to the radio. The town was quiet. We found Brian Maxwell with some friends in the parking lot across from our car. As we approached, they waved a big green-tinted champagne bottle. "Happy Runnin' New Year!" they shouted.

As we climbed into the car, knowing that we would be up until the sun rose, probably with just the sigh of a hangover, it was difficult refraining from the consideration that life had again come around in a complete circle.

We had just taken part in a primitive ritual of welcoming in the new year. We'd done it in a primitive manner: by running with what amounted to mass abandon. We had every intention of watching the sun squeeze itself into the day like primitive sentinels keeping watch on the reindeer herd throughout the night. Everything seemed somehow right with the world at that moment, as though everything were indeed in its proper place.

Somewhere, I was sure, Max Acker was going to be watching the sunrise with us.

Afterword

Return to Running

*T*hings began to break up for Larry around the 18-mile mark, just before the hills. We dropped back into a slightly lower gear and started up the first hill, hoping to conserve some strength for the last miles; hoping to make up any time we might lose on the back sides of the hills.

As a fluke race we threw in as part of our training for the Avenue of the Giants Marathon three weeks down the road, the Boston Marathon was a relatively pleasant experience.

Following a weekend filled with meetings, receptions, hospitality rooms and sessions to finalize plans for our coverage of the world's most famous marathon and even following a session of shooting photos up until 15 minutes before the actual race, running Boston was proving to be something of a vacation.

We'd done our stretching exercises seven minutes before the start, trying to push down the side of a bank building in an attempt to make our Achilles tendons supple while church ladies sold baked goods 10 yards away. The local kids frolicked around the park in Hopkinton, hoping that the hot-air balloon rocking back and forth like an inverted punching bag would let go its moorings and soar into the black skies to join the helicopters that ruptured the air. The grease of hot dogs being grilled in the park filtered through the heavy air, causing many of the runners who'd been abstaining from food all morning to curse as their stomachs vacillated between wanting to wrap around one of the hot dogs or contract in spasms at the thought of food on such a nervous morning.

Dozens of runners sauntered purposefully off to the woods behind the church, while a female runner and her companion crouched down behind a garbage dumpster, going through the last rites.

On the street, thousands of runners were lining up behind ropes that corralled them into sections that were coded according to their best-ever marathon times. Runners in the front of each section, standing against the ropes, looked stoic, almost statue-like, as though they'd fought to get their places there four hours before, and wouldn't give up that place even for a chance to urinate.

With five minutes to go, Larry and I walked toward the absolute back of the pack. Neither of us had numbers and we didn't want to get in the way of runners who did; neither did we want to get in the way of other runners who, like ourselves, were running the Boston Marathon because it was the Boston Marathon.

Boston is one of those sporting events that has turned into something beyond sport. It ranks with the Indianapolis 500 and the Kentucky Derby and the World Series: It is a Event rather than a 'sporting event' with a lower case e. Non-sporting people attend the Boston Marathon just to be there, much as they go to the Indy 500 to be a part of the infield crowd, where they may never get to see even a sliver of the race. They come to watch what happens and to feel part of something magical.

The difference, which all of those unwashed, unnumbered masses in the back of the Boston starting field take advantage of, is that a person at Indy never gets an opportunity to drive one of the Foyt-Coyotes, at the Derby the person never gets to sit on one of the horses, and at the World Series never has the opportunity to field a well-hit liner to right field, while a person at Boston can simply walk to the back of the field and take part. The Watcher can become the Doer by merely stepping off the sidewalk and lining up.

For 1978, with 4212 entries, there were approximately another 3000 runners who were walk-ons for the great drama. High-stepping in the cool air to keep recently loosened muscles from tightening up, we checked our watches to anticipate the start. A minute before the appointed hour, the ropes were lowered and the segregated runners were allowed to walk forward to close up the ranks in front of them. There was a cheer accompanied by an anticipatory twitch in the stomach. It was as though the first flash of lightning in a stormy sky had come and all the anticipation was over. Runners turned toward each other and smiled. This was it.

Four days later, when the color slides that were shot from the helicopters overhead arrived at the office, that moment looked like a dam of multi-colored water about to burst its walls.

The start came faintly, better than a country block away, followed a second later by a roar from the crowd that had formed a sluice through which the freed dam water could rush. Hal Higdon, also running without a number because of his refusal to rejoin the AAU, moved in next to us and we stood together, waiting for something to happen. For many minutes, nothing happened.

Then, a little at a time, we began to take tentative steps forward, occasionally walking over one of the ropes. Again, runners smiled at each other as though in line to see a Bugs Bunny Film Festival. We could suddenly take two steps in a row and then suddenly, seven and a half minutes after the start gun, we crossed the starting line. We pinched our watches and began shuffling forward.

Our whole strategy of using the Boston as a training run for the Avenue of the Giants began to deteriorate. We set what we hoped was an eight-minute-per-mile pace, trying to work around the swarm of runners in front of us when they bunched, trying to avoid dogs and cyclists along the side of the road while still managing to acknowledge waves and shouts from the crowds lining the rural road. Already runners were unashamedly taking pitstops a few feet into the still-leafless woods along the road; they were ignored except by the occasional curious dog.

Larry carried a card in his pocket with all of our ideal splits for various landmarks. The first one was in Ashland; we felt that we would probably be behind schedule because of the tremendous difficulty in maneuvering around the huge mass of runners. However, we found that we were right on schedule and despite the darkening skies our spirits began to pick up. So did our pace as we passed through towns where the crowds were thick and enthusiastic. We attempted to restrain each other, knowing that to expend too much energy at this point would be disastrous.

We'd done a long run the previous weekend; Larry had gone 21 miles and I'd broken at 18½, a mere half-mile longer than I'd ever run in my life. A veteran of several marathons in the New York City area, Larry has a tendency to bounce when he allows his enthusiasm to overcome his reason. He began bouncing in Framingham as the crowds thickened on both sides of the street and as the rain, that had begun after Ashland, continued to come down. Despite the fact that it was only in the high 40s, we decided to begin accepting cups of water. We had arranged with a friend to hand us squeeze bottles of Body Punch at Natick, but with the huge crowd that had filled the area for the race we had our doubts if he'd be able to get through.

Coming through Natick, however, still passing runners at a regular clip, Joe Henderson shouted from the crowd on the left of the road that our Body Punch was a 100 yards ahead. We sipped at the lemonade-flavored fluid until Wellesley where, instead of accepting a cup of fluid from one of the Wellesley girls that lined the street, turning it into a very pleasant gauntlet, I handed the empty bottle to one of the college girls. At places along the course where the gauntlets did materialize, it became harder and harder to keep our pace because it was almost impossible to pass. We were 30 seconds ahead of schedule as we approached Newton.

Newton is sort of like the moment of truth in all the westerns! Where the sheriff comes up against the notorious gunslinger. The problem is aggravated at Newton because there are three gunslingers in a row in the form of a long, a longer, and a longest hill—the last being the infamous Heartbreak Hill.

Coming into Newton, my own moment of truth arrived. I felt relatively good—much better than I'd anticipated. Until that point I hadn't even thought about my legs; we'd just been moving along, with no unusual sensations coming up from my legs to even remind me that they were there. I was worried, however, because the Newton hills come at the point in the race where "the wall" hits many runners. I'd convinced myself that the previous weekend I'd hit "the wall" at the 18½-mile point in our training run. There was a mile of doubt as we went into the first hill; I wondered if I'd be able to go the full 26 miles. As we went up the first hill, Larry cautioned me to slow down a bit.

For the previous 18 miles I'd been running behind his left shoulder; now he was running behind me. He'd eaten meatballs with his spaghetti the night before; I wondered if they were beginning to bother him. My own spirits lifted as I saw that the hills were long but relatively civilized compared to some of the hills I'd been training on for several weeks in northern California.

The waves of spectators began to close in, as though to get a closer look at the suffering of the runners as they faced and fought the hills. I found myself easily passing many of the runners who were letting the hills effect them. Much of what had sustained us to that point had been the enthusiasm of the crowd; it helped again as we began to discern that they were closing in upon us, not to watch our suffering, but to urge us on up the hill.

Moving smoothly down the other side of the first hill, Larry again cautioned both of us to ease back and we did, but we were still passing other runners at a furious rate. We'd been buoyed to this point as much by the crowd as we were by having started at the absolute back of the pack, where we were passing many more runners than were passing us. Since we left Hopkinton, we'd been passed by less than a dozen runners. And they were wearing numbers; they had apparently stopped to make pitstops and were playing catch-up. We passed seemingly thousands of other runners and were still moving well, but Larry was no longer bouncing.

On the second hill, we slowed a bit to save some for the last hill. Again, Larry stayed behind my shoulder. My only discomfort at that point was some stomach unrest, probably due to the variety of liquids I'd ingested along the way; with my eyes closed I could tell which town we were passing through by the taste of the drink.

We rolled off the second hill and saw a little girl beside the road proudly holding a sign: *Heartbreak Hill 1 Mile.*

The crowd was becoming a massive funnel. It was impossible to run more than two abreast. Passing was becoming more and more difficult and we found ourselves using a great deal of energy calling to the runner in front: "Passing on the left" or "Coming through." Some of the runners were too numb at this point to hear us or, hearing us, to respond.

Heartbreak Hill was almost anticlimatic. Longer but no steeper than the other hills, it was heavily lined with spectators. We dropped back a gear and took it steadily, still passing other runners, pulled up the hill by the cheers of the crowd. Where we had been slapping hands extended from the crowd in the early going, we were now merely concentrating on keeping stride up the hill and on passing as smoothly as possible.

At the top of the hill, on the left, a policeman sat in a white cruiser, calling to the runner over the loudspeaker that this, indeed, was the top, and it was all downhill from there. He had his arm hanging casually out the window. I slapped his hand jauntily as we crested the hill and saw the downtown area spread out before us; he smiled and changed his open hand to a thumbs-up.

Again, Larry cautioned against going down the backside of the hill too quickly. There was no longer a smile on his face.

As we hit the tracks where Commonwealth Avenue gives way to Beacon Street, Larry urged me to go ahead without him, that he had to slow down. Reluctantly I moved away, feeling that running together was the only thing that had gotten me as far as the hills.

Still passing runners who'd hit the wall and were moving as though zombies, I promised my stomach not to take any more liquids, both because I was still feeling queasy and because at the point where there were four miles to go, liquids wouldn't have time to do my body any good anyway. The crowd seemed strangely subdued compared to the early part of the course. Perhaps, better than three hours after the race had started, these people were clapped and shouted and enthused out. Perhaps they were more tired than many of the runners. With three and a half miles to go, I approached and passed a young runner who carried a 16-oz. beer in each hand; the crowd cheered him on as he drank first from one and then from the other can.

With a mile and a half left, I caught up to Hal Higdon, who was walking along the side of the route; he had suffered a leg injury several weeks before and he was limping. "Hal, Hal," I shouted to him, "c'mon along." He dutifully joined me.

Unfortunately, he was in a talkative mood. "When they tell you there's a mile left, don't believe them," he said. I nodded, understanding, finding myself becoming heavy and depressed at the thought. My emotions at that point were so tenacious that even the mention that something might be wrong was toppling me. Larry and I had stepped off the curb and into the pack in Hopkinton hoping to run the course between 3:30 and 3:45. I was still running well, but with Hal's running commentary I was finding myself becoming heavy and leaden; suddenly, the Prudential building didn't seem to be getting any closer.

I had decided, when I'd left Larry, that I was going to try to use up everything I had left in an attempt to come in under 3:30. I now realized that it was going to be close.

"It feels better running at this pace than it does walking," Hal said from my shoulder. *Jeeze*, I thought, *all I need is a conversation now when I'm going to force my guts to come apart to get me through the last half-mile.* Hal, who was the first American finisher at Boston in 1964, was still looking fresh.

"Put your arms down a little bit more and come up on your toes," he said as we turned the corner and headed toward the Prudential. "And start smiling. Everybody's going to be taking pictures." I grimaced.

We had heard radio reports at the moment Bill Rodgers had passed this very spot while we were still about 10 miles out. The announcer's voice had been animated and excited. There were conflicting reports at first as to who had taken second, but it came down to Jeff Wells. Each time Larry had yelled to someone in the crowd to find out who was winning, they'd come back with: "Everybody's a winner in this race, son."

At a 100 yards from the finish, I was skeptical. As I crossed the line and clicked off my watch at 3:29:00.48, I was still skeptical. The crowd became a mob and we were herded down chutes like cattle and some people were hugging each other and there were smiles and tears and some people were being taken to the underground garage where they were being treated for trying too hard to be a winner in their own right.

I limped away from the chutes and tried weakly to get away from the crowd that had sustained us throughout the 26 miles; their numbers were suddenly oppressive and I wanted to escape. Joe Henderson had handed me the hotel room key as I passed him a mile from the finish. I wanted very badly to use it. My toes were beginning to hurt now that I'd stopped; always susceptible to toe injuries on downhills, I knew I'd really destroyed them. I was afraid to take my shoes off as I limped back to my hotel, finding that mile the hardest of the day.

In the hotel room, with a beer in one hand and my body under hot water in the tub, the excitement came back.

Each of the major marathons has its own style, whether it is the casualness of Honolulu or the public relations hype of Chicago or the carefully-constructed status of New York; but, I reflected, Boston is Boston, always has been and always will be the benchmark, despite its problems.

And I'd just run it. *Jeeze, I'd returned.*

About the Author

Rich Benyo lived the story he tells here—the story thousands of men and women in their 20s, 30s and 40s repeat in their own ways each year. It's a story of self-neglect and repair.

Benyo had run as a child in Jim Thorpe, Pa., in the ways we all run as children born to the sport. He'd raced with the cross-country team at Bloomsburg State College—but then had stored it away with the other trappings of childhood, as most athletes do when they decide it's time to grow up.

He took a job as a newspaper reporter and editor, and later took a wife, Jill. He "grew up" steadily from his college running weight of 150 pounds. From time to time, Rich vowed to start running again, to get

During his sophomore year in college, Benyo was a mere 150 pounds while running with the cross-country team.

back in shape. But the effort of it eroded his resolve within in few days.

Years passed. His career flourished. He worked as editor of *Stock Car Racing* magazine in surburban Washington, D.C., and published a book on the sport, *Superspeedway*.

But forces were still trying to bring him back to his original sport, even after so much time away. The death of a close friend his age shocked Benyo into starting a fitness program he would stay on. A few weeks after his 31st birthday, weighing 207, he returned to running for good. Shortly after that, he accepted a job as managing editor of *Runner's World* magazine. He came to California in August 1977 and began low-level racing. By the following April, he was fit enough to finish the Boston Marathon.

Return to Running is both an inspiring account of Benyo's fall and rise as a runner, and a valuable collection of advice for fellow returnees.

At the start of the second Switchback Scamper, Benyo exhibits back-of-the-pack form.

Following the 1977 National Fitness Run, Joe Henderson and an increasingly slimmer Benyo compare notes.

Other World Publications Books on Health and Fitness

FITNESS AFTER FORTY   *Hal Higdon*

DR. SHEEHAN'S MEDICAL ADVICE   *George Sheehan, M.D.*
For Runners and Other Athletes

BASIC FITNESS GUIDE   *Joe Owens*

THE COMPLETE DIET GUIDE   *Edited by Hal Higdon*
For Runners and Other Athletes

SKIN CARE   *Cameron L. Smith, M.D.*
For Men and Women Outdoors

Runner's World Magazine

WORLD

World Publications
1400 Stierlin Road
Mountain View, CA 94043